MY MILLION DOLLAR MOM

The Story of the Remarkable Life of an Ordinary Person

By Ross Schriftman

All rights reserved. No part of this book shall be reproduced or transmitted in any form or by any means, electronic, mechanical, magnetic, photographic including photocopying, recording or by any information storage and retrieval system, without prior written permission of the publisher. No patent liability is assumed with respect to the use of the information contained herein. Although every precaution has been taken in the preparation of this book, the publisher and author assume no responsibility for errors or omissions. Neither is any liability assumed for damages resulting from the use of the information contained herein.

Copyright © 2011 by Ross Schriftman

ISBN 0-7414-6713-5 Paperback
ISBN 0-7414-6714-3 Hardcover
Library of Congress Control Number: 2011931496

Printed in the United States of America

Published August 2011

INFINITY PUBLISHING
1094 New DeHaven Street, Suite 100
West Conshohocken, PA 19428-2713
Toll-free (877) BUY BOOK
Local Phone (610) 941-9999
Fax (610) 941-9959
Info@buybooksontheweb.com
www.buybooksontheweb.com

My Million Dollar Mom

The Story of the Remarkable Life of an Ordinary Person

A Grateful Son's Loving Tribute to His Mother, Shirley Schriftman

By

Ross Schriftman

To Sue + Gary,
A mom's love is everlasting.
Best wishes,
Ross Schriftman

TABLE OF CONTENTS

Section	Page
Acknowledgements	i
Tribute to Mom	iii
There Are No Ordinary People	1
A woman of valor, who can find?	2
Ross! Ross! Where Are You?!	3
Shirley Before Me	14
Mom and Roy	32
Shirley and Herb	38
The Kitchen Table	46
Politics, Me and Mom	47
Going to the Races	63
Ama	79
My Mother's Wise Advice	85

Mom Was Mathematically Challenged	90
Dancing Shirley	94
Mom Wasn't Perfect	103
Shirley as Public Speaker	106
Mom's Retirement Story	114
Ambassador Shirley	137
Holidays	142
Letters to Aunt Bettie	149
Tolerant Mom	208
Uncle Eddie and Sister Rose	212
Gladys and Mom	214
Friendly, Helpful Mom	218
Giving and Receiving	220
The Russians Are Coming	224
Parents Without Partners	228

Flowers	231
Shirley the Patriot	235
Shirley Loved All God's Animals	242
Mom's 80th Birthday Party	258
The Movie Buff	263
Vacations—Schriftman Style	266
She Taught Me How to Be a Caregiver of a Loved One	291
Shirley The Teacher	306
Sayings	308
Mom vs. Healthcare	310
The Worst Day of My Life	319
Nora and Shirley	323
I Want to Go Over There!	337
I Want to Die	339

Loss: The Price for Freedom	342
Sunday Morning's With Alzheimer's	344
Peculiar Behavior	347
Are You Sleeping?	350
The Funny Side of Alzheimer's Disease	351
That's a Big House	356
Lasts	357
Mourning along the Way	369
My Mother's Synagogue	371
The Funeral	377
Epilogue	379
Advice for Caregivers	383
Gratitude	388
About the Author	391

"There was never a great man who had not a great mother"

Olive Schreiner
"The Story of an African Farm"

The measure of a woman can be gauged by the level of her interaction among others.
That Shirley Schriftman engaged others often and whole-heartedly can be used as such a yardstick. This everyday woman left a powerful legacy for those she loved. It is in the span of her lifetime that one can take the measure of her character. Unfortunately, it is also through the lens of Alzheimer's disease that one reflects back on where Shirley started out to where the debilitating effects of the disease finally overwhelmed her.

This literary tribute is a son's thoughtful reflection on the joys – the highs and the lows – that he experienced in the life of his loving mother. This is the story of a true woman of substance.

--Pat Frazier

Acknowledgements

I am grateful to so many people for helping make this book possible. The many friends, family and associates who touched my mother's life provided a beautiful mosaic. To Nora and all the wonderful caregivers that allowed me to fulfill my mother's wishes to remain at home to the end of her life, I extend a special note of warmth and gratitude. And a special thank you is extended to my brother Roy of Blessed Memory for putting all our home movies into a format to produce a videotape and spending untold hours splicing it all together and to Taylor Made Transfers for their assistance with his project. His efforts provided a means for total recall of so many good memories when we were children, which helped tremendously in my research.

A special thank you goes to Pat Frazier of Frazier Enterprises who took the time to carefully review and edit this work, making thoughtful suggestions to capture the spirit and essence of my mother, Shirley.

Also thank you to Michael Heayn for the beautiful portrait he did of Mom and me for the cover of this book, to April Zay of Hummingbird Art for the Portrait of Mom with her pets, Victoria of Assembly Image Management for her assistance in placing the pictures throughout this book, SomeLifeBlog for the stunning photo of Haleakala, and to the Old York Road Historical Society for finding Mom's letter to the editor in the Ambler Gazette during the U.S. Bicentennial. Also, I extend a special thank you to Mrs. Basenberg, my high school teacher, who helped me learn how to type.

Finally, thank you to my Mom, whose letters, stories and articles contributed immensely to this collection of windows into her life. She also taught me many of the writing skills that I have in order to tell a good story like this one. Her rich life and the rich life she helped so many others achieve was an inspiration. She truly was *My Million Dollar Mom*.

Tribute to Mom

By Ross Schriftman

Mom, I have always loved you since
I was a little boy.

Mom, you have been my friend and my support through all of my life.

Mom, you are the brightest star for me and always will be.

Now you can't express yourself the way you used to, but your love still shines through.

I will be your voice to break through the clouds covering your mind.

I will sing your song for you and
with you every chance I can.

There Are No Ordinary People

It is extraordinary how extraordinary the ordinary person is.
George F. Will

Every person is unique and has his or her own story. On the surface my mother may have seemed like any other ordinary person. She was a mother. She was a wife, a daughter, a sister, a grandmother and a niece. She worked. She took courses. She went to synagogue.

Her life was anything but ordinary. Her accomplishments included raising four sons which was her greatest joy. Caring about others, whether human, animal or flower had its own unique style.

To me, Mom was like a Forest Gump of her generation—touching, at different points along the way, the lives of people we are all familiar with. She was right there in the middle of it all. She was a shining example of the best of what they call "The Greatest Generation"—those who grew up in the Depression, fought World War II and started families with kids who are known today as the baby boomers.

The last years of her life, too, could have been considered ordinary. Five million Americans have Alzheimer's disease. Families are struggling with this issue and focus their lives on making sure that their loved ones are safe and well cared for. Much of this part of the story is the unique relationship between me and Mom and how we faced her disease together with our love for each other still intact. It is the story of how we got through this difficult period with grace and appreciation of life's beautiful and yet simple gifts.

This was my Half Torah Portion at My Bar Mitzvah and is so appropriate to describe my Mom:

A woman of valor, who can find?
Her worth is far above rubles.
The heart of her husband trusts in her
And nothing shall he lack.
She renders him good not evil
All the days of her life.
She opens her hand to the needy
And extends her hand to the poor.
She is robed in strength and dignity
And cheerfully faces whatever may come.
She opens her mouth with wisdom.
Her tongue is guided with kindness.
She tends to the affairs of her household
And eats not the bread of idleness.
Her children come forward and bless her,
Her husband too, and he praises her:
"Many women have done superbly,
But you surpass them all."
Charm is deceitful and beauty vain,
But a God-revering woman is much to be praised.
Place before her the fruit of her hands;
Wherever people gather, her deeds speak her praise.

-- Proverbs 31

Ross! Ross! Where Are You?!

"Ross! Ross! Where are you?!" It was Labor Day weekend 2007, and my mom's Alzheimer's disease was now fully overwhelming her. Just the Sunday before, she and I had traveled to the Washington, D.C., area to visit her high school friend Gloria and her husband George. Although she had an obsessive attack the day before, she was fine most of the time it took for the three-hour trip from our house north of Philadelphia to visit one of her best friends. My only concern was managing Mom's visit to the ladies' room at the rest stop on I-95. I stood by the door and decided if she didn't come out I would ask someone to go in and check on her. She had done well. We had a nice visit, including lunch at a Chinese restaurant. We took a picture of Mom and her friend. Clearly the picture showed Mom clutching a tissue in her left hand, something which she did most of her life. (Shirley with the runny nose is what she said they called her as a child.)

Now just one week later, she was screaming, angry and frightened. Alzheimer's can be frightening for family members, but imagine what it must feel like to the person with the disease. They feel anxious, unsure about what is happening and everything seems wrong.

Each time I would try to leave her bedroom and go downstairs, Mom would yell, "Don't go anywhere. Stay here. Come back now!" Up until this time I had been managing, although there were many difficult events and I was constantly cleaning up and doing things for her while I tried to keep up with the workload and stress of my job selling insurance.

I felt tremendous stress. I felt like I was trapped. If I tried to leave to go grocery shopping or go to work at my office, she would chase after me banging on the garage door as I drove my car down the driveway. I also felt I could not leave her alone. My life and her life were becoming impossible.

"Ross! Ross! Where are you?! Don't go anywhere!" she shouted. It was the worst feeling I had ever experienced.

"Ross, Rossy bossy, come in for lunch." It was the summer of 1955 at our home in Baltimore. Mom was a young mother of 30. I was her second child just about to turn three. My brother Roy, who always looked after me, was now six.

Dad was at work. Mom, Roy and I sat on the front steps of our little one-story suburban-style house and ate what she called "Jewish Chop-Suey." I am not sure why she called it that. It was a bowl of sliced cucumbers, chunks of tomato, cut up radishes and gobs of sour cream and cottage cheese. Maybe it was one of those neat little treats her mother invented and gave to her during the Depression. I always liked it and still make it occasionally today.

We were a happy little family. Dad worked for the Army as a chemist testing antidotes to gases used in war. He worked at the Edgewood Arsenal in Maryland. Mom was a homemaker and a great mother. We had only one car, but she would take us places. We didn't have a lot of money, but she always figured out a way to have an inexpensive and fun outing. Once we went on the bus to Pimlico Race Track. Mom loved horses. She didn't have money for the price of admission, so we stood at the end of the track outside the fence on the side of the highway and watched the horses run around the track. We would go to downtown Baltimore on the bus. We would have a hotdog at a stand or just go into the stores and walk around.

One winter I almost got traded in for a little girl, as Mom told it. She had dressed me in a snowsuit and we went to a downtown department store. She had gotten distracted and I had started to walk off. Mom looked around and didn't see me. In a mother's panic she started running around looking for me. She saw the snowsuit and picked me up, but my weight didn't feel right. Just then another mother came running over. The other woman had picked me up and Mom had picked up her little girl. Both mothers had dressed their child in the same kind of snowsuit. Mom loved to tell that story.

At our home, we had our own swimming pool, not the kind that many people have to day. It was a plastic wading pool, but it even had a sliding board attached to it. Roy and I could splash and enjoy our pool.

In our house there was a beautiful candy dish that I would climb up on a chair and take candy from. It was round with very thick glass and a gold metal cover. I still have that dish.

My brother Roy was protective of me. Mom used to love to tell the story of how Roy had some friends that wanted to play with him. They wanted Roy to send me home because I was only three. He told them, "If you don't play with my brother you don't play with me." Mom was a good teacher of how her children should relate to one another and how important family is.

Roy and I put Mom in a panic one day. There was a Nike base (not the athletic shoe, but the missile base) about two miles from our house. One afternoon, Roy decided to go visit the base and he took me with him. Mom could not find us for three hours. Roy was seven and I was four. Can you imagine what we put her through? I wasn't scared and neither of us at our young age thought about how our mother would take our disappearance.

I always remember Mom as being happy. She would sing and dance throughout the house, playing music on the Victrola (record player). She loved show tunes and the catchy Cole Porter songs of the time. I remember her whirling around while she danced. She also had a beautiful singing voice. She would sing "Summer Time" from the musical, "Porgy and Bess", "Fish Gotta Swim" from "Showboat", or "Someone to Watch Over Me" by George Gershwin. Judy Garland was her favorite. Mom would sing "Somewhere Over the Rainbow" and other Judy Garland tunes. Later Mom would sign up to perform in community musical plays with other parents at the elementary school in Springfield, PA, in Delaware County, and much later at Beth Tikvah Synagogue in Springfield, PA, in Montgomery County.

Mom was always inventing ways to give her family interesting and enjoyable times. Family trips were wonderful experiences.

When I was five years old, my dad got a job at Wyeth Laboratories in Radnor, Pennsylvania. We moved to Springfield, Delaware County, Pennsylvania. I remember that trip driving along Baltimore Pike and coming to Springfield. Playland Park was an amusement park along Baltimore Pike, and I remember passing it just before we made a left turn and went into our new neighborhood. My impression was that this seemed like a fun place to live. It was 1957, and until 1963 we lived in that little white house on the corner of Powell and Lynbrook. My brothers and I began our growing period there and the wonderful memories of the families and community there are always with me.

Our life in Springfield included elementary school, parades down our street, July 4th fireworks in Media at the park at the end of the Red Arrow trolley line, birthday parties, holidays, Cub Scouts (Mom was a Den Mother), going swimming and playing with other children in the neighborhood including my best friend Freddie Peifer. We had wonderful next door neighbors; The Matlocks. One time, Roy and I and several other children in the neighborhood decided we were going to dig to China. After a few hours of this my mother happened to step outside to see what we were doing. There in the middle of her backyard was a four-foot deep, four-foot wide hole in her lawn. She was not very happy about this and our quest to reach the other side of the planet ended abruptly. Mom scolded us, but I don't remember her yelling at us. She made us fill in the hole and then she covered the area with grass seed.

As a child I never said, "I'm bored. I have nothing to do." If I didn't have a friend available to play with I would go exploring around the neighborhood. The park was across the street. There was a wooded area next to it and lots of things to do. There was also a Springfield Athletic League for baseball. These were not well organized games. However, they were better because every kid was put out in the field. Sometimes there would be 20 or 30 boys on the field. Every kid got a turn at bat. There were no try-outs. Mom and Dad would be there and help out. All the parents were there cheering their kids and just having a good time. When we were done, we would go back to the house and have chocolate milk. I don't even remember if they kept score in the game. It didn't matter. We all had lots of fun.

We were a family that loved to eat. There would be dinners at the Alpine Inn on Baltimore Pike, pizza at Mar's Restaurant or the time we went to Center City and went up to the Penthouse Restaurant overlooking Philadelphia and had a fancy dinner with a violinist playing. There were picnics with deviled eggs, hotdogs, lobster pots and Japanese restaurants. You name it. We loved to eat.

In 1963 my father got a new job with Rorer Laboratory in Fort Washington. We left Springfield and moved to a ranch house on Greystone Road in Whitpain Township, Montgomery County. Back then, this seemed so far away from Springfield. Today it is about a 30-minute drive down the Blue Route. We were all sad to miss the friends and the neighborhood. We were renting in Whitpain and only lived there one year. The memorable times were good and bad. We saw the movie about John F. Kennedy in World War II at the Ambler Theatre. It was "PT-109." We also experienced JFK's assassination. I was in class and the teacher was called out of the room and came back in to tell us. Some children thought Nixon would now be President. I told them that Vice President Johnson would become President. Mom was very upset. We watched the funeral on television. It was a very sad time for our family and our nation.

The next summer saw our move into our new home that my parents had bought. I am not sure, but I think all previous homes we had lived in were rentals. It was 1964 and my mother was very happy. The house on Dillon Road had a large backyard. The lot was three-quarters of an acre which seemed huge to me. There was a swim club just three doors from our house. It had opened the previous summer and everyone on the block got a membership with a free bond if they would join and pay the annual membership. My mother, being a Pisces, loved the pool. She also loved the shade when sitting outside and claimed the one scrawny little tree by the fence near the snack bar to sit under.

When we moved in everyone helped. Mom and I washed the new wallpaper that had been placed throughout the house. She swept the dust off the back porch and hung plants on the front porch. Dad and I planted trees, including one narrow branch 30 feet past the back door. (Now that beautiful pin oak tree is over 100 feet tall and provides shade over the entire fenced-in area of the backyard.)

Dad, my brothers and I laid a walkway in the front and planted bushes. We all worked very hard so that we could have a very special new home. We had our own place. Mom was beaming with joy.

In the morning we would awaken to the wonderful sound of cowbells down the street at the Levin dairy farm on the corner of Limekiln and Dillon. The Levin Family had purchased a portion of the land from the Dillon Family. The Dillon Farm had been a much larger farm decades before. The street was named after that family.

Since Dad had the only car and needed to go to work everyday, if Mom needed to buy groceries, she would put Barry in the stroller and Roy, Lee and I would walk beside her up Dillon Road to Welsh Road and then two miles to the A & P at the Upper Dublin Shopping Center. Each of us would carry a small bag back to the house and one bag would be tucked underneath Barry's seat in the stroller. This round-trip trek was about six miles. Mom thought nothing of it. Today I wouldn't walk along Welsh Road because it is a dangerous highway with people driving too fast, talking on cell phones and texting.

One Saturday afternoon several people riding horses came up the street and Mom had them ride their horses right up our driveway. Each of us got to sit on a horse and Mom kissed each horse and told them how pretty they were. I have a recording of this event on film taken by our home movie camera.

Our first summer was 1964 and that was the year the Phillies became known as the *Wiz Kids*. We were all into baseball and very disappointed when the Phillies didn't make it to the World Series. The last game of the season happened to be a day that Mom had invited Rabbi David Wice from our synagogue, Congregation Rodeph Shalom, and his wife Sophie over for a Sunday dinner and a blessing of our new home. Mom instructed us that we couldn't watch TV while the Rabbi was at our home because he was blessing our new home. When Rabbi Wice walked in he announced, "Let's watch the game." He and his wife were wonderful people.

There were many sweet memories of those days in our new home. Roy and I had our own rooms. Lee and Barry shared a room. We had a family room and a play room downstairs. Our split-level house was full of activity. There was Friday night family game nights, Sunday afternoon dinners in our dining room, parades down our street on July 4th, the swimming pool, trips to Center City Philadelphia and Valley Forge, visits to our grandparents in New York and Washington and evening dinners where we all sat together around our kitchen table. (Now I am not sure how all six of us sat there, but we did.)

There was also the Civil Air Patrol which became a big part of all of our lives. One of my junior high teachers was Robert Taylor. He had become active in the local squadron and would tell his students about how much they would get out of participating in the Civil Air Patrol. I joined and then my brothers joined as well. There were encampments, parades, rescue missions for missing people and downed airplanes, flights to other parts of the country, and even a trip to Germany, Italy and Israel that I won through the International Air Cadet Exchange. My parents hosted parties for the squadron with an afternoon swimming event at the pool. Bob and Suzie Taylor and their children Roger and Michelle would have the squadron over to their home in Roslyn. We all became good friends and did many community projects together. There was Blair Allen, Joe Hildebrand, Duane Quenzel and his sister Lynn and Bruce Goldstein and his sister Wendy that became friends. When I was cadet commander of Squadron 902, we had 60 cadets. My parents were very proud when the squadron had an awards dinner with the School District administrators and township officials in attendance and I gave a speech about leadership and community. I was 17 years old at the time. Mom's face was glowing.

In the summers, we each had jobs to do before we could go to the pool for the afternoon. Mom had a schedule worked out so our cleaning or gardening duties were not overly burdensome. She wanted each of us to know the importance of work and the joy of being rewarded after doing our tasks.

Mom was in charge of all arrangements, with the other five of us (including Dad) assisting her with whatever project she came up with. She always ran the activity with the goal to make things enjoyable for everyone.

Mom made sure we did our homework and that we tried our best at our work. As we got older each of us was responsible for getting to school on time. In high school if I missed the bus I would then have to run the two miles to get to class on time. No one was going to drive me there.

There were so many pleasant memories of my childhood that I could spend years remembering all the great things that happened. My mom was the one in charge of all the work and good times. I will always be thankful for the childhood my parents gave me.

Shirley Before Me

My mom, the former Shirley Goldman, was born in Springfield, Massachusetts, in 1925 to Harry and Freda Goldman. Her parents had immigrated to the United States in the early part of the 20th century with their parents. Harry Goldman came from the Ukraine countryside outside of Kiev. Freda came from Riga in Latvia.

Harry and Freda were loving parents of their two daughters, Shirley and Miriam. My Aunt Miriam was born 11 years earlier than my mom, so she truly was Mom's big sister.

Little Shirley. Bags packed. Let's go! (Probably her father's joke.)

Mom imitating Shirley Temple.

Eating ice cream.

There were many siblings of my grandparents and my mother would tell me all kinds of stories of her time growing up. The family moved from Springfield to Brooklyn, MA, in the Boston area when she was still a small child. Mom attended Edward Devotion Elementary School in Brooklyn.

The school was a few blocks from where the Kennedy children grew up. Mom used to tell the story of how she was playing at recess and a boy was on the other side of the fence. She asked him why he wasn't in school. He said it was a Catholic holiday. She swore the boy was Robert Kennedy. In fact, it could not have been Robert as the Kennedys lived in New York when Robert was in elementary school. However, John F. Kennedy did attend Devotion a few years before my Mom.

Elementary school picture.

From the stories she told me, her childhood was a happy one. Despite years struggling through the Depression, the family remained together and worked hard to make ends meet. This proves that money isn't as important as love and devotion to family. Harry worked as a shoe salesman. My mother said he worked so hard that one time he fell asleep on the streetcar coming home and rode to the end of the line before the conductor realized it and woke him up.

My grandmother, Freda Goldman, would play the piano in movie theatres as there were no "talkies" or "music" soundtracks in the films. The story goes that she quit one day when a mouse ran across the piano. She then worked in Filene's Basement department store in Boston.

The family made the best of the Depression years which began when Mom was only four. All the family lived in one house owned by my Aunt Bettie and her husband Harry Eisner. Sunday dinners were important with everyone in the family in attendance. Harry Eisner was an inventor and a founder of the New England Automobile Association. (Here are some pictures.)

HARRY EISNER CO.
Ignition Specialists
907 Boylston St.
BOSTON

Official Service Station for Popular Magnetos and Generators

HARRY EISNER, for 17 years the foremost ignition expert in New England, announces to his friends and to the automotive trade the opening of new and larger quarters for the more convenient and expeditious handling of customers who desire skilled service in the repair and adjustment of Magnetos and the various types of ignition, and Generators and Starters.

The new location at 907 Boylston Street, made necessary by constantly increasing business, is at a most convenient place. The stock of parts and supplies is the largest to be found in the New England States.

Quick Work on Any Job—Satisfaction Guaranteed

Mr. Eisner has surrounded himself with a large staff of specialists, including men who are especially trained to handle the various types of ignition to be found in foreign-built cars. The quickest service in the city—the best service—and satisfaction guaranteed.

The basement of the Eisner quarters, entered from the rear of the building, is arranged as a service station, and is so laid out that 16 cars can be accommodated at one time.

Dealers and Service Men—Get Our Prices

A cordial invitation is extended to dealers and representatives of service stations and garages throughout New England, to visit the new quarters, to make use of the unlimited facilities, and to present any special problems for treatment. The Eisner Company is in a good position, with its broad trade connections, to stock dealers with parts at attractive prices, and invites consultation as to terms, discounts, etc.

Special Fittings to Install Magnetos on Cars with Battery Systems

Harry Eisner Co.   907 Boylston St., Boston
Telephone Back Bay 8254
                   4062

MOTOR-AMBULANCE, WHICH WAS THE GIFT OF CHAUFFEUR EX-DOUGHBOYS T COLONEL GIFFORD FOR BOSTON'S SALVATION ARMY HOSPITAL.
Reading from left to right are: Captain Burke, Hospital Staff; Dr. Raymond Hoope terne; Mr. Harry Eisner, Vice-President, Massachusetts Association of Automobile Operators tain E. R. Gifford, Supervisor of Hospital and Dispensary, and Miss Amy Clark, Superir of Nursing Staff.

My mother said he invented the magneto. A Google search confirmed that he did invent certain components that he sold to Ford. Harry had been born in Austria. He had a heavy accent. According to my mother one time he was dictating a letter to his secretary and when he got the draft he was puzzled. "Vat is this word here?" he asked his secretary. "It says 'the pants'." She responded, "Well Mr. Eisner, I thought that was what you said." "No, I said it all 'depends,' not 'the pants'."

Aunt Bettie was my grandmother's sister. She was a wonderful, exciting woman 20 years younger than her Harry. She was the life of the party and always out having lots of fun. She spent the last two years of her life living with Mom and me.

Family home, Brookline, MA.

Harry and Bettie lived upstairs with Bettie's brother Jack. My grandparents and their daughters lived downstairs. Also, my mom's cousin Lydia was her roommate. Lydia's parents were very poor and so there was room for their daughter to live with my grandparents.

Mom said that for birthdays my grandmother would make special "birthday cakes." Since money was tight, she would take a loaf of bread, slice it open and put peanut butter and jelly inside and birthday candles on top. My mother really thought this was a special treat.

My mom, who loved animals, used to tell me stories of riding the milk wagon. The driver would let her take the reins of the horse. She really thought she was directing the horse. Of course, the horse had the same route every few days, but it was great fun for my mom. Mom's favorite book as a child was *Mr. Jolly's Hotel for Dogs*. She said that she wanted to run a hotel for abandoned dogs when she grew up.

When she was a child the family had several dogs, including Scrapsy, Jigsy and Rexy Bozo. They were Boston Terriers with cute pug noses and short feet. Picture Spanky and our Gang.

Bettie and Jigsy.

Bettie's house was on Winchester Street, a long road near Coolidge Corner. Behind the house was a steep hill. In front of the house the hill kept going down. From the second floor balcony you could see Fenway Park. Bettie and Freda would go to the Red Sox games a lot. Boston was and still is a big sports town.

Mom was an active child. She told me that she would run down the side streets which went up and down the hills. She thought she could run so fast and flap her arms and fly.

Since my grandparents both worked, my Aunt Miriam would have to "watch" my mom. Miriam was already old enough to be interested in boys and didn't always want the role of big sister. However, she tried her best. One time, Miriam made a chicken for the two of them but didn't know how to cut it up. Each of the sisters took a leg and pulled;

they both ended up on the floor holding the legs with the rest of the chicken falling on the floor between them.

When she was a little older Miriam went into "show business." She got a part in a radio broadcast. She was the murder victim. She would practice by screaming at my mom who would hide under the bed. When the broadcast came on, everyone waited to hear her performance. But they never heard her voice. Upon arrival back at the house, everyone asked her what she had done. "Didn't you hear the scream at the beginning of the program? That was me."

Sisters, Shirley and Miriam.

Miriam was an actress of sorts. The story goes that when boys would come to call for her when she was a little older, she would go into the parlor and play the piano. When they came in, she would go, "Oh, I am sorry. I didn't hear you come in. I was just playing my concerto." Miriam was grace and elegance. She did want to go into show business, but my grandfather wouldn't allow it. She never forgave him for this and resented his decision of her "career" choice. She married a wonderful man named Harry Kandall who went into the furniture business with my grandfather. They raised two daughters—my cousins Lisa and Deedee.

One summer my Aunt Bettie arranged for my mom to stay on a chicken farm in Upstate New York. Within weeks, the farmer asked my aunt to pick her up. My mother had named all the chickens and wouldn't let the farmer slaughter, "Sara or Alvin or Frank."

My grandfather was a kind man with a deep love for his family. He took care of his wife like she was a queen, although my grandmother worked very hard. Harry was devoted to his daughters. Once, he took my mom fishing off a pier. (It could have been anywhere in the Boston area.) He wanted to make sure she got a fish, so he went under the pier with fish he had bought from the market, tied them to my mother's line so she thought she was actually catching fish.

When she was a little older my grandfather decided to teach my mom how to drive. My mom hit a tree with the car and damaged the fender. Several hours later they returned home. "Harry, where have you been?" my grandmother inquired. "Freda, I had a little trouble with the car so I took it in to the shop to check it out." My grandmother never knew about the accident.

There was another incident with the car. My mom was playing on the roof and slipped off. She fell on her arm and broke it. The roofs of cars were much higher in those days.

During the Depression years, children were taught to behave. If you did something wrong at school your parents would find out by the time you got home. Neighbors would report bad behavior by a child. One time, my mom and some girlfriends were having ice cream sodas in the drug store at Coolidge Corner. When they got to the bottom of their drinks, their straws made a sucking sound. A lady came over and remarked to them, "I never have seen such rude behavior. I will be telling your mothers about this." My mom said she was very upset about this "incident" and hoped she wouldn't be punished. What a difference in how things are today.

As the Depression got worse, more close relatives moved in with the family. There was a man they called Uncle Al, but he wasn't a relative. His wife had committed suicide when they lost everything in the stock market. His name was Al Ziemer. I used to tease Mom that his name was "Alzheimer." Little did I know that this particular disease would end my mother's life.

My mom bunked with a "cousin" named Lydia. They became good friends over the years. Years later, they would get together to watch me run the Boston Marathon.

My Uncle Jack was an instigator. The family would get together every Sunday for dinner and they would argue politics. Jack would throw oil on the fire by popping in with comments like, "I don't think Roosevelt is doing a good job." He would then wink at my mom while everyone's intensity of debate would rise.

One time, there was a huge argument about baseball by the uncles and cousins. They decided to settle who was a better player by going out to Boston Commons and playing their own game. They took my mom along. She said they were terrible players.

Mom went to Brookline High School for her first three years before the family moved. World War II had just begun. Before and during the war my Mom's family helped rescue Jews from the Holocaust. My Mom would go to the movie house, and they would show newsreels of the atrocities of war in Europe and Asia. They would also show the local high school football game highlights. Brookline's big rival was Newtown, the hilly neighborhood just up the road from Cleveland Circle.

Many of her friends would end up in the war. Newt Goldman, a neighbor, would die when he got sucked out of a bomber on which he was the navigator. Another student would die years later after being wounded parachuting into France. Because so many of their children perished, it was a very difficult time for every community.

There were also many happy times despite the difficulties. My grandparents loved to go out and to travel. After my grandfather got a better job selling Berkline chairs on the road, he would sometimes take his wife and daughter and Bettie and Harry Eisner with him to dinner or a show between business stops. They would go to Worcester, MA, to a seafood restaurant or somewhere in Upstate New York or down to Manhattan. Having been through such times, it must have been a real treat to just go somewhere and have a nice meal.

At one point during his career in the furniture business, the owners of Berkline asked my grandfather if he would be willing to buy in to the business by purchasing stock in the company. They were expanding and needed capital. My grandmother was afraid because so many people had lost money during the Depression. "Harry, don't buy stock. Lend them money." Of course, a loan could also default if a company goes bankrupt. If he had bought part ownership, finances might have been different for my mom in her adult life.

I SAT IN THE MILLIONTH BERK-LOCK!

Chicago Furniture Market
January, 1956

When the United States entered World War II, Americans made great sacrifices. There were wage and price freezes and rationings for many items. Gas rationing was a particularly hard thing for sales people, especially. By then, my grandfather's territory was all the major department stores from Boston to Atlanta. He started looking to move the family south in order to take better advantage of gas rationing. The first choice was Pittsburgh. At the time, Pittsburgh was a drab, dirty city. Not only didn't this choice work out, Miriam and my mother ended up being left by the bus at a rest stop, probably because Miriam was taking her time talking to some boys.

The choice came down to Washington, D.C. This would give my grandfather access to both the North and South of his territory. They bought a house on 16th Street and took the trip down from Boston. The weather was not good on the trip and my mom was feeling sick. By the time they got to Washington, she had full-blown pneumonia and a collapsed lung. She was very sick and nearly died.

After her recovery, she went back to school. She was now a junior and entered Theodore Roosevelt High School. Years later the Class of 1943 had a 65th Reunion. We had planned to go when they first started talking about it, but by the time it took place, Mom's Alzheimer's disease had completely overwhelmed her. I sent the class organizers a note expressing how she would have wanted to go.

High school is where Mom met her friend Gloria. Gloria was also from "up North" having grown up in Frogs Neck, NY. They became best friends. Later Gloria would marry George Falk who worked in the Foreign Service for the State Department. They were stationed in Havana when Castro took over. Gloria, who was always a spunky person, and another wife of an embassy employee were out taking pictures in the middle of the Cuban Revolution. They happened to take a picture of the front of a very interesting building. It turned out to be Communist Headquarters. They were picked up by Castro's henchman and were being driven to an interrogation point when the car stopped at a red light. Both women jumped out and ran into the U.S. Embassy a block away. They were quickly transported out of the country. Gloria and George showed me the news articles about the incident years later.

My mother, who liked languages, became very interested in Spanish and took classes both years she was in high school. She continued studying Spanish and loved to learn about other cultures.

After high school, my mother got a job at the State Department as a Spanish translator. Even back then, any position with the government required investigation. Two FBI agents showed up at her door one day and asked her a bunch of questions about her background and her beliefs. She told me it was a little unnerving, especially talking about her parents' backgrounds as immigrants from Eastern Europe. The agents also questioned their Jewish religious preference. Nevertheless, she must have answered correctly as Mom got the job.

Her work for the government involved translating State Department press releases into Spanish. The releases concerned the activity of the War Department and what the United States was working on in building the coalition against the Axis powers and reports from the various war fronts. These releases would then be forwarded to the various embassies.

At one point during her work, Mom was asked to go to South America for a meeting. At the vary last minute she got bumped off the trip when an Ambassador's daughter decided she wanted to go.

The organization she worked for within the State Department was the Office of Inter-American Affairs. Its director was Nelson Rockefeller—heir to the oil fortune and a future New York Governor, Presidential candidate and Vice President of the United States. There are two Rockefeller stories my mother loved to tell. The first was that when she was working in the office and had some papers around her desk, someone came by and shook her hand. She was still looking down. After the person left, one of her co-workers said she had just shaken Rockefeller's hand. The other story goes like this. Mom was in the cafeteria line. Nelson Rockefeller asked her if he could borrow a dollar for his lunch as he had forgotten his wallet. I guess wealthy people can forget to take their wallet sometimes. She never saw him again. So the Rockefeller estate owes Mom's estate one dollar plus interest for 60 years.

While working in Washington, she had the opportunity to do a number of other government-related activities. She helped edit Vice President Henry Wallace's book, *Sixty Million Jobs*. It was a book about how to achieve full employment. Henry Wallace would run for President under the Progressive Party banner in 1948 against Harry Truman. She met Eleanor Roosevelt at a function at someone's house and helped her edit some papers. Mrs. Roosevelt was a tremendous inspiration for my mom. She claimed she met Eleanor at the same function where she went to see the "Hope Diamond" and had been asked by the President's wife to help her do the edits. I was never able to confirm this as my mom told me these stories years after her time in Washington.

Late in the war, President Roosevelt had become very ill. The day he died, Mom was riding the bus home from work. People getting on the bus were saying they heard the President had died. She got off the bus and ran back to the State Department. Mom worked all that night helping the staff with press releases to our Latin American allies.

Throughout the war, my mother was a USO hostess. I found many pictures of her on trips with soldiers on leave. Some appear to be at Haines Point in Washington. Others could be from a trip to Ocean City, Maryland, which, at the time was a small community of houses and a beach. The trips were chaperoned, so there would be no "funny business" between the hostesses and the men. The pictures I found show a very happy group of young people enjoying themselves. One shows three soldiers standing with Mom sitting on the grass. They all were smiling.

Mom's Hostess Training book.

Mom also visited Walter Reed Medical Center many times during the war. Some visits were to boys she had known growing up in Brookline; they had been badly wounded in the war. One visit she remembered was to a boy named Bernie Schwartz who might have been Tony Curtis, the actor. Of course, there could have been a different Bernie Schwartz.

Mom with Marvin and Zach at Walter Reed Army Hospital.

During her time in Washington, Mom also became active in Young Judea. The establishment of the State of Israel became an important issue for many Jewish Americans. My grandparents had joined Washington Hebrew Congregation in Washington's Northwest section. My mother loved to study her religion and did so throughout her life.

Growing up as Shirley Ruth Goldman was an experience that my mother talked about many times. I am fortunate that I remember so much of her stories. One joke about Mom was that she would tell the same story over and over again. I am glad she did so that I can now tell you. Her story is part of the American story . . . the immigrant family coming here. It is a story of hard work, love of family, good times and hard times. From 1925 when she was born to the end of World War II in 1945 there were a remarkable number of challenges faced and great changes made. They shaped the beginning of her life, which would change even more over the years that followed.

I remember when Mom's mother died suddenly. We were driving back from the funeral in Boston. Mom was sitting silently looking out the window up at the sky. I could tell she was thinking about all her parents had done for her. She loved her mother very much.

When her father died while living with us I remember how she kissed him on the forehead as he lay peacefully in his eternal sleep. He had done so much for her, and Mom had returned the favor to him by caring for him at the end of his life. My mother was a blessing to her family and they were a blessing to her.

Edward, alias "Bubbles" Cohen – a cousin.

Mom and Roy

At the end of World War II, my mom started dating a soldier named Joe. Pictures of her at the time showed a thin, pretty girl with long, dark hair and an engaging smile. Years later she would look at those pictures and say, "I didn't think I was pretty, but I guess I was." It was true. She was a very pretty young woman and her friendliness must have attracted many a soldier when she was a USO hostess. Shirley loved to dance as well. She would tell the story about how one night at an event she was having so much fun when a serviceman she was dancing with stepped on her foot. She kept dancing and didn't realize how badly she had been injured until she got home and took off her shoe.

So Mom met Joe. They fell deeply in love and moved in together. At that time, it was not the thing to do, but Mom trusted Joe and loved him very much. He said they would marry soon. My mother was afraid to tell her parents because

Joe was not Jewish. This was in the late 1940's. In today's world mixing religions is very common and accepted, but it was not the custom when my mother was growing up.

At some point, my mother became pregnant. When she told Joe, he had to admit that he was already married and that he could not marry her. He left. Shirley Ruth Goldman was devastated. She would tell me years later that she felt like committing suicide. She had thoughts of walking down the middle of the road in Rock Creek Park in Washington, D.C., and hoping a car would hit and kill her.

Now she had to decide what to do. She could not face her parents, so she entered a home for unwed mothers. At this institution each girl had to work and support the community. She worked in the kitchen lifting and cleaning heavy pots after her son's birth. The staff in the nursery took care of her son whom she named Roy. My brother Roy was a smiling baby with a round face. He was now the love of Shirley's life. My Mother did not want to give him up for adoption. She didn't think about that. She was a dedicated mother even though she knew she would face enormous hardships. She now had no loving man, no job and very few prospects. She felt she could not go to her parents who at the time lived in Miami Beach, Florida.

My grandmother, Freda Goldman who was a very loving woman, could not accept what her daughter had done. She would tell my grandfather, Harry, "Shirley can come home to us when she gets rid of it." "It" was Roy.

So what was to happen to Shirley and her baby Roy? Harry Goldman is the hero of this story. A loving man who was devoted to his family, Harry knew his wife would fall in love with her grandson the moment she saw his face. Those pudgy cheeks. That happy smile. "Freda, just see the baby. You have a grandson," my grandfather finally convinced her. Shirley and Roy went down to Florida, and the story took a remarkable and happy turn. Harry Goldman was right. My grandmother fell in love with Roy. My mother came home, thanks to her wonderful father.

Mom lived with her parents in Florida with Roy until she met my dad, Herbert Schriftman. She never mentioned her past to her other sons until each one was old enough to understand.

Mom and Lee visiting Mom's parents home in Miami Beach many years later.

I remember at age 13, my mother called me into her bedroom and said, "I have something important to tell you about my past." She then explained the story. I only knew Roy as my older brother, and he was, in my mind, always my full brother, never my half-brother. When my mother told me the story, I asked her what was the name of Roy's father. She said, "Joe," and she started to cry. So many years later she had feelings for this man, even though she loved my dad.

When my grandmother died, among her papers was a letter from Joe to my mom apologizing for his actions and hoping that she could forgive him. My grandmother must have intercepted it when it arrived at their home in Florida. She probably did not want to upset my mom or affect the relationship that Mom now had with my dad.

Life can be challenging. My mom could have given up her son, walked away and lived a less difficult early life. It was pure love that kept that thought out of her mind. One small act of kindness and love can change everything. The love between my Mom and Roy and between her parents and my mom saved an entire family and every generation to come thereafter.

My brother Roy died the day before Thanksgiving only six weeks after his mother died. He had cancer. He was only 60. I will never forget Roy and Mom and their special bond.

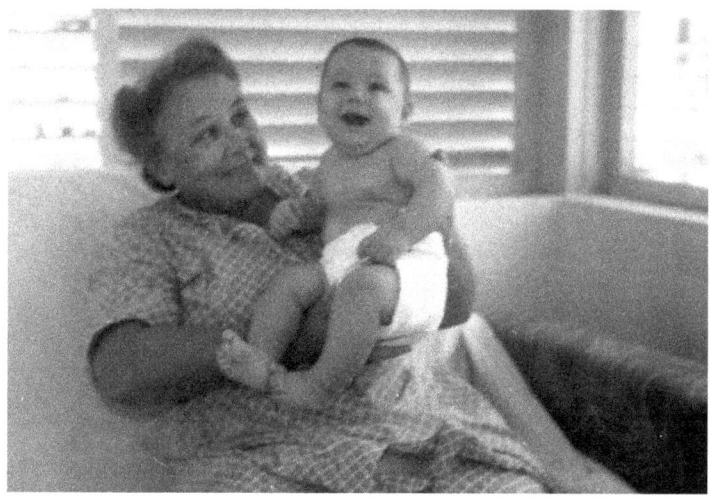

Roy and his Grandmother, Freda Goldman.

Roy and his Grandfather, Harry Goldman.

Mom and baby Roy.

Mom and Roy with Grandma and Grandpa Schriftman.

Roy at play.

Roy holding Micah. Deena peeking underneath.

Shirley and Herb

Shirley Goldman and Herb Schriftman's first meeting was on a double date; but Shirley had a date with Herb's friend Sy Tenser and Herb's date was another woman. So how did they get together? Sy gave Herb Shirley's phone number. Herb must have been very interested in Shirley. Shirley was not happy about Herb getting her phone number. She told me years later how inappropriate she thought it was that he had gotten the number from Sy. But Herbert Schriftman was persistent and kept calling her.

Herb was a graduate student in chemistry at the University of Miami. He was a Brooklyn, New York, kid raised by Shirley and Abe Schriftman. (Yes my grandmother and my mom had the same name.) Herb was in the Army during World War II, but had developed Ileitis (Chrohn's Disease) from eating the Army's food. It was nothing like his mother's cooking. He received a disability deferment after then, but went on with his education and attended City College of New York. He had a bright mind and a great curiosity.

My mom had met Sy while living in Miami Beach with her parents after my brother Roy was born. I am not sure how she met Sy, but I remember him as a big friendly teddy bear kind of a guy. Years later we would visit him and his family when we would go on our family vacations to Florida. We would always have a lot of fun going out to eat, going to the Hollywood Beach or the pool at Coral Gables.

Shirley finally agreed to go out on a date with Herb. They were going to go to the Orange Bowl, but instead they spent the evening at Wolvie's, a popular restaurant in downtown Miami Beach. Shirley was disappointed. Herb already had two strikes against him. The first was getting her number and the second was not taking her to the Orange Bowl game on New Year's Eve.

What eventually sealed the deal is when Shirley told Herb about Roy. My future father told her that he would love her son and would adopt him if she agreed to marry him. My dad clearly saw what a good mother my mom was to her son and felt he wanted to be part of her life and to raise a family together with her. Herb loved Roy very much.

Their wedding was a small affair with close family and friends. I don't know where the ceremony was held, but I do know that their reception was held at a table in the Sorrento Hotel for the evening show. They were entertained by Sammy Davis Jr., Dean Martin and others. Mom used to tease about what a fancy wedding party they had with such famous entertainers.

After getting his master's degree in chemistry, Herb got a job with the Army at the Edgewood Arsenal in Maryland. Mom, Dad and Roy moved to northern Baltimore. Their first home was an apartment on Loch Raven Boulevard. And then soon there was me. Years later Mom and I were going through some papers and we found the hospital bill for my birth. It was $120 for four days. That wasn't a deductible or co-pay; that was the entire bill for both of us.

One day my dad came home from work and my mom was crying. "What's wrong?" he asked. "Sara died!" Mom wailed and sobbed. "Who is Sara?" Dad asked. "*On Guiding Light*, she got hit by a car." She then felt silly since this was just a soap opera story. She had really gotten "involved" with the characters.

Soon after my birth, the family moved to a house on Hanson Avenue in northern Baltimore. That house contained my earliest memories. I still have the glass candy dish that I used to take candy out of by climbing up on a chair.

Then my brother Lee was born. I remember sitting by an elevator watching the pointer go up and down for each floor and waiting with my dad and my grandparents for my new brother to come down in that elevator. There were now five of us.

When I was five, the family moved to Springfield, Delaware County in Pennsylvania. My dad had gotten a job at Wyeth Labs in Radnor, Pennsylvania. He also began to work on his doctorate in chemistry at Temple University.

Soon there would be another Schriftman. My "baby" brother Barry was born at Bryn Mawr Hospital. I remember standing on the lawn outside the hospital building with my dad and my brothers looking up to the window of the maternity wing to see Mom holding Barry and waving to us. (No, she didn't hold him out the window Michael Jackson style. Actually, Mom was very gentle with all of her children, except she could raise her voice or be silent and give you that look when she was upset about something.)

Although my dad worked hard between his job and his courses, he was told it would be difficult getting a Ph.D. as a part-time student basis. Mom would help him in the evening by organizing his reports and editing them for him. They would get into arguments as she had her ideas about wording, and he had his scientific jargon. Eventually, he was not successful in getting his degree. This was a great disappointment to him. At times, he would express his regret that his family made it hard for him to achieve his goal. This, I believe, was the beginning of the marital problems that would result in their separation in the early 1970's and divorce in 1973.

My parents would argue about the bills and other issues. However, throughout the ordeal, they were great parents. My mom would direct events and my dad would take us to the scheduled events—Cub Scouts, field trips, vacations, school activities. We would go to Sunday school at our Synagogue. All four of us were in the Children's Choir after school on Sunday. However, we would go home hungry after choir practice. All the other children would bring lunch to eat before practice. Mom always would have a big Sunday dinner, which would begin around 2:00 p.m. On the way home from Rodeph Shalom in Center City Philadelphia, we would stop by Pechter's Bakery in Drexel Hill to pick up dinner rolls and a dessert such as butter cake. Dad would give each of us a piece of a dinner roll. "Don't tell Mom I gave this to you," he would say. Mom didn't want us to "spoil" our dinner by eating anything beforehand. I never understood how you spoil a meal by eating something before you get started.

Our Sunday dinners would include soup, a meat, two vegetables, rolls and dessert. We would then play games, watch TV and then go to bed. Of course, if anyone's homework wasn't done yet, that had to be accomplished before TV or play time.

When Roy was 13 and Barry was two, my father suffered another bout of Ileitis. Mom would be constantly running back and forth to Bryn Mawr Hospital with him. My father had a series of surgeries. A lot of his gastro-intestinal problems were probably related to stress and disappointment with his career and education. Roy became our protector and caregiver, especially for Barry. He would give us meals, read to us, make sure we all did our homework, and he also played with us. For a 13-year-old, he did it all. While my father's illness was going on, two-year-old Barry actually called Roy Dad for a while.

Herb and Shirley's divorce was not a fiery, finger-pointing event. My father had filed for divorce and, since by 1973 they had been separated for awhile and had managed their lives, it wasn't "messy." It was difficult on several levels. My mother now faced the prospect of supporting her children and maintaining our home in Maple Glen, PA, on a secretary's salary. In the settlement, she received $1,000, the house and a car. I remember going to the New Jersey courtroom with my mom. There were only a few questions from the judge and the "matter" was resolved within a few minutes. They each paid their own attorneys and then it was over.

My dad disappeared for awhile, but when my brother Roy married his first wife Tobey in Chicago, my dad showed up with his new wife Sylvia, someone he met in Texas where he had gone to live. This was a very difficult surprise for my mom who focused on the happiness of her first son's marriage. Later my dad divorced Sylvia and moved to Palm Springs, California. We wrote and called each other over the years.

In the mid-1980s I had become active in the Men's Club at Congregation Rodeph Shalom. I was selected to represent the group at the national meeting in Los Angeles and invited Mom to come. I had told Dad that I would be visiting California, so he drove into Los Angeles from Palm Springs to take me out to dinner. So on the evening of our get-together Mom and I were standing in the lobby when this man came over and started talking to us. I thought it was someone from one of the other brotherhoods and I tried to remember where I had seen him because he looked familiar. Neither of us recognized Dad. Instead of the Schriftman receding hairline, he was wearing a toupee. Finally, we recognized him. We also drove to San Diego and then to Palm Springs before we headed back to Los Angeles to get our return flight. Mom was friendly to Dad during the visit. She never was one to hold grudges. I guess she always knew that Herb Schriftman was there for her when she needed someone to step up and help her raise her son. She also had so many wonderful memories of the six of us to make the pain of divorce that much easier.

My dad lived in Palm Springs until his death. I got to see him for the last time when I had a business meeting in Phoenix, Arizona, and had rented a car and drove out to see him the year before his death. He had gotten very thin and old for 70. We had a nice time together. When I hugged him and drove off, I was pretty sure that would be the last time I would see him. We stayed in touch by phone. In fact, the day he died I had called him and there was no answer. I had a strange feeling that something had happened.

While she had Alzheimer's, one night Mom was looking at the pictures of her sons. She said to me, "Was I married?" "Yes," I told her. "You were married to Herb Schriftman." She thought for a minute. "What happened to him?" (Yes, people with Alzheimer's can still reason at times.) "He died," I said. "But you had been divorced from him many years before he died." Then she asked, "Did I divorce him or did he divorce me?" "He divorced you, Mom," I answered. She thought for another minute. "I must have been upset!" she responded.

Mom and Herb holding Roy.

Roy and his new Dad, true love.

Mom, Herb and Roy.

Family expansion with baby Ross. Loch Raven apartments.

The Kitchen Table

In the 1960s at our home in Maple Glen, the kitchen table was a center for our family. Even though the kitchen was not very large, the six of us would sit around the table and have dinner together almost every evening. My mom's dinners included soup, a meat or fish, two vegetables (one usually being a starch such as potatoes or rice), and dessert.

The black and white television would be on during our meal. The TV was placed in the doorway between the kitchen and the dining room. Instead of some kind of entertainment shows, we would watch the evening news with Walter Cronkite.

Our dinner conversation included each of us telling about our day, whether it was about what we did at school, work or around the house. We would also talk about events that we would see on the TV news report.

I now look at that table and wonder how we all could sit comfortably around it. I eat breakfast at that same table sometimes with my dog Happy Girl watching me carefully and waiting for her sample of whatever I am eating. I eat dinner upstairs in the TV room. Though I enjoy eating as I watch one of the news channels and mull over the day's events in my mind, it would still be nice to talk with Mom and discuss the day's events. Of course that can't happen anymore.

I wonder how many families today still have the kitchen table ritual in their homes. This was the place our family came together almost every evening when my brothers and I were kids.

Politics, Me and Mom

My mother grew up during the Depression. Most of her family became big supporters of Franklin Roosevelt. Most of them were Democrats. During her childhood there were many discussions about politics.

Having been an employee of the State Department in Washington, D.C., during World War II, my mother came in contact with many of the people who were well known to Americans. She worked for Nelson Rockefeller in the Office of Inter-American Affairs. She met Eleanor Roosevelt. She helped edit Vice President Henry Wallace's book on job growth.

In the 1950s she was a huge fan of Adlai Stephenson who ran twice for President against Dwight Eisenhower. She was impressed with his intellect and would tell me stories about how he campaigned with a hole in his shoe, which had been worn out from all his campaigning.

By the time I was eight years old, I was aware of politics and John Kennedy was running for President. That Halloween my mom dressed me up in a costume consisting of a paper Mache hat setting on top of my head with a sheet over me. I had crutches and a sign that read, "It Doesn't Pay to Fight over Politics." My brother Roy was dressed as a ballot box. He and I had taken the Red Arrow train to Upper Darby and got posters at the Kennedy-Johnson Headquarters. The kids at school tore the posters off his ballot box. That was mostly because we lived in a Republican community in Springfield.

After Kennedy was elected, we stayed at home for the Inauguration of the President. We had egg salad sandwiches in our little white house while we watched on TV as the new President paraded down Pennsylvania Avenue to his White House. Later that year I would announce to my family that someday I would become the first Jewish President of our nation. I had decided at eight years old to become a politician.

My interest in politics continued and I did my first campaigning in 1965 handing out local Democratic campaign literature in Maple Glen. The local committeewoman was Elizabeth Larkin (Bogle). The Township Chair was Sue Felix. My district at the time was 7 to 1 Republican. There were maybe a dozen active Democratic workers in the whole township. There were Sue, Elizabeth, Del DiFeo, Catherine Barone, Tom and Janet Minehart and Kay and Chuck Mulvany. That was about it for campaign workers. Mom became Inspector of Elections which meant she helped people sign in at the polls in the big binder with all the voters' names.

The voting district consisted of one-quarter of the whole township. As I got older, Mom would drive me around the district and we would use flashlights to find the houses of Democrats. I would get out of the car when we found a house and encouraged the residents to come out and vote.

In 1968 I would walk the halls of Upper Dublin High School with a big Hubert Humphrey (HHH) for President button. I was very impressed with Humphrey who had been the hero of the 1948 Civil Rights Plank at the Democratic National Convention in Philadelphia. This, of course, was before my time, but I read all about his efforts and his style of campaigning, which was upbeat and hopeful.

Mom and I would go to all the local meetings. By 1970 we had both become very active. However, there were still few Democratic workers. One evening we went to Larry and Shirley Curry's home. Larry was a candidate for State Representative. There were candidates and workers from all over the area meeting for a planning session. The statewide Senate candidate, Bill Sessler from Erie, was there as well. He was running against Hugh Scott, the senior Senator. After a short period of time everyone realized that each worker in attendance had a voluntary position with each of the campaigns. Some people were doing six jobs, including their local committee post. It was a real fledgling organization.

In 1971 the Commonwealth of Pennsylvania enacted a law allowing 18-year-olds to vote. I was the first person under the age of 21 to register in the county at the Voter Registration Office at the County Annex in Norristown. That same year my brother Roy, who was studying for his master's degree in Education at Michigan State, ran for School Board. Roy loved the discussions with voters but hated walking the neighborhoods. We went out campaigning together. If he found a voter at home he would spend a half hour talking with them in their living room. We were not successful that year as we were still outnumbered three to one.

The next year there was a reapportionment of the township voting districts. Mom and I prepared a challenge and an alternative to the map to keep one community intact. I was successful in convincing the commissioners to alter their decision. Janet Minehart, whose husband Tom was a Chair of the State Democratic Committee at one time, told my mom that she was so impressed that she was recommending me to be a delegate candidate for the Hubert Humphrey Campaign for President in 1972.

Mom and I got to work going to all the meetings, knocking on doors and calling voters. During the Primary campaign in April, Muriel Humphrey, the wife of the candidate came to the Philadelphia area to campaign. My mom was recruited to be her driver since we had a long station wagon and there was room for her staff and local party leaders. Mom went all over the area one day driving to various meetings. I was out knocking on doors, so I was not with her for those events. She came home very excited about having the opportunity to go to all the events and spend a wonderful day with Muriel.

Despite our best efforts, we were out-campaigned by the McGovern supporters, many of which were young people who opposed the Viet Nam War and would not support Humphrey who was Lyndon Johnson's Vice President. In June I went to New Jersey for the day to help the Humphrey delegates/candidates in New Jersey. Although Humphrey did well in New Jersey, he lost in California to McGovern. California was a winner-take-all primary, meaning that whoever got the most votes won all of the delegates. The only hope now for Humphrey would be a challenge at the National Convention in Miami in August.

That summer I was working as a relief cook at Linton's Restaurants in Philadelphia. I went all over the city filling in for people on vacation or out sick. I would work the graveyard shift at 28th and Passyunk and then have to be back working at 3:00 p.m. the next afternoon and into the evening at the restaurant in Germantown. Even though I was a healthy 19-year-old, I was exhausted when August arrived. One day, I had had enough. I quit. I came home and when Mom arrived I said, "Let's go to Miami and go to the Convention." She was very happy and told her office the next day that she was going on vacation the next week.

We took my little 510 Datsun and headed for Florida. It took us two days of almost straight driving. As we approached Miami the radio was reporting that the Rules Committee had just determined that Humphrey's challenge to the California delegate seating had failed and that Humphrey was just about to make an announcement at his hotel headquarters. I pulled up to a parking spot along the street two blocks from the hotel and ran into the hotel lobby. Mom was following down the street. As I entered the lobby, supporters were coming out of the news conference crying. Humphrey had ended his campaign and thus ended his efforts to ever become president. The 1972 nominee would be George McGovern.

Now, here was Mom and me, 1,200 miles from home, ready to help convince delegates to vote for HHH and the plan was over. What do we do now? Obviously, we decided to stay. We met a delegate and his wife from Erie who arranged for us to get a room at a motel in North Miami Beach. We went to Wolfie's Rascal House Restaurant that night with this couple. Wolfie's was the place where Mom and Dad had had their first date so many years earlier. The restaurant was full of political types. We met a State Senator from Philadelphia who was there with his daughter. The more moderate Democrats we spoke with were disillusioned and concerned that the very liberal McGovern would hurt the party in the fall against the Republicans.

The second day of our trip to the Convention I got active with the Vice Presidential campaign of Endicott Peabody, the former Governor of Massachusetts. The convention was such an open event that at least a half dozen people were campaigning for Vice President. McGovern selected Tom Eagleton of Missouri but then pulled the plug on the VP candidate after the convention because of Eagleton's past history of mental illness. This further hurt McGovern's chances, and he got buried by Nixon in the fall. Today, few people would think that Eagleton's past history would be a scandal or a problem compared to the real scandals of infidelity, lying and corruption that occur frequently.

Mom was not only a supporter of my efforts in politics, but she also spoke out when she got the opportunity. She spoke in front of the Township Commissioners and successfully got the Township to petition the Commonwealth of Pennsylvania to install traffic lights at the intersection of Dillon Road, Limekiln Pike and Meeting House Road. This was a dangerous intersection with many accidents; some fatal. She was never afraid to speak out and express her views.

In 1973 Mom and I helped elect Walt Rosen to the School Board. Walt, who had a bipartisan group of supporters, was the first Democrat ever elected.

Right after the 1973 election I announced that I would run for State Representative in the 151st District. Some party leaders were skeptical of my candidacy as I was only 21 when I announced. The incumbent, Chuck Dager, decided to retire and so this became a race for an open seat. Two other Democrats got into the primary—State Committeewoman Margaret Geoghegan of Springfield and Ambler Councilman Charles Quinn. It would be a logistically difficult election since I was finishing my senior year at American University in Washington, D.C., that spring. Every weekend I would come home and my friends from the Young Democrats would help me canvass the district. Mom was right there pitching in as well. She made phone calls, knocked on doors and helped stuff envelopes.

My college graduation was three weeks before the primary. The School of Government and Public Administration held its graduation at Washington Hebrew Congregation, which had been my mom's synagogue when she lived with her parents in Washington. The commencement speaker was Lowell Weicker, the U.S. Senator for Connecticut. When my name was announced to receive my diploma, Mom jumped up and yelled, "Hurray for today and May 18th." May 18th was the primary election. Mom never got embarrassed about being up front.

I won the primary, garnering 47% of the vote in the three-way race. Our victory celebration took place at our home. It was very exciting for all of us. But, it was just the start.

In the fall I knocked on 11,000 doors introducing myself to voters. Mom and my brothers and Nan, Lee's future wife, and Tobey, Roy's wife, also knocked on doors, along with our other volunteers, including Jules and Ruth (Jules eventually would serve many years as a Township Commissioner and Chairman of the Board), Ruth's brothers and sisters, Ira Forstatter, Bruce Goldstein, Ken Ryesky and his brother Matt. Connie Layman who was my press assistant, Mary Brown of Horsham, Phoebe Driscoll of Lower Gwynedd and Marty Reddington and Dennis Dougherty of Abington, Colleen Alexander of Springfield, Jack Dean and Bob Russell of Ambler, Sue Felix, Kay and Chuck Mulavany and Del DiFeo of Upper Dublin and many other active Democrats. Our living room and family room served as the mail stuffing and sorting facility. The house phone was our campaign communications center. Hand-addressed envelopes with a rubber stamped listing the polling place location were used. We sorted by precincts first to get the right stamp on the envelope and then resorted by zip code to fulfill the bulk mailing requirement. In the end, the general election campaign cost $2,000, a lot of money in my view in 1974. Today, of course, legislative campaigns sometimes cost $1 million, which I think is a waste.

Election Day came. We did very well. As a Democrat in a district with only 28% Democratic registration, I got 46% of the vote. I lost 9,000 to 10,400. The Watergate scandal helped, but our message of open government and change resonated with voters, even with some more conservative ones. We were all disappointed, but I had achieved a remarkably high vote for a young politician. Mom was very proud of me. We needed a break and I needed a job.

In 1975, it was Mom's turn to run for office. She became the Democratic candidate for District Justice for Ambler and Upper Dublin. Many people will recognize this position as Justice of the Peace. It is the first place minor civil cases go to. It is also the place were people being charged for criminal offenses are arraigned. This would be a new experience for my mom, but she felt that if she were elected she would be fair judge. I teased her that after she got elected I would introduce her as "Here Comes Da' Judge" like they did on the "Flip Wilson" skit on the TV show, "Laugh In." Mom worked hard to learn everything she could about the law and if elected she would have gone through a training course. In the election she won in the Borough of Ambler and came close in Upper Dublin. She got 44% of the vote against the incumbent. Again, there was disappointment, but this time I got to be proud of her stepping up and taking on the challenge.

Although Mom did not win, we did have breakthrough success in 1975 with the election of Ed Heller and Norton Freedman to the Township Board of Commissioners. Interestingly, when they were installed the Republican leadership put them at each end of the board table like bookends. Ed said to Norton someday they would meet and shake hands in the middle. Ironically, the board now has six Democrats and only one Republican.

I would run again for State Representative in 1976. In the spring of that year, I walked to Harrisburg with a petition signed by voters encouraging more open government and the creation of district offices so that citizens could voice their concerns locally and get help with matters of state government. A gathering of volunteers were at our house to send me off. Others met me in Ambler including Councilman Jack Dean and his sister Florence Henderson (Assenheimer) and then at County Democratic Headquarters in Norristown. That evening I was one of two speakers at the Pottstown Young Democrat's Dinner. The other was Tony Campolo who was running for Congress in Chester County. Tony is a minister, a professor and a world renowned commentator on religion.

The next morning, I awoke to stiff legs. The rest of the trip was more challenging. Mom and Barry drove up to Reading to look for me, but I had taken a short-cut through Birdsboro and Shillington. Eventually, they found me. There was a Martin Luther King Celebration in Harrisburg and Colleen Alexander, Party Chair, had told my mom she thought it would be good for me to go. They could pick me up and then drop me back off wherever I stopped walking. That was on the Lebanon County/Berks County border. I have a memorable picture of C. Delores Tucker, the Secretary of the Commonwealth of Pennsylvania, fixing my hair, which had been blown all around my head from my travels across the state. Mom loved that picture. I now have it on my wall.

Again in 1976, we all worked very hard to achieve a victory. I had met Kass Fesi (Hermann) during the campaign and she was an expert at bulk mailing and handled preparation of the mailers which freed up more time for me to do the door to door campaigning. There was also Eileen McCaul who joined the campaign to help coordinate the effort. Jimmy Carter was running for President and Bill Green, former Mayor of Philadelphia, was running for the U.S. Senate. Carter won. Green lost to John Heinz. I lost to the incumbent, Vern Pyles. The vote was 12,400 to 13,800. I got 47% of the vote. It was another disappointment for me and my family. Although my friend Joe Hoeffel won in the next district over. However, Mom was always able to shrug it off and keep a happy spirit about her. She never dwelled on what might have been or blamed anyone. I guess I was the same way.

I had been selling insurance for the two years after the 1974 campaign and continued to do so. I also was hired as an Auditor in the Auditor General's Department. Money was now tight as the 1976 campaign cost $8,000 and contributions were only about $3,000. I had a loan to pay off, college loans and living expenses. I became a "work-a-holic". I would go to my job with the Commonwealth of Pennsylvania auditing the books at state institutions like Graterford, Byberry, Norristown, West Chester University and Cheyney University. In the evenings I would go out and sell insurance. After appointments, I would return to the insurance agency office of my friend Gary and complete the applications and other paperwork until midnight. I would then do the same thing the next day. Mom was very supportive but concerned about my health and my well being.

In 1979, I again ran for office. The Democratic candidate for Montgomery County Controller had dropped out of the race. I made the mistake of telling Colleen, the County Chair, that I would run if no one else stepped forward to fill the vacancy by the August deadline. I became the candidate. This would be a real shoestring campaign. I spent $400 mainly on printing handouts. Marie Romanick, the Clerk of Courts candidate and a friend of mine, would go to the community college and do voter registration with me. We would hand out our literature. We went to every event we could throughout the county. If any handout cards left on the table still remained in useful condition, we would pick them up on the way out and use them at the next event. On Election Day I got 42,000 votes. My opponent Bob Godshall got 83,000. Bob is now a State Legislator and has been since 1980. As always, Mom was right there throughout the campaign pitching in, going to events and talking with voters.

Recently, I found a letter from Walter Mondale to my mom. Mondale had run against Ronald Reagan and had lost badly in 1984. The former Vice President had not only written to my mother in response to a letter she, sent but he took the time to write a note on the letter. She had reminded him of their common background, which he appreciated.

Here is the letter. I have not found the letter my mother had written to him.

Mondale Letter

WALTER F. MONDALE
50 SOUTH SIXTH STREET
SUITE 1500
MINNEAPOLIS, MN 55402
(612) 340-6307

November 22, 2002

Ms. Shirley R. Schriftman
1576 Dillon Road
Maple Glen, PA 19002

Dear ~~Ms. Schriftman~~ Shirley:

I am sorry that I am so late in responding to your wonderful message. Joan and I were blessed with ten wonderful days to make our case for justice and decency. We have no regrets. Thousands of people worked for us and inspired us every minute of the way.

We are truly grateful for your kindness.

Sincerely,

Walter F. Mondale

Thanks for your letter that reminded me of so much of our common history.

Politics became my excuse not to do projects around the house that Mom would constantly come up with. "When are you going to XXX?" she would ask. "After the next election" would be my response. This became our little joke back and forth over the years.

In January of 1993, Mom and I went to Washington for Bill Clinton's first inauguration. We stood at the corner of 12th and Pennsylvania Avenue for hours in the cold just to see the motorcade go by. Mom was never one to complain about cold weather so long as she was having a good time. She talked to everyone who was standing around us. We stayed with Gloria and George that evening and drove home the next day.

After 1979 there was a long period that Mom and I helped all sorts of campaigns, but I was not a candidate again until 2004 when I ran for State Representative. By this time Mom couldn't campaign the way she had for so many years. At the kick-off fund raiser we held for my campaign, I introduced Mom as my producer. She had a broad smile on her face. The picture on the cover of this book is from that campaign. It was used on the campaign literature. Mom was already 79 years old, but some people who didn't know us thought she might be my wife. She did look young for her age. Little did either of us know that within a very short period of a few more years, illness would change both of us so much.

Local Democrats.

Getting Ready

Kay Mulvany, Ross Schriftman, Shirley Schriftman, Ted Weathers and Marie Zaengle of the 151st Democratic Committee look over some of the political campaign memorabilia to be displayed at the Annual Winter Social to be held Sunday, 4 to 7 p.m., at the Woods Clubhouse, Butler Pike, Ambler.

I was not successful in 2004 even though I knocked on 19,000 doors. The Republicans had selected Sue Cornell, the daughter of long-time representative Roy Cornell. He had died on New Year's Day 2004, and there was a special election only a few weeks later. Roy was very popular and well known among voters, and Sue benefited from a strong Republican organization. Hardly anyone came out to vote in the Special Election, and I received only 29% of the vote. It was very frustrating. The rest of the year our campaign was pure retail. Door-knocking was the only way we could try to break through. In the end I received 43% of the vote (13,000 to 17,000). Even though Mom was much older now she still knocked on neighbors' doors to support my candidacy and proudly wore the campaign sticker on her clothes when she went out. Neither of us "seasoned veterans" was disappointed this time.

In 2006 I briefly became a candidate, but I had not intended on running and the party leaders had already lined up another candidate. After his endorsement by the committee people, I bowed out and helped the campaigns as usual.

Then on the Saturday before the election, Mom and I, along with 1,200 other Democrats, packed into the Keswick Theatre in Glenside for a get-out-the-vote election-day rally. Coming to support Ed Rendell for re-election as Governor and Bob Casey Jr., who was running for U.S. Senate, was the U.S. House Minority Leader, Nancy Pelosi, and the Junior Senator from Illinois, Barack Obama. After the rally Mom and I went to dinner at the Chinese restaurant next door to the theatre. She said to me, "Barack Obama will be the next President of the United States." "Mom, he just got elected to the Senate," I explained. "I think he probably won't run next time. He is too new to national politics." "Oh no," my mother accurately predicted. "He will be our next President." She called the election of 2008 before anyone I know. (Personally, I believe the Democratic Party leadership has made a sharp left turn and is not confronting runaway government spending.)

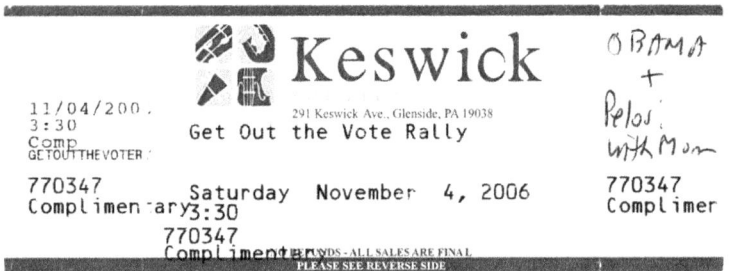

In the 2006 election Rick Taylor won the election for the 151st Legislative District, which was the old seat I ran for in the 1974 and 1976 elections. His campaign arranged a bus trip to Harrisburg for his inauguration. I took Mom with me to witness this event. She was already having some problems with memory and reasoning. I had to watch her while we were in the State Capital so she wouldn't get lost. She was sitting in Rick's office next to Rick's mother. Somehow during the event my mom put her false teeth in Mrs. Taylor's pocketbook. Rick's mother also was having some dementia issues. Mom told me later, "That lady was wifty. She didn't know what she was doing." It took a little while to get my mom's teeth back as Rick had to explain to his mother what was in her pocketbook.

The next year was the County Commissioner election. Mom still wanted to help the campaigns, but she was already developing dementia. In the fall of 2007 she still went to a public forum that was held at Temple Sinai, the synagogue down the street from our house. She sat quietly and listened to the candidates and the questions.

The day before we got a caregiver, I took her to the Ambler Train Station early in the morning to campaign for Joe Hoeffel and Ruth Damsker, the Democratic candidates for County Commissioner. Both of them knew Mom well. Joe had been to my house many times during the Young Democrats days. Ruth was the Honorary Chair for my 2004 State Representative Campaign.

While Joe, Ruth and I were talking to voters about their campaign, Mom sat on a bench. When the first train arrived Mom got up and started walking with the other commuters to get on the train. Just in time I reached her and said, "No, Mom, we aren't going on the train." Joe and I thought it could have been a real problem if she had gotten on and disappeared down the tracks headed to Philadelphia on the train.

This was Mom's last campaign day. On Election Day in 2007 she missed her first vote in her entire life as she was in the Abington Hospital psychiatric ward for striking a caregiver the day before the election. It was a tough way for me to see her involvement end, although in January of 2008 I took Mom and Nora, Mom's caregiver, to a model Presidential caucus held by the local Democrats, and she got to sit and see what was going on. In August 2008 Nora and I still took her to the local party's picnic down the street in the park. We kept feeding her so she wouldn't get up and interrupt the speakers.

Politics had been so much a part of her life, from her early childhood right up until the year before her death. Her last patriotic date was July 4, 2009, at the Oreland Parade. That would be the last time Mom ever came downstairs in her home.

Going to the Races

Walking is like talking. Running is like singing. For me flying down a road is like singing a beautiful song. Running races has been one of my joys throughout my life as far back as my childhood. Mom was my biggest fan and supporter. Over the years she had gone to dozens of races to watch me. She was my driver and my assistant, handing me water or tissues by the side of many roads in many races. After marathons I would lie down in the back of the station wagon with the seats down and sleep as Mom drove me home.

Today, running has become a very common activity for millions of people. Back when I started running, there were few of us doing it. In 1962 there was a film entitled "The Loneliness of the Long-Distance Runner." Nearly 50 years since, one of the more recent Philadelphia Broad Street Run events boasted having more than 30,000 participants.

My first recollection of running was actually with my mother chasing me. I don't know what I had done wrong, but my mother kept saying, "If you don't stop, I am going to pull your pants down and spank you in front of your friends." We were living in Springfield, Delaware County, and I was probably five or six at the time. The house was on the corner of Powell Avenue and Lynbrook Road. Mom ended up chasing me all around the block. She was boiling mad. Yes, she did spank me in front of my friends right next to the little log cabin my parents set up in the backyard for us boys to play in. I was more embarrassed than hurt. Mom's idea of spanking was one *Patchka un Tuchus*, a Yiddish term translated to mean "pat on the butt."

As a child I was always active. I never sat still. Another Yiddish term, *Schpeilkiss*, (ants in the pants) describes the way I acted then and probably still do. I don't sit around for long, even today. When I do it is usually in my recliner in front of the TV before bed and half the time I fall asleep.

My childhood was filled with biking to the firehouse four blocks from our house when the fire alarm went off, to see a posting of where the fire was and biking to see the fire, playing baseball with the Springfield Athletic League, playing basketball, or going swimming.

By the time I was in sixth grade and we had moved to Whitpain Township near Ambler, I had gotten into running around the block. Mom had told me stories of her childhood in Brookline, Massachusetts, of how her father would put her on his shoulders at Coolidge Corner to watch the Boston Marathoners run by. The Marathon was a big event in Boston. It was held on Patriot's Day, a Monday state holiday commemorating the start of the American Revolution in 1775. The event used to be called Bunker Hill Day. Bostonians were big sports fans. They were fascinated with the athletes who could actually run 26.2 miles without a break. Coolidge Corner was and still is denoted as Mile 24.

One day my sixth grade teacher decided to punish the entire class for an offense, the nature of which I don't remember. She made everyone run the perimeter of the playground three times. After the third time around I decided to keep going. My classmates were angry with me and some of the boys tried to stop me. I just loved to run and didn't want to stop. For me, running was not punishment at all.

The next year we moved to Maple Glen in Upper Dublin Township. I was now in junior high, which started with seventh grade. I played football in the fall since there were no running sports in junior high during the autumn. I was not a great player as I was only 4 foot, 7 inches and weighed a slight 75 pounds. I was on the 115-pound team, which was for kids weighing less than that. I was given the position of third-string linebacker. I never got to play in a real game, only in scrimmages. With my speed, I could cut off a runner and be lucky to tackle him by getting in the way so that he would trip over me. In the spring I would run track, usually the two-mile. Mom would come out to watch whenever she could. Dad was working in Northern New Jersey, and he usually drove the car to work, so sometimes my mother would walk the two miles to the high school to watch me run. Mom never thought about the distance. It was her son, and she wanted to be there in support.

    By the time I entered high school I had not grown that much. However, now I could run cross-country. The courses were usually in the ball fields behind the high school. The distances were between two and three miles. Endurance as well as speed was now essential. In the spring I was a two-miler for the track team. Even though football would draw large crowds to watch, each year there would be one early evening track meet where many parents and supporters would come out to watch. In my senior year Mom and Dad watched me run a 10:36 in the two-mile against Upper Moreland. I believe I took third place, which gave Upper Dublin some points. We won that meet.

    My final track meet in high school was against Methacton. The coach dropped me down to the mile run, with only four times around the track versus eight times. I won in a time of 4:54. Today at age 58 that is a personal achievement I will never see again. Since Methacton was about 15 miles away, Mom didn't travel to watch me run. When I came home I got a big hug. She was as excited about my winning as I was.

During the summer after graduation in 1970, I finally started growing to my current height of six feet. I worked that summer at College Settlement Farm Camp helping in the kitchen. This is a getaway camp for inner-city youth coming out to the "country" in Horsham, Pennsylvania. Interestingly, today the camp is surrounded by large developments of homes and office complexes but it still has its original streams and wooded areas. I would run to work from the house and be there all day for breakfast, lunch and dinner. Then I would run home in the evening. If it was early enough there would usually be a note on the table from Mom: "I am at the pool. Please come over and join me." Sometimes I would swim with her at the community pool three doors from our house. Sometimes I would just watch her swim laps back and forth. At age 45, she was not very fast in the water, but she would slowly swim lap after lap. On occasion she would stop swimming if she saw a neighbor in the pool and would chat with them for awhile before she resumed her swim.

After she was done and dried off we would walk together back to the house through the two backyards between our residence and the pool. We would talk about our day. We would join my brothers and we would have ice cream, watch TV, and enjoy each other's company.

In the fall of 1970 I entered Montgomery County Community College. I continued running cross-country. I also ran my first marathon in November of 1970. It was the first Philadelphia Marathon. The circuit started in front of "Boathouse Row" on East River Drive (now Kelly Drive). It continued on the lawn up the steps from behind the Art Museum. It then circled the building on the road at the top. We would then return down the hill and then up East River Drive to Falls Avenue. The course crossed the bridge and went down West River Drive (now Martin Luther King Boulevard) for about 200 yards. Runners then turned around and ran back down East River Drive to Boat House Row. We did this three times to complete the full 26.2-mile distance.

Mom was very concerned about my health since I was on a bland diet for a peptic ulcer. The ulcer was probably caused by internalizing the rocky time my parents were having in their relationship. Dr. Robert Yost, our family doctor who epitomized Dr. Welby from the television series, told me and Mom that running would not be a problem for my ulcer. In fact, the exercise and activity may be good for relieving stress. (Even today, I believe that to be true.) Mom and my brothers Barry and Lee came along to watch the race. There may have been 25 or 30 other family members watching the 60 or so runners venturing out to do this crazy thing called running a marathon. (What a difference running is today. In 2007 I tried to enter the Philadelphia Marathon before the deadline, but got an e-mail message that the race was "full." There are now about 20,000 people entering the Philadelphia Marathon.)

After the first lap I looked pretty good. However, at the second lap, Mom said later that I looked tired. She was very concerned, but I plodded along. One of my fellow runners from community college gave me a pat on the butt as I went by and yelled encouragement. By the time I got to the Falls Avenue Bridge at Mile 22 my legs felt like iron blocks. I had never experienced this kind of feeling, but it is common in running when the tightness and cramps start to set in. On the way back I stretched at a tree around the Hunting Park Avenue exit. Three more miles felt like 20. Despite the tightness I finished with a time of 3:24. I had done my first Marathon. Mom looked relieved. I lay down on the ground for about 30 minutes and then we went up to the second floor of the University of Pennsylvania Boat Club for donuts and coffee. They handed out the awards while we all sat on the floor (yes, all of us, the entire group of runners and their fans). Stiffly I got back downstairs, lay down in the back of our Ford station wagon and fell asleep. Mom drove us home. I got into bed and stayed there until the next morning.

In the spring of 1971, I went to Massachusetts to run my first Boston Marathon. Mom had to work. I found another runner who was going, and we shared a room in downtown Boston. Aunt Bettie, who was living alone in the Winchester Street house, came to Coolidge Corner to watch me. As I strode by I stopped and gave her a hug. In true Boston sports fan tradition, she yelled at me, "Keep going. Keep going!" There were 887 entrants and I finished in 333rd place with a time of 3:07:55. (Now the race attracts tens of thousands of runners and only the elite finish in the top 500.) That night the other runner drove us all the way back to Philadelphia. Awaiting my arrival, Mom was still up at 2:00 a.m. when I came home. She was thrilled that I had done so well.

In 1977 I broke three hours in the Philadelphia Marathon running 2:58 on the same three-loop course. Mom and Barry came down to watch me, but I was dating a girl named Ruth who had an apartment along the Ben Franklin Parkway. I stayed at her place that night. Mom was disappointed that I didn't come home with her after she had come down to watch, but she did understand.

I made it up to her when both of us went up to the Boston Marathon in 1978. We stayed at Aunt Bettie's house. I decided to run to get the bus, which was almost three miles from the house. In this race I ran my personal lifetime best of 2:57. I finished 1,800 out of 4,000. It was remarkable how marathoning had progressed in such a short time. In 1970 male runners were even signing petitions to allow women to enter the race. Today, running is a universally accepted sport for everyone.

The 1978 race was my most memorable. All the way from Hopkinton to Heartbreak Hill in the hills of Newton I kept up a steady pace. There was no pain, no fatigue and no stiffness. I ran up the hills with little effort and then down the other side past Boston College through Cleveland Circle and Coolidge Corner. The CITGO sign was in front of me. I passed Fenway Park and along the river, turned the corner and charged down to the finish line as fast as I could run. I couldn't wait to see Mom and Bettie. They had decided to watch near the finish line, which is difficult because of the crowds. Bettie had on her coat which Mom said was flapping in the wind as they ran down the street to find me after I finished. The three of us were so excited.

We took the trolley back to Coolidge Corner and walked up Winchester Street to that two-story house where Mom grew up. After a hot bath and something to eat we said good-bye to Bettie and headed home. As soon as we got on the Massachusetts Turnpike my car got a flat tire. I changed the tire and then drove home in six hours. I guess when you are 25 years old you can do just about everything. Today when I run a marathon in another city I usually stay overnight after the run just to rest up before I drive home.

Over the years since Boston 1978, Mom and I would go to many races together. There was the New York Marathon with its international flavor. We would stay at my Aunt Bea and Uncle Paul's house in Brooklyn. We would get up very early in the morning, drive into Manhattan, park on a side street and I would get the bus to the runner's camp at Fort Lee next to the Verrazano Narrow's Bridge. Mom would sit for hours in the lobby of a hotel next to Central Park waiting for the runners who would be arriving at the finish line in the mid afternoon. Don't worry about Mom, though; she would have had dozens of conversations with complete strangers in that lobby and the hours would fly by for her.

One year, the temperature was unusually warm for early November. By the time I entered Central Park at Mile 22 my electrolyte count must have dropped off a cliff, despite having consumed lots of fluids along the way. As I came by Mom just before the turn at the end of Central Park, all my leg muscles cramped up at once. I was glued to the pavement. It took several minutes to get my legs to loosen up enough to finish the run. It would take another hour before we would find each other after the runners were crammed through a chute to leave the running area. I struggled back to the car, and we drove back to Bea and Paul's. Throughout, I constantly had to use the bathroom because I was so nauseous. Heaving with my head over the toilet sounded like I was dying. Paul said to Mom, "Why do you make him run." She said, "I don't make him run. It is something he likes to do." Mom never told any of her children what they should do or who they should become. She was simply supportive of whatever we wanted to do so long as we tried our best. She never was concerned about whether we came in first. She was more interested in whether we had a good time and that what we did was rewarding to us and to others.

For several years there was no longer a Philadelphia Marathon. Then for a while there was a "point-to-point" run that would go from Temple University's Ambler Campus to Independence Mall in Philadelphia. It was appropriately called the Independence Marathon. It was very convenient for me as the start was just one mile from our house. In fact, in the summer of 1969 (yes, like the song), I was the "pots and pans" man in the dining room when they had all the music students in for a summer semester. I used to run to work every day that summer.

Mom would drive the car to Fort Washington Avenue to watch me run by at the beginning of the race. One year, I decided to toss my runner's hat off after only running a half mile. Here is a picture of me yelling to Mom to go back and get my hat while all the other runners are looking forward and sprinting down Fort Washington Avenue. Mom snapped this wonderful shot. With wit and sarcasm she wrote, "Rossy Bossy, Speaking!…at Philadelphia Marathon."

She then got in the car and drove to Stenton Avenue in Whitemarsh to see me run by. She then drove down to Chestnut Hill to the top of our climb at Mile 13. She then drove to Independence Mall, parked the car and waited for me to finish. The runners went into the Bourse Building across from Independence Hall to recover from the race. The place looked like the Atlanta scene in *Gone with the Wind* when the Confederate troops injured in the fighting were all lying around. People were moaning and groaning. After my recovery, Mom drove me home as she had always done.

There were many Broad Street Runs that Mom would take me to. She would drive to Broad and Olney which is right before the start. She would then drive down to the southern part of Philadelphia to JFK Stadium to watch me finish. Sometimes I would get there before her. She was afraid to drive on the Schuylkill Expressway, so she tried to work her way from north to south through the city. The problem is that many roads don't cut through. One year I ran this 10-mile race in 61 minutes. Today I am happy when I break 70 minutes.

Mom and I also would go to Washington for the Marine Corps Marathon. We stayed with my Cousin Lisa and Mom and I would drive down to Arlington. She would stand on the side of the road and watch at the start, at the seven-mile point and at the finish. She only did this the first time I ran this race. Standing at the races had already become difficult for her in the 1990's, so she would go with me and stay with Lisa and see me after the run.

Another year, Mom and I went to Boston and we stayed at a motel along the route in Brookline. Her cousin Lydia came to watch the race with her and we went to dinner the night before with Nan's cousin Sam. We really enjoyed this trip as it was a chance to see family and to have a first-row seat for Mom near Mile 24.

After running for State Representative in 2004 and knocking on 19,000 doors in the campaign, I qualified for the Boston Marathon by completing the Philadelphia Marathon that November. My time was 3:32. I had to complete the course under 3:35 for my age group. My brother Lee came down to encourage me and we decided to take Mom to Boston the next spring for the marathon.

In April of 2005 Mom was still in fairly good health both physically and mentally. The weather on race day turned out to be warm and I struggled after the halfway point in Wellesley. Just past the sign that reads, "Welcome to Brookline," I found a medical tent. I felt like I was dying. My chest was tight and I felt like I was exploding. My hands were tingling and red. It turned out that I was merely having a panic attack from fear of leg cramps that I experience many times in the past after I have finished. Mom and Lee had seen me run by in Natick at Mile 10. We were supposed to see each other again at the top of Heartbreak Hill at Mile 20, but we never connected. It was hours later that the hospital emergency room personnel let me use a cell phone to call Lee. Mom was relieved that I was O.K. This would be her last Boston Marathon.

In 1978 I discovered Sea Isle City, New Jersey, as a great shore town. One of the employees at the Woodhaven Center in Northeast Philadelphia had a brother who was an amateur impersonator. I was an auditor for the Commonwealth of Pennsylvania and she told me about the event. He was in a contest at the Ocean Drive Hotel and Bar (the O.D. as they call it). I went down to watch him perform. That is when I saw a flyer for the Island Run, a half-marathon race in August of each year. (It is now a 10-mile run.) The race starts on the Promenade, runs north to the end of the walkway and onto the beach. There is a turn-around and you run back down the Promenade past all the spectators and then down on the beach again to the inlet across from Avalon. It then turns around and returns to the starting point. It is a great race for runners' families to see the start, the middle and the finish. After the first year I ran it, Mom would go most years until the last time, which was 2007. On several occasions, we took Mom's friend Gladys who was deaf and blind. Gladys loved the trip because she could smell the ocean and feel the breeze, and she was with her friend Shirley and me.

One year Mom got a little extra entertainment while waiting for the start of the race. She got to see two streakers come out of the Springfield Hotel, run down the Promenade and back into the bar. She was not embarrassed at all. For a long time after the incident, she would tell everyone the story of the streakers.

Another year, we had decided to visit Aunt Bettie in Boston after the run. I figured we would drive up the New Jersey coast for a while after the race and stay in a motel to be closer to Boston rather driving back to Philadelphia right away. The problem was that everything was booked on a nice summer weekend. At 3:00 in the morning we finally found a place in Red Bank, New Jersey, just south of New York. We were both exhausted.

Many times my brother Lee would also run the race in Sea Isle City. I didn't even know he had taken up running until one time Mom and I were sitting on the benches in front of the Springfield Hotel waiting for the race to start and Lee came over. It was nice having him share running with Mom and me. This little trip became a tradition for Mom and me. We would leave around noon and get down to Sea Isle around 3:00 p.m. on the Saturday of the run. The race would start at 5:30. Mom would cheer me on and wave at the start. At the halfway point I would give her a hug. Afterwards we would go out to dinner. We usually would go for seafood. Then I would drive back to Philadelphia.

The last time I took Mom to Sea Isle City was August of 2007. I was concerned that there may be a problem leaving her alone while I ran. The year before she had argued with me and didn't stay where I told her to in order to pick her up with the car after the race. This last trip she was less mobile and I figured she would stay on the bench to watch as always. I gave her a hug at the halfway point. However, when I finished she was no longer on the bench. I asked people if they had seen a lady with white hair. No one had. Before I could panic, I heard my name announced by the person at the awards platform one block away at the Beach Patrol. There was Mom. "I couldn't find you. Where did you go?" she asked. "I was still running the race," I told her. Mom was beginning her frantic panic attacks whenever I wasn't right there with her.

As was our tradition I had planned on having dinner before we headed home. One of the couples from the Ambler Running Club had a summer home at the shore. Everyone from the club had been invited over after the race. However, Mom wouldn't get out of the car to come inside. She just wanted to get home to the animals. I went upstairs for a short while, had a beer, and then came back downstairs. We drove back home and ate a very late dinner.

On New Year's Day while other people slept in, Mom and I would get up early in the morning and take our dog K.C. to Carpenter Park in Horsham. I would run a 5K sponsored by the Hatboro YMCA. Mom would be bundled up in a coat and so would K.C., but Mom would be game to be there and cheer on the runners. She would also enjoy talking with the other spectators.

K.C. howls on New Year's Day. Carpenter's Park, Horsham.

    Sea Isle City 2007 would be Shirley's last race to watch me run. However, I continued to take her to the Ambler Running Club's activities such as meetings and wine-and-cheese events in the lobby of the Ambler Theatre. "I like those people. Everyone is so friendly," she would tell me. During one wine-and-cheese event, a young couple brought their baby. Mom was still walking. She went over and asked them, "What is the baby's name?" The mother said, "His name is Mitchell." For the rest of the evening my mom walked around telling everyone, "The baby's name is Mitchell." Everyone smiled. Here is a picture of Mom and me at one of these events in 2007.

    The morning of her death, I was preparing to leave for Scranton to run the Steamtown Marathon. Mom had seemed comfortable and calm but weak the last couple days, so I wasn't expecting the end to be so soon. Maybe she knew I would be away the next day and decided this was the time to pass from this world. If she had died the next morning, I would have been out of touch for at least five hours and in no condition to jump in my car and drive the two hours trip back home. Two years before her death, she wanted so badly to go with me to Scranton. Obviously there would have been no way for an aide to control her for hours during the run as well as the difficulty of staying with her in a hotel. Mom was out of control. She was very angry with me for going to the Marathon without her. "I have always gone with you. You have no right not to take me," she said. I made it up to her by taking her to breakfast at Lancer's Diner in Horsham the Monday morning I returned. It was my birthday and she was happy to be with me. We went to my office for a while after breakfast and she forgot about being left behind on my trip to the marathon.

  The year before her death, she had less awareness and I didn't even tell her I was going to Scranton. As I was leaving to go, I heard her calling out my name. Tata, who was filling in for Nora who was on a break that weekend, was a big woman with a big smile. I was in the laundry room. I heard my mom say, "Ross, where are you?" Tata then said, "Shirley, can you help me fold this sheet?" "O.K., here I come." Tata had smartly distracted Mom. I could now safely leave. During that race, I was more relaxed than the previous year concerning Mom's condition. However, leg cramps were a difficulty from Mile 22 to Mile 24 and I dropped out at 24.5 miles, just a mile and half from the finish. That is the closest to the finish I ever dropped out. I didn't want to get sick or injured, as my primary job then was caregiver. Now I can run any race or participate in any event without having to worry about what I would do if I could not physically help Mom. I can run Antarctica (which I used to tease her about doing) or Kilimanjaro or anywhere. Mom no longer needs my help. But I am grateful for all the races she shared with me as my biggest fan and supporter. I will continue to run races in her memory and will always think of her when I am running those contests she shared with me over the years.

  This past August we sponsored the first Shirley's Run and Dog Walk in honor of her memory. A special website is devoted to our efforts: (www.shirleysrun.org).

Ama

Shirley Schriftman loved her grandchildren. She wanted to be with them and help as much as possible. She was very proud of her grandchildren and their accomplishments. Sometimes she would travel long distances to be with them and to share in their joys and their life events.

My mother was called Ama by her grandchildren. How did she get the name Ama and not Grandma, Bubby or Mom Mom? It started with her first grandchild, Deena. Deena was a very smart little girl and talked early. She couldn't say Grandma, so my mother became Ama. The name stuck when everyone in the family would refer to her as Ama when mentioning her to the grandchildren.

Deena was the first child of Roy and Tobey. After Deena was born, Mom would babysit a lot. Tobey had a rough time physically and Mom was more than happy to help. She loved Deena so much and wrote to her own Aunt Bettie about how smart, sweet and cute this new baby was. Mom liked to make what we fondly termed as "fish face," which involved turning her lips together. She made the "fish face" especially for Deena, which would make the child laugh. (There were many letters that had devoted entire sections to describing Mom's interactions with Deena. Excerpts appear in the chapter titled Letters to Aunt Bettie.) Deena was a very smart young girl. She is now a wonderful mother of two children with her loving husband Dan.

Roy and Tobey had a second child, a son they named Micah. Mom now had two children to babysit. Deena, as big sister, would help Mom take care of her baby brother when their parents were away. Micah grew quickly. He is now a tall and friendly young man, just like his Dad was.

Lee and Nan named their first child Seth. Then they had Daniel. Mom loved going over and sitting for them.

They both were very smart. Seth is now a lawyer and Daniel works for Lee in his dental practice. Then along came Ilana, Lee and Nan's third child. Ilana had no inhibitions about entertaining. At five years old she got up in front of the entire Seder at Temple Sinai and sang a Passover song all by herself. My Mom *kvelled* (a Yiddish word for a parent or grandparent's joy at the talents of their child or grandchild). As a young lady, Ilana with a beautiful singing voice, would perform in high school plays. She landed the leading role in *The Fantastics* at the Jewish Y in Northeast Philadelphia. Shirley Schriftman and the entire family were overjoyed with her singing, her stage presence and her acting talents. Ilana is now working in a post-graduate program in the field of psychiatry.

When Roy married Lera he embraced her son Sasha as well. Eventually Roy adopted Sasha, who was seven when he came with his mother from Sevastopol in the Ukraine. My mother, Shirley, would go over and play with Sasha whenever she could, even though she was much older by then. My mother enjoyed watching Micah and his new younger brother play video games.

Mom took special joy in each family event. Volumes of pictures show her dancing with Daniel at his Bar Mitzvah. There are wonderful memories of her at Seth and Ashley's wedding in Chicago and Daniel's destination wedding in South Beach, Miami, Florida. When Deena and Dan were married in the Allegheny Courthouse, Roy took Mom to this special event. Mother would later tell me how a man was sitting next to her in the courthouse before the wedding ceremony. Mom said this man was waiting to be arraigned for a crime (as Mom told it). When he began to cry about how wonderful it was that Deena and Dan were getting married, Mom put her arm around his shoulder and told him everything would be O.K.

My Mother would travel to Texas and Virginia when Lee was in the Air Force dental program. After the Texas trip, Mom would laugh about how Seth and Daniel were picking up Texas accents. They would ask Nan in a semi-drawl, "Ma'am. I'd like some Meeilk."

Thanksgiving at Deena and Dan's in Pittsburgh with Dan's parents would become a tradition in later years. Mom and I would get up early on Thanksgiving Day and drive to their home on the North Shore of the city. It is a long trip, taking five to six hours with stops, but it was something my mother enjoyed immensely. We would have a wonderful dinner and travel back to Philadelphia the next day.

It even got better when Deena had her first child, Owen. Now Mom was a great grandmother. She joked, "I always knew I was great; now it's official." Owen was born when Lee and Mom accompanied me when I ran the Boston Marathon in 2005. Two years later when Mom had already developed mild dementia, Deena had planned a birthday party for Owen to be held on a Sunday morning late in April. Mom was very excited about going. Unfortunately there was a freak mid-spring storm. At 3:30 a.m. that Sunday morning I got up to check the weather map on the computer and to see if Mom was awake yet so that we could get ready to go. To my surprise, she was already fully dressed sitting in the TV room waiting for me. She really wanted to go. When I looked at the map, the entire state was pink and white meaning the roads were covered in ice and snow. Consequently, it would be far too difficult and treacherous for her to travel across the state. If the roads were closed, or if we had trouble with the car and got stuck a blizzard, the highway would be no place to be with an elderly person with dementia. Although Mom was disappointed, we called Deena later in the morning and mailed them Owen's gifts. Sadly, this would have been her last trip to Pittsburgh, a trip that my mother did not make.

There would be three more great grandchildren. Seth and Ashley had Noah. Daniel and Erin had Zachary, and Deena had another child, Elaine. Mom got to meet Elaine at her last Mother's Day celebration at Barry's house in 2009. Although she was agitated that day saying things like, "I hate your guts" and "You're a nut!" when Deena brought Elaine to Mom, who was in her wheelchair, and showed off Elaine to Mom, my mother blew a kiss to her new great granddaughter. Soon after Nora and I laid Mom down on Barry's sofa, and she fell asleep until it was time to go home. She had one more Mother's Day similar to the kinds we had when my brothers and I were children. Almost everyone was together again. I think it was the last time. Soon after that Roy's illness got worse and Mom could no longer travel.

Shirley Schriftman was a blessing. Her grandchildren and great grandchildren are a blessing to her memory. She will always be Ama.

Deena visits Ama.

Deena's Bat Mitzvah.

Deena's and Dan's wedding at Allegheny Courthouse.

Ilana's 5th birthday with Seth and Daniel.

Mom, Micah, Deena and Bettie.

My Mother's Wise Advice

My mother was one of the wisest people I ever met. Many of the suggestions she made to me have been useful throughout my life. One of her favorite little books she read to us when we were children was *The Little Engine That Could*. It was a very simple story about a steam engine trying to pull a train up a mountain track. "I think I can. I think I can. I think I can," said the engine as it worked its way up the mountain. Mom taught her children to think they could do something and keep trying. "So long as you try your best" is what she used to say. Persistence toward a worthwhile goal is a virtue. I think I have that virtue and have always taken each difficult step along the way toward some goal in my life. Thanks, Mom.

When I was in high school, Mom suggested I take a typing course. "You never know when you will need to type," she said. I was the only boy in the "Home Economics" typing course with Mrs. Basenberg (may she rest in peace). I learned to type 70 words a minute and that was many years before word processors. I learned to type on one of those old manual typewriters that you bang away at. Who knew that 40 years later I would be writing a book about Mom using my own typing skills? Thanks Mom.

When I was at American University I was able to get a job in the office of Senator Alan Cranston from California. It was a typing job in the basement of the Russell Building which used to be named the Old Senate Office Building. It was affectionately called the "Old SOB." I worked from 5:00 p.m. to 10:00 p.m. four days a week. I got the job because it was hard to find women willing to work up on the Hill in the evenings and have to walk home or back to their cars at night. (This was before the Metro was built.) I could type while few men could. The job helped me pay for tuition. Thanks, Mom.

Mom taught me not to insult people and to think before you say something that you might not even think would be hurtful. When I was about six we were riding the trolley from Springfield to Upper Darby. As we came near a station the driver shouted out, "Next stop, Drexel Hill." "Mommy, he said drecky hill!" I yelled out. (*Dreck* in Yiddish means shit.) My mother quietly took my hand and put her mouth to my ear. "Don't say that," she told me. "People live here and you're insulting them." I always remembered that lesson and tried not to say something without thinking what the reactions would be first. Thanks, Mom.

Mom could act in a crisis, too. When I was about seven, Mom decided to take her sons for clothes shopping in downtown Philadelphia. I didn't like these trips because it meant standing in a department store where there was no place to sit down and waiting for my brothers to try on clothes. It was boring and tiring. (I still hate buying clothes.) The trip would involve taking the Red Arrow trolley car from Saxer Avenue in Springfield to the 69th Street Terminal and then transferring to the Subway for the trip to Center City. This one time as we went down the stairs and Lee and I got on the subway car, Mom with Roy beside her was moving slower than the rest of us. She was early in her pregnancy with my Brother Barry, and Roy was helping her down the stairs. Suddenly the doors of the subway closed and the train started pulling out of the station with Lee and me on it and Mom and Roy outside on the platform. With a panicky look on her face, Mom kept her presence of mind and yelled to us. "Get off at the next station and wait!" The next station was Melbourne. We got off and waited for the next train. After 10 minutes it approached. Mom was in the front with the engineer. She was waving to us. She had commandeered the train. "Get on the first car!" she yelled out the window as the front of the train roared past us and then stopped. We ran up to the first car and jumped on. Mom came down the aisle. She hugged us and she was relieved. But she was smart enough to know what to do. She gave us confidence as children that she could make good decisions and we learned from her. Thanks, Mom.

In elementary school each student was given the opportunity to play a musical instrument. "Why don't you take up the violin?" Mom said. "You have long fingers." I learned to play and continued doing so through high school. At our Synagogue I got to be the fiddler when the children's choir put on "Fiddler on the Roof." I climbed up on a ladder with Morris Goldberg holding my legs while I played the violin behind a paper mache house. I really enjoyed playing the violin and plan to take it up again soon and even compose music. Thanks, Mom.

Family was very important to my mom. Every Sunday we would call our grandparents. Each one of us would get on the phone and talk. My mother taught me the importance of being close with your family and to stay in touch even over long distances. I still stay in touch with my cousins who live in distant cities. Thanks, Mom.

"Treat everyone fairly and hold no prejudices." Mom never said this. She didn't have to. She lived it and I learned by the example of her life. She was kind and considerate of others. She was almost always cheerful when she met a new person. They became her friends immediately. One time we went to visit my brother Barry who had a summer place in the Atlantic City area. At one point during our two-day stay Barry turned to me and said, "There are only seven people left in Atlantic City that Mom hasn't talked to yet." He was pretty close to the truth. There were people walking along the Boardwalk, in the restaurants or along the street. If they stopped by a store window, she would be there talking with them. To some, she spoke in English. If she thought they might be Latino, she would ask, "Habla Espanol?" and then she would switch to Spanish. They would get a broad smile on their face. She taught me to open myself up to others. Thanks, Mom.

Atlantic City with sons Barry and Ross.

"Learn as much as you can about a subject. Really delve deep into it to better understand it." Again this statement was never spoken but practiced. Mom taught her students to gather an enormous amount of information on a subject from books, maps or other reference guides. Her students loved her. She was so proud to tell me one night when she came home from Adult Night School that her class stood up and applauded her when she finished. They really enjoyed learning from her.

I guess throughout my life I have had the same desire, taught by Mom, to really try and understand a subject. That is probably what attracted me to public policy and the frustration I have when some politicians only superficially try to understand difficult issues such as health care reform, education, poverty or the environment. Mom taught me to look at all sides of the issue and understand the root causes, the history and the potential solutions. Teaching is actually a process of learning how to learn and inspiring others to learn and then teach others. Thanks, Mom.

"It doesn't matter if you win. It matters if you did your best." Both my parents would repeatedly reinforce this statement over the years for their sons, especially when we didn't come in first in some sports event or school contest. This was something that appeared to be taken from the Cub Scout Motto, "Do your best," and revised for family use probably by my mom. The theme of trying your best has followed me all my life and has gotten me through when I didn't win, whether it was in a track meet or in a political campaign or in business. Whatever the outcome, I always felt good that I "did my best." Even when it came to caring for Mom, at the end I have a good feeling that I did my best for her and have no regrets. Thanks, Mom.

Mom Was Mathematically Challenged

My mom was not very good at math. We used to get into big fights when I tried to do her bank reconciliation. She would add one column and subtract the next. I called it creative accounting.

But somehow she managed to pay her bills, pay off a mortgage and raise four sons. She never had an income of more than $1,300 per month in her lifetime. That included her Social Security check when she was older. She never had more than $15,000 in savings at any one time.

How did she do it? She had her priorities right. She knew the difference between things you want and things you need. She loved going to the swim club, but due to her financial situation, she gave up her membership and got her bond money back so that she could pay for basic needs. She would still walk the dog along the fence at the pool and at least peek into where she used to swim every summer. It was hard for her to miss the simple pleasures of going for a swim, but she needed the money.

During my last two college years while I was at American University in Washington, D.C., she somehow managed to give me $60 per month for expenses. After college, I had just started working and didn't have any money. One day she gave me $3 just so I could take a date out for pizza.

Even though she wasn't good at math, she could give good advice on finances. One time while working at Temple University one of the students who was working part-time in the office came over to my mom's desk and showed her the paycheck the University gave her for the week. It was more than $3,000. This was 1969. My mother called payroll and was told that the computer doesn't make mistakes and that maybe this student worked over-time. Of course that would have meant she worked about 1,500 hours in one week, which is impossible. So my mom told this girl to put the money in her bank account, earn interest, and that eventually someone would discover the mistake and she would have to return it. At least she would receive the interest.

When my parents divorced in 1973, she received $1,000, the house, and an old car. The lawyers got more money than my mom did. It was a tough time financially.

Despite her finances, Mom helped me buy my first car. It was a Datsun 510. The purchase price was $2,300. Mom gave me $1,000 as a gift and I took out a loan to pay the rest. The gift was for my graduation from Montgomery County Community College. I was very grateful to her, considering her finances.

To help pay her bills, Mom rented the spare bedrooms in our house. The guests were customer service engineers who were training at Univac's Headquarters in Blue Bell, PA. These men were literally from all over the world. They were from Japan (Hiromishi Maida), Taiwan, Persia, Czechoslovakia and the Caribbean. There were men from Georgia (Mike), California (Bob Kelly), New York (Neil Silverstein) and Utah (Mike Roundy) who stayed at our home over several months. Mom rented rooms for about a decade in the 1970's and early 1980's. It helped keep her going financially. It also created wonderful friendships with some remarkably wonderful people. We would all eat many meals together as a family. The men would take us out to dinner. Bob Kelly and Mom drove all the way to Western Pennsylvania to pick up Jules Mermelstein, me and my car after I had an accident on Route 80 coming back from a Young Democrats National Convention in St. Louis.

For many years Mom would correspond with these men after they returned home to their families. At Hanukah she would string together dozens of holiday greeting cards from all over the world and hang them as decorations in our living room and dining room.

While staying with us many of these people helped Mom with repairs. Their backgrounds lent them to be very good at these tasks, as I was not. They would fix her car, work on the plumbing and the electric or fix the hinge on a door. Mom was very grateful. Recently Mike Roundy sent me an e-mail with a poem my mother wrote to him when he returned to Utah thanking him for fixing a light in the kitchen. It reads:

When we open the front door we will think of you.
When we turn on the kitchen light Mike will be there.
The sound of music will bring you near.
Let's all hope that you'll be back next year.

Mom was a big gambler. She would insist on my picking up $2 worth of lottery tickets each week. God forbid I would forget to get the tickets. Her dream was to win big, buy the houses around her, one for each of her sons and their families, and have a "Kennedy family compound" like that famous Boston family who had lots of money.

How was she able to get by as she did on so few financial resources? She made it work through determination and self-sacrifice. She hardly ever bought clothes for herself unless there was a family wedding or other event coming up. She only spent money on holiday dinners, which she worked very hard to prepare. She kept a positive attitude about her situation almost all the time. She tried to be strong for her children.

Mom never spent money to install central air conditioning in the house. As she got older she would either sit in the TV room with the door closed, keeping herself cool from the air conditioner that Mike Healy and I would place in the window or she would sit downstairs in the family room, which was the coolest place in the house, where she would splash water on herself.

If the weather was very hot and I didn't have afternoon appointments, I would leave work and take her to a local Chinese restaurant for lunch. The place would be air conditioned and she would get a break from the heat.

Mom managed to keep plugging along despite the financial hardships. There was only one time that I found my mother in despair. It was when my parents were going for marriage counseling in the early 1970s. She had been driving back to the house after one of these sessions. Obviously her mind was on trying to save her marriage. She received a traffic ticket for running a red light. She claimed it was turning red as she went through the intersection. She went to court to fight it, but lost. She didn't feel she had a chance to tell her side, as the judge kept telling her to be quiet.

That afternoon she came home from the hearing and was sitting in a chair on the front porch crying when I got home. We sat and talked for hours. She let it all pour out. She told me how difficult things were and how hard she was trying to keep it together. I was glad I was there for her.

But she made it. She survived. She lived out her life in her own home and on her own terms. Despite being mathematically challenged, Shirley lived within her tight budget and made the right decisions to support her family. She never had a million dollars, but her love and caring made her *My Million Dollar Mom*.

"A generous person will never be poor for his wealth is not in money or possessions, but in his heart of gold!"

              Bill Montague

Dancing Shirley

Mom loved to dance. It didn't matter if no one got up to dance with her; she would dance anyway. Mom didn't dance in a quiet corner of the room; she would dance right up front next to the band and the singer. She would sway. She would whirl. She would sing along.

You would think that the band would be annoyed at the competition. I only saw smiles and acknowledgement of appreciation from the stage.

It didn't matter the occasion. There might be a trio and singer at a comedy night during the reception before the main event at a synagogue fund raiser. It might be at an outdoor summer festival in Evanston, Illinois, the afternoon before the wedding of my Nephew Seth to his bride Ashley. Or, it might be at someone's Bar Mitzvah or a wine-and-cheese fund raiser for my firm's charitable foundation. Mom would dance. Mom would sing. Mom loved life. As the words of the song say, "I hope you dance." Mom was the music. Mom was the song. Mom was the dance.

Mom used to tell the story about how she and my dad would win dance contests in the Catskills. My dad was tone deaf and had great trouble with the Rabbi training him for his Bar Mitzvah. He would get slapped across his knuckles with a ruler because he couldn't chant in tune. But Dad had great rhythm. He couldn't sing, but he could dance. My parents grew up in what is now referred to as the "swing" era. Back then their dance was called the Jitterbug. The story goes that after one contest, other guests were asking them which hotel they danced at professionally. Mom was always proud of her talents and abilities.

Then there was the rumba, the cha-cha, the mambo and all those Latin dances. Miami Beach is where my parents met at the beginning of the 1950s. Latin was a big thing, and there were great bands to listen and dance to where they lived.

In the 1950's and 1960's my mother joined the parents at the elementary school for musical shows they would put on for the community. In the 1970's there was disco and Parents without Partner events. Shirley was always on her feet—dancing.

In the 1980's she was invited by a fellow committee person to become involved in the players' group at his synagogue. I went to pick her up one night and ended up being recruited by the director, Rosemary Fox, to perform a "little part" in one of her productions. There is never a little part, so it became a regular activity with rehearsals almost every night. Mom and I were in "Bells Are Ringing," "A Funny Thing Happened on the Way to the Forum," and "Lil' Abner." Mom was in her 50's already, but she was up there dancing and singing with the rest of the cast. It was a lot of work, but it was great fun.

**Mom as concubine in,
A Funny Thing Happened on the Way to the Forum.**

**Mom as a eunuch in,
A Funny Thing Happened on the Way to the Forum.**

Once she went with me to the Variety Club camp in Worcester north of Philadelphia. The Montgomery County Association of Insurance and Financial Advisors was sponsoring a dance to raise money for the camp which helps children with disabilities. My mom spent the entire evening dancing with the children and loving every minute of her time with them.

As the years went by, Mom couldn't whirl like she used to, but she could still move her hips and sway to the music. At her surprise 80th birthday party, she was up dancing with so many members of her family and friends that she almost didn't get to eat. My brothers and I had hired a band that played 40's, 50's, and 60's music. She loved it. It was a perfect gift. At 80 no one could have imagined that two years later her disease would make it even hard to walk.

In a note to my mother at her 80th birthday, my sister-in-law Nan's mom, who is also named Shirley, wrote that at a party at Lee and Nan's years earlier my mom got up to dance. The note said, that she asked Mom "Do you like to dance? I love to dance—I just love to dance."

In her final years, Mom still enjoyed watching others dance and was a fan of "Dancing with the Stars." She thought the TV dancers were really looking at her and asking her to call them. She would get me to dial the number on the screen.

Toward the end of her life, "Happy Feet" was one of Mother's favorite movies. We went to see it before her disease got bad; she would watch this film on DVD in the TV room. "Savion Glover did all the dancing," she would tell me.

Till the end of her life, she was still listening to music and enjoying it as much as she could. Life is a beautiful dance through time and Mom was right there swinging to the music.

Mom dancing at Ilana's Bat Mitzvah

Mom, Dancing with the Stars audition?

Mom and Ross at Ilana's Bat Mitzvah

Mom dancing with Barry at Roy and Tobey's wedding.

Mom dancing with Daniel at Deena's Bat Mitzvah.

Julie's wedding.

Julie's wedding. Just one of the bridesmaids!

Mom Wasn't Perfect

Reading this book, one might think that my mom was a kind of saint. She was not. She was an ordinary person with faults. She would have flare-ups of anger for no apparent reason. (In later years they might have been early signs of her illness, but I hadn't recognized it yet.) As the kids say today sometimes she would just "lose it." Or she would become silent with her jaw jutting out and her eyes staring off into space. Then she would gradually let it go and be back to her happy self, without holding on to her angry emotions. She would not hold grudges. She would have her "episodes" and then they would be over.

One Mother's Day when we lived in Springfield, Delaware County, she became so upset at something that someone had done (I don't remember what it was) that she threw an entire set of cups and bowls across the room. They were a cute gift we had all bought for her for Mother's Day. As she threw them and they shattered, everyone kept saying, "No, no." Afterwards she felt so guilty that she went out and bought the same set to replace the ones she had destroyed.

Mom loved to be dramatic. One time just before a vacation to Florida, Lee and I were playing leapfrog on the sidewalk outside our house in Springfield. As I jumped over Lee, he stood up. The collision knocked him back down and he hit his chin on the sidewalk. He was bleeding profusely. Mom came running out. She administered first aid and then announced, "Now we can't go away. The vacation is ruined." I felt terrible. It was my fault. But of course other than a bruise, Lee was fine, and we went on vacation.

On trips, she would get upset, jump out of the car, and walk down the highway. My Dad would be following her begging her to get back in the car. "Shirl, come on!" he would plead. Finally, she would get back in the car, with her arms folded and looking out the window. Later all would be forgotten.

When I first got in the insurance sales business, I had an appointment one morning and Mom had made breakfast for me. I was running late and ran out of the house. She was shouting. "Eat your breakfast. I made your breakfast. Eat it!" "I got to go. I'm late!" I tried to explain as I rushed out of the house. As I got into my car in the driveway, Mom came out with the plate of sunny-side eggs she had made for me. She tossed the eggs off the plate onto my windshield and then went back into the house. This was not a great way to get ready for a sales presentation.

There was another egg story. I remember when my older brother Roy was about 10 he had a face off with my Mom one morning at breakfast. Roy hated eggs. Mom insisted he eat them because she made them. Mom shoveled a spoonful in Roy's mouth. Roy kept those eggs inside his cheek for almost 30 minutes. Mom would not let him leave the table. I don't remember who eventually won but I do know that both Mom and Roy could be stubborn in their own adorable ways.

Another time on a hot summer Saturday afternoon, she got so angry at one of us (again I don't remember who she was angry at or what happened) she ran out of the house, got into her car and started to drive toward Allentown. For some reason, that northerly direction was her escape route when she wanted to get out and get away for a while. When she got to Quakertown, she realized that she had no shoes on and had left her pocket book at home. She drove back to the house and was laughing about how silly the whole thing was. She completely forgot what she was angry about.

In later years if there was a group of the family together talking and she felt she wasn't being heard, she would shout out, "I'm talking and no one is listening. I don't know why I bother." She always wanted to be right in the middle of a conversation.

Everyone has their moments. My mom was no different.

Shirley as Public Speaker

While Mom was working at Univac she joined the Toastmistress Club (now known as International Training in Communications). The organization teaches people public speaking but does a lot more. It teaches how to present yourself to others, how to listen and how to improve your human skills. Mom not only enjoyed participating, she made many friends. They included Bunny and Vi who became her friends. Kay Mauchley Antonelli who had been married to Univac founder John Mauchley became a friend.

The group of women traveled to ITC conferences throughout Pennsylvania. They had a monthly meeting and each person was responsible for some phase of the organization. Mom became a fairly good speaker on top of her fabulous writing skills.

One of the exercises they did was to try and remember other people's names. Most of us seem to have this problem. So the group was taught name association. The person would introduce herself and relate a word or phrase to describe a trait. For example, "My name is Betty, and I like butter" or "My name is Sheila and I like sugar." Mom would laugh because she would see Betty and think of butter but she could not remember Betty's name. Mom was always friendly with everyone she met but always had trouble remembering names.

She experienced so many good times with interesting programs and trips with this group. The club's activities were something she looked forward to. Recently I found her first speech. Here it is:

"November 17, 1976
Madam Toastmistress, members and guests, today is my ice breaker before you and by the time I have finished, I hope

you will be closer to the answers for these two questions – Who is Shirley Schriftman and how did she come to be standing here before you today? Most of you have seen me at the last seven or eight meetings of this chapter of Toastmistress Club. Some of you share or have shared similar study interests – writing classes, supervision classes, programming classes. Some of you have seen me while I have been at my work area or in the cafeteria. But do you know Shirley Schriftman or do you know only that a woman who answers to that name appears with her lunch tray each Wednesday and takes a seat at the table where she proceeds to partake of both lunch and the scheduled activities – all at one hurried forty-five minute period.

Firstly, I am a mother of four sons, ages 27, 24, 20 and 16. I also have a ten-month old granddaughter. Pride in these offspring is a strong factor in my character. My family has been my chief motivator for everything that I am. As a single woman, my life centered around my parents, my sister and my other relatives.

Psychologists say that in the first six years of a child's life every factor that will form this child's character will be experienced. So a look into the past will give you some idea of my traits. Unfortunately, my ability to recall these first six years is just non-existent so I will have to begin sometime later.

I grew up in Boston, Massachusetts in a very close-knit family situation. For many years we lived in an apartment which occupied the first floor of my maternal aunt and uncles' home in Brookline. My grandmother and other aunt and two uncles shared the larger apartment upstairs. My paternal relatives lived a few blocks away. On Friday evenings and again on Sunday afternoon and evenings, the entire family got together for Sabbath dinner and Sunday conversation and listened to Lux Radio Theatre, The

Shadow, Jack Benny and Fred Allen. When we weren't eating or listening to the radio, the conversation around which I grew concerned the Red Sox or the Boston Braves, or about politics. Since there were differences on both topics, the conversations I heard would become more than just lively. Altogether, it was a happy time for me.

Because of economic conditions, the Goldman Family (my maiden name) moved to Washington, D.C. in 1939 and I started my sophomore year of high school. Although we were away from the larger family now and my dad's work kept him away from home 4 or 5 days a week, my mother filled her time with charitable work. The phone was constantly busy with organizational matters for various charities. There were a few years where her arthritis was quite severe and Dad sent her to Florida for the winter. In these years, it was very quiet at home as I was alone there. My sister had married and returned to Boston. My mother become president of our sisterhood, president of the City of Hope, etc., and did not allow the loneliness for the rest of the family to keep her down. I learned from her that one should not mope but fill one's time creatively. So this experience was a strong influence on my character.

When my dad would come home on Thursday or Friday evenings, all his attention would focus on us. Our social activities included the three of us. Dad and I would go over my homework for the week. My handwriting was and still is atrocious and we had no typewriter so this was a big concern.

Meanwhile I made some very good lifetime friends in school. The atmosphere was exciting as the school was located in an area where many of its students were children of government employees, diplomats and congressman. All the earlier conversations I had heard in Boston became more alive and real as I actually felt the nearness of my country's government. I still have the 48 star flag that bedecked my bedroom wall. The radio blared forth all the newscasts and press interviews. My mother had the facility to turn on two radios at a time on different stations and listen to both. Our synagogue was regularly visited by officials who spoke on current matters of those days.

During the time Anne Frank wrote her famous diary, I also kept one while I attended the New York World's Fair. My mother and I went from one amazing exhibit to another with great excitement. However, we were all terribly worried over the events in Germany, Austria and Czechoslovakia.

I remember December 8, 1941, when my classmates and I gathered in the high school auditorium to hear President Roosevelt talk of the Pearl Harbor attack. I saw many of my classmates leave for World War II before graduation. Some of them never returned. Charles Collingwood's sister was in my English class and was looked to by one and all as a news authority by virtue of her bloodlines.

My parents gave blood at regular intervals during the war. Plasma was a new medical advancement, as was penicillin. My mom rolled bandages each Wednesday and became a Senior Hostess at a Servicemen's Center. Now that I was in my teens, I was able to join her as a Junior Hostess and attended twice weekly plus the weekend picnics and trips to the shore etc.

After graduation from high school, I was faced with a choice. My parents wanted me to go to college, just as my sister had done. However, patriotism won out and I took an accelerated business course at Hickok in Boston, returning to Washington with my certificate as a bi-lingual secretary.

I began working for the office of the Coordinator of Inter-American Affairs, directed by Nelson Rockefeller. My first meeting with the future Vice President was when I worked in the Purchase Department. I handled the orders for supplies from our officers in the other American Republics. It was a few days before Xmas and I was on the telephone taking a rush order for #2 pencils from "our man in Rio" when I saw several hands extending across my desk. Without looking up I switched hands holding the phone and shook each hand beneath my eyes while I tried to memorize the order being given on the phone. After the phone call and the visitors had left, my boss astounded me by telling me who had been there. Talk about dedication!

My second meeting with the VP indicated another facet of my character. It occurred three months later just after my top security clearance and my transfer to the Guidance and Policy Planning Director's office. I was sitting on the floor with the door of the safe open and was concentrating on returning to the inside shelves the envelopes which had been given to me for safe keeping. So intent was I that I never noticed the office door swing open. A half second later, Mr. Rockefeller fell over me scattering all my envelopes. Since I hadn't looked up the first time I met him, I did not know his face. I had no idea who was helping me to a standing position (albeit it was a clumsy situation.) While he was pulling me up and I was trying to gather my papers, he was apologizing for bursting in so fast. At this point my supervisor, hearing the excitement came rushing out with great embarrassment. He introduced his new administrative assistant to the Coordinator for the Office of Inter-American Affairs. Speaking of this facet of my personality, I have one more brief example.

One day Mr. Rockefeller's secretary called to say that there was a top secret document in their office to be picked up, immediately scanned by my supervisor and then transferred to the Secretary of State who was then Cordell Hull. I hung up the receiver, jumped from my seat and dashed down the corridor of the Commerce Building on my way to the Coordinator's office. Meanwhile, the Coordinator had decided that the document was so important that he wanted to bring it to my supervisor himself and spend some time conferring about it. Well, he came running down one corridor while I was on my 500 yard dash down the other. Within seconds we collided and the documents were scattered all over the hall. While we both hurriedly picked them up and my face became beet red, Nelson Rockefeller roared in laughter. "Well, Miss Goldman," he laughed, "One of us has to slow down or we are going to kill ourselves." So now you know, Shirley Schriftman is a klutz – but a conscientious one.

This possibly answers Question #1 – Who is Shirley Schriftman? But what about Question #2 – How did she come to be standing before you today?

Well, by this time you may have figured out that I have a deep love of people and spend a lot of my time doing, in a much smaller fashion, what my mother used to do. I was Vice-President of the Northeast Chapter of Parents Without Partners, Inc. I organized the Buxmont Chapter about 18 months ago. I used to be quite active in my congregation and in the Sunday school and I was a Den Mother for eight years. I attend classes after work, am a Committeewoman in my precinct, Vice-Chairwoman of the Legislative Area, have worked hard in both of my son's campaigns, served as coordinator the workshop for committee people and poll workers this past September. While I love being with people, it has been years since my public speaking courses at George Washington University in Washington. I feel that I need to develop more as a communicator as I tend to ramble – not knowing when to end. This is one reason for joining Toastmistress – the chance to develop these special skills.

But it also brings to attention the other reason. Although I have many friends outside of Univac, I never really feel satisfied that I have my fill in the area of friendships. I feel that, perhaps, Toastmistress will open more doors, both within its membership and out of what I can learn at its weekly sessions.

After all, each experience in life is a learning experience and I suspect that Toastmistress will afford me both the training and the opportunity for friendships that I seek. I thank you very much for the opportunity to speak to you today for the first time and hope that it has given you some added information that will help you to see me as a whole person."

Shirley preparing for Toastmistress presentation.

Shirley addressing Toastmistress Chapter.

Shirley speaking at Sperry Univac.

Mom's Retirement Story

Recently while going through boxes in my office I came across a story written by my mom. It looked to be part of a Toastmistresses (International Training in Communications) project. Although the names were different, it definitely was my mom's own story of working at Univac. It would have been written around the time of her retirement in the mid 1980's. She had taken an offer the company made that they would pay health benefits for life for anyone who took early retirement. She took the offer at age 60. The company would later renege on their commitment when Univac combined with Burroughs to become UNYSIS. She was the retiree willing to go on TV with Larry Kane of Channel 10 and allow an interview in our home to talk about the difficulty of now having to pay for her health insurance benefits for herself and her children. She was never afraid to speak up for herself and her friends. Here is the story my mother wrote:

> I can almost see the horizon in the distance and there—the road appears to drop off to nothingness, as though the car would soon give a leap into the air and then sink down into . . . into, what? Where did it all begin? This road to nowhere. Why do I feel so compelled to stop the car from its onward motion, to turn off the ignition? Why do I have such a strong need to get out and turn back down the long, torturous pathway to the place of origin for this disappearing pathway? Where is that place? It was such a long, long time ago, I can't remember.
>
> Seven nights ago (only 7 nights?) I sat at the head table, the place of honor. The time had finally come for my retirement. Who would have thought it! I would be free now to do whatever I please. I was so

lucky. This is what Irene the young secretary kept repeating all day at work. What did she mean "whatever I please?" I wanted to remain at my job. I wanted to be with my co-workers. So many of them had been with me through all the lean years, as well as the good ones. Others had joined me at different stops along the way. They were all a part of my "work family." But now, I would no longer be needed. Like the proverbial race horse, I was being put out to pasture. I was supposed to be thrilled at the prospect of having "all this free time". To munch on hay I suppose and nibble at the farmer's apples! For many years I had planned for the time when I was no longer to be considered a productive member of society. Somehow, it was to be sometime in the distant future. Never did it ever come to my consciousness that future becomes today and that the time would come for me just as it had done for others.

How many office luncheons and dinners have I attended in 19 years with the company? How many times have I shared the inside jokes and reminisces with my fellow workers? The anniversary parties, the farewells to those going to other jobs or moving to other areas, or the young mothers-to-be starting on their new careers, and the retirement parties, all of these brought tender moments but; once over, these people faded away . . . brought back only occasionally in a memo pulled from the file or a chance meeting in a shopping center or on a bus. Once on vacation I happened to see a retiree who had settled in Florida. He seemed so different, no longer excited by the latest development in our industry. He was now more concerned with the quality of his hibiscus that season. Not that I malign the hibiscus. There was a time many, many years ago, when I first got married and lived in Florida when I planted a hedge of hibiscus along the property line between my parents' home and the home next to it. How I cried when the tiny plants lay floating in the emendation which followed a hurricane, their tiny branches broken by the wind. But Charlie had been such a vibrant person. His voice could be heard booming over the partitions when he would stand by his blackboard shouting out his ideas to those gathered in his office. By placing the clock at this position on the schema, he would bellow; we could save so many nanoseconds in transporting the message across the bus to its appointed register. His mind had been so keen and so sure. Now instead of the quick-moving, hand-waving, shouting Charlie, there was a quiet, slightly bent, sun-burned and wrinkled elderly man who spoke to me of flowers and sunshine and tropical breezes. When I had spoken of developments in the industry, he simply shrugged them off. He chuckled because he remembered his part in what he called "that old rat race still going in circles." Wasn't he proud of all his accomplishments during the years he was a part of the company! Was that all it was to him now?

    This dinner was different from any of the dinners I had ever attended at work. This time I was the object of all the jokes, of all the gentle reminders of by-gone incidents, the object of all the warmth and congeniality. Yet, gnawing at my emotions like a dog savoring his fresh soup bone was the sudden understanding that now I was with my office family, a family whom I had loved, had sat beside for 19 years, had worked with, and sometimes fought with. All the warmth and tenderness, like the sweet wine and delicious food and the mellow music of the orchestra, was too precious to let go of. I wanted to hold on to that evening, just like the dog who buries his delectable bone so that he can bring it back time and again to enjoy it with the same fervor as the first time his tongue curled around the marrow. Each gag gift, a token put together with love by some member of my group, drew laughter from the assembly and I choked with emotion as it brought back a distant memory of some project long since completed. Each impromptu speech as momentum gathered to say something that I could take with me, brought the blood to my cheeks. Why does our society say that when we reach a specific age, we must stop in our path and make a turn away from everything that has come to be a part of our very breath! Why can't retirement come as a natural winding down! I am not ready to leave. All the preparation, the seminars given by my office, the small talk from friends about all the wonderful mornings I could sleep late and the end to struggling with the car on snowy mornings, and the sudden downpours of rain in which I had to run along the parking lot to or from my car and the building where I spent most of my waking hours, not one single thing had prepared me for this dinner. My eyes saw everyone, my ears heard everyone, and my fingers ran back and forth on the gifts. In a few days I would be packing my clothes into the beautiful luggage handed to me by my supervisor. I had planned a wonderful trip for myself. I was not going to let myself pine for my old routine.

During the past three months, I had worked closely with the travel agency that had been handling the travel for "my men" for 19 years. I knew the people in the agency as well as I knew my own workers, for it was the nature of my office to send its people on trips to other locations on a regular basis. In fact, three of the employees of that agency were at my farewell dinner. Our phone conversations over the years had made us friends even though I had seen only one of these three people before. This was Stella whose job it was to deliver the tickets twice daily to our front lobby. I used to think she had a really neat job. She would travel from one company to another all day delivering tickets for the employees who went on business trips. After seeing her two and three times a week for so many years, we became close friends. Stella was eight years my senior and had retired some years back but we had remained friends. She had moved in with her daughter in Chicago after her retirement and our friendship had continued via the U.S. Postal Service, but tonight she was there at my retirement. It was such a tremendous surprise! She had not said one word in her letters to me of the past two months. She was not a very happy woman. Her daughter had a business of her own and was rarely around. The grandchildren had not grown up with her in the same city and after the initial visit lengthened into a full-time stay, they had ceased to pay any attention to her presence. No one was unkind. No one was resentful. They simply had their own lives and were busy with their own activities. Stella did not have hibiscus to care for and her grandchildren did not need her presence. Her son-in-law was in Europe much of the time for his company and so she spent much of her time reading. Since it was not her own apartment, she did not spend much time on shopping trips once she had settled in. She had no friends in Chicago, had tried some senior citizens' organizations for social outlets but found that most of the people she came in contact with there were having problems of one sort or another, either with their families, or their health, or income. Mostly it was a loneliness brought on by lack of direction that made them pass their days in somewhat depressed states. The trip home to attend my retirement dinner was something that had occupied her for three weeks. Stella, who had arranged other people's trips for years, had become in awe of the newer techniques in travel. It was an adventure for her. It tore my heart to see her so changed. We would spend five days and nights together before her return to Chicago. I would pack them with activity. There was so much we could do together and we would sit up and talk all night and make plans for future trips together. She would have time to visit with her former friends. How grateful I was for her attendance at this dinner. In the eight years since she had been retired from the travel agency, they had hired a series of young girls to take her place. The first gal had two accidents the first month and it was decided to move her to an inside job. The second left after three weeks. The third remained 14 months but left when she became pregnant. Another displayed temper and annoyance with a degree par excellence. She thought her fellow employees were something less than perfect and as for the secretaries for the various companies it was her practice to visit, they were totally inept, if she were to be believed. She was caught up in her time schedule and lacked patience to wait even as she could hear their quick steps down the hallway as they ran to pick up the tickets after receiving the call from the receptionist noting her arrival. Many a secretary would storm back into her office and reach for the phone to call Denny or Paul to tell them to send her back with the tickets, once a plane was missed because it was scheduled to leave too soon after her return and the man had to change his flight, rearrange the meeting time, etc. Her temper flared far and beyond one day when she walked out on her job because an irate secretary had snapped back at her that it was her job to deliver the tickets and return unused ones in whatever way necessary service the customers. The secretary really let her have it much to the amusement and pleasure of all the other girls who heard the battle. It was the talk of the ladies' restroom for weeks. Terri told her off in no uncertain terms. "Your salary depends on your efficiency and pleasant attitude," she whipped out at the uppity young miss. With a huff, the travel agent threw the entire caboodle of tickets on the receptionist's desk and stormed out to her car, never to return to our office or the agency. Eventually a suitable young lady took on Stella's position and did a commendable job. However, no one could ever take Stella's place. Her quick wit, her beaming smile, and her efficient manner and intelligence added to everyone's day. She loved people and we all felt it. "My men" were able to do their work better because Stella did hers so well.

 I never noticed how tiny she was until now. What a power-house she had been! My eyes scanned that tiny 90-pound frame as she stood up at her place at the table. She was talking about me, about the time my boss in my original organization had to leave for Sweden within three hours of the time I had called to make the reservation. What a mad-house that day had been! Phil had been at the staff meeting that morning when a call came in from the office in Sweden. There was a problem at one of the installations and the customer wanted his assistance not immediately, but yesterday! He came flying out of the meeting to ask me to make the arrangements. I called the agency and requested airline tickets, hotel reservations, etc. Next I called his wife to let her know I would be dropping by shortly. Then a quick call to the limousine service. Following this I hopped into my car and drove to the cleaners to pick up his suit on the way to his home where his wife threw his suitcase in my trunk. Then back to the office. Stella was at the reception desk waiting for me with his ticket and the details as to his hotel reservation and car rental in Sweden. What a sigh of relief I let out as I slid into my chair and prepared to ease back and catch my breath. Then the phone rang again. It was the company office in Sweden. Plans had changed. The customer had decided to wait a week before arranging with his people to have a conference with Phil. The crunch had been lifted. I called the agency and before Stella arrived the switch in tickets had been arranged. The next morning she was back with the appropriate stickers and new itinerary. With a pleasant laugh and a shrug of the shoulder she transferred the old ticket to the new and there had been nothing more than laughter over the entire situation. It had just added a little spice and excitement to our daily existence. Many times as the years went by Stella and I had laughed while enjoying a cocktail with dinner over similar such incidents. This kind of thing would happen time and time again. How boring life would be if it were not for the unexpected changes in plans!

After she finished talking, Denny rose and took out a handsomely wrapped gift for me. It was a tiny toy airplane. Instead of a retirement card in the attached envelope, there was an airline ticket, with five sticker changes attached. Changes included time changes, city changes, hotel arrangement changes, and finally a notation that the ticket had been cancelled "on the customer's request." All of these years and this was the first time I had ever seen Denny. All the laughs we had enjoyed together via Alexander Graham Bell's masterpiece. He looked about 55 now but we had known each other for at least twelve years. A tall man weighing about 230 pounds, he had a middle-aged paunch and a shiny bald head, but his eyes twinkled with enjoyment as he handed me my gift. He used to love to embarrass me on the telephone with his double-meaning innuendos. It wasn't what he said. They were perfectly normal requests. It was the way his voice would rise or fall that would leave me laughing. "Oh yes," he would say, "a double-room for Messrs ____ and ____. They will share . . . a car?" Once we had a terrible time getting reservations for two men in my organization. The town to which they were going was the scene of a State Fair and a Sports Car Convention the same weeks as their business flight. Absolutely nothing was available. We finally got them two rooms at a hotel nearby to the plant. Lo and behold, when they arrived, neither man found his room waiting. Someone in the hotel had written it down for the previous week. A neat trick since we had not made the reservation until the day after it had been incorrectly reserved. As the two men attended their meeting, leaving their baggage outside the conference room door, Denny and I called every hotel in the area. I even got to meet the travel agent in that town who handled the same hotel for the first night—on the other end of town I might add. The second night one of them was to move to a second hotel closer in where he would stay for the two nights. On the third night, the first man was to move to the same hotel. On the final night both men were to return to the hotel of the first night. Sound confusing? It was. How would they ever be able to travel back and forth with their luggage, etc? Denny simply replied with a twinkle: "Why I have a sled dog waiting. He's been trained to pick up the luggage and toss it on the sled. He makes regular trips between the hotels." The sled dog was, of course, the fellow from the local travel agency. So this was Denny, my telephone friend of twelve years.

Paul sat beside Denny at my retirement dinner. A much quieter man whose voice had always been very pleasant but very reserved, he had been with the agency about five years now. He seemed to be about 35, with corn-blonde hair, blue eyes and with impeccable taste in clothing. Ours was a comparatively new friendship and one that was quite business-like. He offered the regrets of the others with whom I had been in close contact at the travel agency over the years and jovially informed me that he was there to represent those guys and gals who were unable to arrange their schedules to come to the dinner. I loved them all. I was happy for the chance to meet Paul in person at last.

Also at the dinner, and it was quite a surprise for me to see him there, was Jack Popofski. When I first came to the Company, he was one of the inter-office mailmen. I was working at a location away from the main building at that time and Jack would come by three times daily laden down with mail for the 60 or so employees at that site. In the beginning he was very job-specification conscious. If the mail was not properly stacked in the appropriate bin, he would not pick it up. He would never carry anything over a few ounces. "Call shipping," he would snap at Alice when she would ask him to carry a pound carton of manuals. When he would leave, Alice would shake her head and grumble: "Something is wrong with that man!" But Alice was not one to let anyone remain angry or sullen. In time she broke him down just as she did everyone else in the office. Before I realized it, we came to know Jack as a man with a very dry sense of humor. His arrival was always good for a few minutes of friendly insults between the two of them. Since her desk was located opposite to mine, I enjoyed the few minutes to eavesdrop as I typed away without looking up. Within a year, I had moved to another location and did not see Jack anymore. A few years later when I finally came to work at the main building, Jack had been transferred to the Maintenance Department. He was now a carpenter and painter for the Company.

On one of the many days that I found it necessary to stop down at the cashier's office, I discovered that the particular section to which I was directing my footsteps was undergoing improvements. My curiosity got the better of me. I wanted to get a closer look at the carpets which were being place on the tile floors and inspect the new lowered ceilings and attractive light fixtures. The old, ugly green partitions with the plastic shadowy windows were being replaced with modern magnetic walls in various bright colors. Work went on as usual. Nosily, I poked my head through the old opening in the single remaining green partition which stood there between where I stood and the cashier's desk. It was no longer attached to anything else and seemed so unnatural. Just as I stretched my neck to see what was holding it up, a head popped up from what seemed to be under the kneehole of the cashier's desk. It was Jack. Forgetting his snappy retorts I remarked with stupid innocence, "What are you doing down there?" Without a smile but in a voice loud enough so that it could be heard above all the hammering and tapping of calculators Jack came back at me: "Oh, just screwing around." The cashier jumped away from her chair with a shocked, "Not with me." An elderly bookkeeper who had heard the proceeding let out a gasp and turned to her neighbor to say, "Did you hear what he said?" "Well, I am," Jack calmly said and pointed his screwdriver at her. Again the bookkeeper gasped. This time she grabbed her pocketbook and asked her neighbor if she wanted to take a break. As they hurried away, I heard her say, "What is this world coming to? Imagine a man talking like that!" I began to laugh and Jack came around the partition and gave me a gentle hug. The other maintenance men began to guffaw at the poor soul who had left the room for parts unknown. It was good seeing Jack again. Now that we were again working in the same building there would be plenty more times of laughter for me because of this man's humor. What was his gift to me? You guessed it—a screwdriver.

Of course, Alice was there. She had retired four years earlier. She spent much of her time taking trips to Europe. She had always been a part of the Company group trips and her retirement did not end this phase of her life. She still had many friends in the company and was always being invited to join in on a planned vacation or a special occasion activity. Alice had become my closest friend at work on the very day that I had interviewed her nearly eighteen years ago. At the time, I was serving as the Administrative Assistant at the location away from the main building. It was my job to see that things were operating in a smooth fashion in this remote site. My responsibility included maintaining the supplies for both office activities and conferences and classes (there were eight classrooms in that site). Arrangements for large meetings of from 30 to 80 people also fell into the line of my responsibilities. Just this one time, I was also called upon to select a receptionist.

Before my arrival, the previous receptionist had left in a somewhat unseemly fashion. I had heard all kinds of stories related to the time she was a member of the staff. Apparently her extra-curricular activities had somehow spilled over into the work-day with some personal repercussions. I do not know what was exaggerated and what was true and so chose not to believe everything I heard. However, no one seemed to want to take on the responsibility of replacing her in a hurry. Although Personnel had sent over several applicants, no decision was made to hire any of them. Meanwhile, we made do with a series of part-time temporary girls. Needless to say, things were in somewhat of a dither because of the lack of familiarity with the particular needs of that installation. Since each girl in her turn was only there for a temporary period of time, no one wished to take the time to familiarize her with the bare minimum needed to do an adequate job. So each week, the agency would send a new girl. Each week, I would show her how to work the switchboard, use the duplicating equipment and even how to answer the phone. Some could type, while others could not. They were not employees of our company and so their hours were somewhat different so they could not be counted on to complete any but the shortest of projects.

Finally there arrived on the scene a girl by the name of Terry Ann Walker. I remember her as "arriving on the scene" because from the moment I saw her I could imagine her waltzing on to a Hollywood set in the manner of Loretta Young, complete with full skirt and flowery patterns. Of course, when Terry Ann did first arrive, she was a pudgy girl not more than five foot two, with a round face and warm brown saucer eyes to match. The roundness was completed by her size 44 bra. Terry Ann was in her mid-20s with a musical voice and a very affected quality to everything she would say. Her make-up accentuated her eyes, making them look like the eyes of a cat glowing in the darkness. The effect was heightened by using the special light on the wall which backed her desk. The relief which adorned the wall behind her stood out in glimmering silver over a deep blue background—a pictorial world showing all the places where our company had installations. To add to the theatrical appearance of Ms Terry Ann Walker, she wore a different wig each day of the week. She must have owned sixteen or seventeen of them. Oh yes, I suddenly remembered her nails. Each day they were colored in the same shade as her dress to go along with the same shade of eye shadow.

Although she had graduated from college, Terry Ann was not interested in a career in the business world. It was merely a stepping-stone for her. Her interests fluctuated between a desire to go on the stage but at the same time to marry and travel. As soon as she realized that there were close to 70 men in that location and that many of them were in their late 20s or early 30s, the job became quite interesting to Terry Ann. Her big mistake was that she ignored the female employees her own age and chose, instead, to find an empty seat with some of "the guys" when coffee break or lunch time came along. As a result, she became the target for all the "meowing" and "purring" that single girls can put forth when put to the test. It was of special interest to them each time she left her receptionist desk to personally deliver the message to a single male employee. Personnel had decided to hire Terry Ann the day she went to them and told them she enjoyed working with our company and how much she wanted to stay. Once considered a permanent employee, Terry Ann went on a diet. Her determination to have the willowy figure of a Loretta Young was caused by her driving force to capture a budding young junior executive for her very own. Unfortunately, the other girls had let the word out to the available and desirable young men and they, in turn, attempted to stay clear. None of them wanted to be snatched away from their singlehood. So strenuous was her diet, that Terry Ann began to be sick more often than well. When she did come in to the office, she was an ideal receptionist. However, any work beyond greeting people and answering telephone was definitely ignored and this caused much consternation among the girls. After several months, Terry Ann began to remark that the men in that building were really nothing much and more and more of her time was spent on the telephone calling friends on the outside. I think the final blow came when Terry Ann took a two week, non-paid vacation less than three months after she had been hired. Never mind that Personnel had agreed to it at the time of her hiring since her plans had been made while she was a temporary. This made no difference to the young single girls. They chose to think of this as some kind of favoritism for the "Princess" as they called her. Their imaginations had no limitations as they pondered this "favoritism." Poor Terry Ann; when she returned from this vacation, she was very excited and wanted to talk to everyone about her trip but no one wanted to listen. Being a captured audience, I was given a run-down of the trip from the moment she left her home until she arrived back at the office. For awhile she acted as though she didn't notice that her circle of "friends" had dwindled. All the while she kept taking "sick days" and spending her time talking on the phone. Finally she didn't show up for five days in a row. I called her home and she told me she had found other employment and had no intention of returning.

 About two years later, I met her in a department store one day. I was walking through the junior department when I heard a voice over the racks of sports clothes. Sure enough, there she was standing before a three-way mirror admiring her appearance in the latest gaucho-pants, with leather jacket and satin blouse. She was bubbling with excitement about her latest "boy friend" and how he was really going to be "bowled over when he sees me in this." I called out to her and after appropriate displays of woman-like affection, complete with hugs and embraces and kisses and standing apart to see each other and appraise each other's appearance, I told her how very beautiful she looked. She really did. She attained the figure she wanted. She still pranced around like the

Blue Ribbon Philly in a horse show, but gone was the pudgy girl, and instead I was looking at "Loretta Young." She told me that she was employed by a modeling agency and had even done some television advertising. She seemed quite happy in her new career and I wished her well. I wondered, now that I sat at my retirement dinner, what had happened to Terry Ann. I used to watch for her on TV and listen to see if I could recognize her voice on radio, but I never ran across her again. Had she ever found that perfect husband, or was she involved with the theatrical business?

It was my task to find Terry Ann's replacement. I took to Alice instinctively. While she did not have the appearance of the usual receptionist for a front-office position, I felt that she would be more likely to stick with the job. Being an older woman, she would not be so concerned with the young single men, nor would the young girls consider her a threat. She seemed personable and willing to learn and adapt to office procedures. Also, there was a plus. Since she lived in the adjoining building to our location, she always arrived early and before anyone else had arrived, got the duplication equipment ready for use, cleaning the insides, adding paper and toner, etc. She loved plants and soon all the grateful supervisors and managers were giving her plants, which she placed in attractive pots. By the time the rest of us began to arrive, Alice was sitting at her desk bright-eyed and bushy-tailed. Always a joke or sly innuendo greeted each of us and each remark was especially geared toward its recipient. The only fault I could ever find with her technical knowledge of office routine was her inability to learn how to load a ribbon in a typewriter. This was a blind spot for Alice and she generally wound up covered with yards and yards of carbon ribbon in her lap and on the floor. At her retirement she had received a necklace and bracelet of twisted carbon ribbon braided with loving care by the girls who by that time worked under her supervision. Apparently the legend had been passed down from one generation of office workers to another. Typically, Alice, she wore this old necklace and bracelet to my dinner. At the appropriate time, she presented me with a dozen boxes of ribbons to recall the days I repaired her typewriter when she reached the end of a reel.

All during my career with the company and from the time I had transferred out of the same area where Alice and I worked together, Alice and I managed to meet one day a week for lunch. Sometimes just the two of us would go out and have time to talk alone. Other times she would bring current work buddies; still other times, I would bring one or more of my own associates. But we remained friends all through the years. Never having married, Alice was a single woman just as I was a single woman by reason of divorce. Although I had a family of four fine sons, Alice had her two nephews that she adored. We had a great deal to share. No retirement dinner for me would have been complete without Alice, and she had been invited by my boss, who knew most of my friends.

As for my boss, Tom Hunt was by far and large the finest man I had ever worked for. I would miss him most of all. His kindness and understanding were known throughout the company. He came to the company fourteen years before my job interview for the first position I had with the company. His knowledge of the history of the company and the development phases of most of the company's product line was well renowned. He came to the Company when he was just out of trade school. Not yet an international corporation, Tom was a part of its infancy, arriving shortly after the birth of the data processing industry. Having attained his place of leadership after struggling through each pang of agony as he climbed the ladder in the company, he had never moved up by virtue of pushing anybody else off that ladder. Many times, he had been pushed down, but his ability and know-how were so great that he could not be kept back. As I listened to what he was saying as he prepared to present me with my farewell gift, my mind again wandered back to the time when he had been replaced in his job by a man from Chicago. He had over fifty people working for him at that time and the inspiration he instilled in his young engineers came through the example he set. No matter how difficult the problem, the entire group worked together in a spirit of fruitful cooperation. Yet, he was being replaced. The entire department was in an uproar. No one was able to concentrate on his own task. Everyone stood in groups trying to decide if there was anything anyone could do. Of course, the men did not know what went on at the staff meeting that lasted seven work days. For days they kept gathering around my desk to find out if I knew anything. I was not at liberty to say anything and played dumb the entire time, but I prayed that all their work was not to have been done for nothing. So much of themselves had been put into this product. Tom had fought hard for his dream. All the skill he had developed in the years with the company, all his ability at training his men and watching them develop their own skills and techniques on this project, everyone's sense of accomplishment was at stake. Yet, upper level management had not been convinced. Inevitably another manager had come up with another approach for the project. Internal politics had been working for months and gaining momentum was the determination to scrap Tom's approach in favor of the idea being proffered by the other manager. Not ever having been a politician, Tom was sure that by showing them an accurate test when the time came, the problem would itself disappear. However, outside developments in the industry, plus the internal politics towards scrapping the present approach, led upper management to reevaluate their goals. It was their decision to drop our approach in favor of giving the other manager time to develop his theory. For six days, Tom tried to show through architectural plans, specifications, product descriptions, projected job controls, etc., which all indicated that this would be a marketable item showing promise to change the entire industry. It would save the company huge sums of money to produce. It was less costly to maintain and would not require the lengthy service contracts. Finally on the sixth day, he had to make his last plea and on this day, it was decided that the project as it was, was to be temporarily halted. Instead, Tom's department was to be reorganized, some of the men being pulled out of the department and assigned elsewhere; the rest to remain with Tom but now they would work on the development of a testing machine that would check what had already started, in its present state, before it was finished; before it had been refined; and before it was truly serviceable.

Ludicrous as it seemed, Tom finally recognized after seven days of meetings and conferences that there was no way to receive permission of the power players to complete the project as originally scheduled before developing the testing equipment. It could come down to scrapping the approach altogether and starting all over with the other manager, thus, discarding two years of work. The original time frame had been five years to complete the project and one year for testing before putting it on the market. He settled for testing now to attempt to prove its future worth. Now two-fifths of the way into the project, it was to be tested.

On this seventh day, Tom asked me to call the entire group together. He introduced the new man that upper level management had decided to place in Tom's place. Hereafter, Tom would report to him and would concentrate on the testing of his incomplete dream. The new director would make the decision as to the approaches and methods for further development of the project itself. By his tone of voice and his gentle mannerism, the men never knew how close they had been to being laid off. Those being transferred felt bewildered, but he reassured them that their new departments would expect the same quality of output as they had thus far produced. Those remaining, he tried to instill with a feeling of excitement for this new development—an opportunity to test what they had been working on thus far. His introduction of the new director was accomplished as though it was the most natural of things. After the departmental meeting, he immediately called his supervisors together and got started on the new assignment—without any bitterness or show of disappointment. I never forgot this magnificence. As I sat listening to him talk of my experiences with the company, I remembered more.

I thought of the day the mail clerk brought me a letter from the Board of Excellence. For four years it had been giving out certificates to those people who the Company believed deserved special commendation for the extra service or expertise far and beyond their job descriptions. This occurred a few weeks after the reorganization. I decided Tom Hunt should get that award. In fifty words I was to summarize all the years that Tom had given of himself to the development of equipment which had taken a small company and led to its becoming a part of a multimillion-dollar corporation. As I thought about it at that time and then again at the retirement dinner, I knew that he had never been another cog in the machine. From a few hundred people, it now employed thousands upon thousands of people all over the world, but in my opinion Tom Hunt was deserving of distinction. I wanted everybody to know. I wanted upper management to know that if he had a dream, it was worth pursuing. I wanted them to know how much the people who worked for him, or parallel with him, or immediately above him, were inspired by him. This quiet man, a man above all others although only five foot eight, who never raised his voice beyond that of normal conversational tones, who loved his people as though they were an extension of his family deserved to be noticed and I was going to do my best to see that he was. I can remember how I pondered over the fifty-word maximum. How to sum it all up on a few lines of a form! I wrote it on scratch paper first, covering it with my hand so no one would see it. Time and again I started afresh. Finally it was done and I put it in a personal envelope and sent it on to the Board of Excellence. Four month later I received a letter from them. He had been given a nominee number of 4078. How many nominees did they have? What chance would he have? I was told that each nominee would be investigated during the following ninety days and any further correspondence would be referenced as to the number and not the name. Finally six months later, I received another letter. "We are pleased to inform you that candidate 4078 has been selected to receive the Citation for Excellence Award . . . Especially noteworthy, in the judges' opinion, were those qualifications which demonstrated that "extra" measure of dedication and performance which are the marks of true excellence."

"For fourteen years," Tom was saying, "we have worked together. Diane came to work for me after recovering from a broken back. Her secretarial work always demonstrated that "extra" measure of dedication and performance which made her invaluable to me." My God, I wondered, did he have any idea that I was the one who had put his name in for that award that year? He used almost the same words about me as the Citation of so many years ago. Every employee had a chance to nominate someone, but the winners never had any idea who had placed their names in nomination. Was it a coincidence or had he suspected all these years. My face flushed with even more redness as his blue eyes pierced across the table into my own brown eyes. His wife smiled and gave me a wink. In another 14 months, Tom would be retiring. Why, for God's sakes! He was as good at his job today as he ever was. Why this ridiculous policy? Did he not have more in that head of his to put out for all the world to use? Could not many men and women benefit because of his expertise in his chosen field?

As I sat in my car thinking back to that retirement dinner and the people in attendance, I wondered what was right and what was wrong. Yes, there are many young people needing jobs, needing a chance to develop their skills, but why must the senior citizens move aside and become gentlemen gardeners or rocking chair enthusiasts? If this is what we want, then by all means we should be allowed to retire. But if we still are desirous of continuing along the same road, why must we be made to sit on the roadside? The greater majority of people, I suppose, look forward to the day when they will no longer have to work. But what about the rest of us? Many retirees have stopped working with enough money that they could use it to start a business of their own—some pet project that they always wanted to get into. Unfortunately, most retirees find themselves living on pensions so small they can barely survive. If they try to work part-time, they have to be careful or the income will exceed the maximum allowable and they will lose their Social Security benefits. Why should this be? They earned this security. It is theirs. What difference does it make if after a certain age they wish to continue to work; they should be assisted with this money. A choice to accept a lump sum might help get a senior citizen into a small business that will keep him active and productive and able to find his measure of happiness. What was ahead for me? How would I survive? How many more years could I move about with ease and comfort. How well could I survive on my retirement? So many of these questions had been discussed at the Company workshops for the approaching retirement employees. I read through dozens of pamphlets and brochures filled with suggestions to help prepare me, but somehow the workshops and literature had never really comforted me. I had not worked all through my adult life. At least I had not worked at a wage-earning job and so the Social Security payments and the retirement benefits were quite moderate. As I looked through the window at the road ahead, I was afraid. Would I be a Stella or an Alice? Would I be the same adaptable Diane I had always been? Could I settle for this new route? I was determined not to let my fears take hold and was reminded of the song sung many a year ago in a musical called "The King and I". I began to whistle but my eyes were fixed on the horizon ahead. Finally I decided it was time to stop driving. I didn't want to see what was beyond. Approaching on the right side of the road was a diner. Slowing down, I turned my wheel to the right and pulled in. It was time to stop for refreshment."

Ambassador Shirley

My Mom was very connected to the entire world. Whether it was her students from Asia and Europe or guests who rented rooms from her while training at Univac, or her interest in languages and other cultures, Shirley Schriftman was an ambassador of good will. With all the people from around the world who lived in our home, took classes with Mom or came to visit, she truly ran Shirley's International House.

Mom and I joined the World Affairs Council of Philadelphia and attended many events to listen to various speakers. They included Ambassador Joe Wilson; Secretaries of State Colin Powell and Madeline Albright; Labor Secretary Robert Reich; and Hotel Rwanda hero Paul Rusesabagina. After each event Mom would try to speak with the guests or talk with people around her about what she just heard. Our discussions would continue over lunch or dinner. We would go to Chinatown or stop at Michael's Diner in Wyncote on the way home. She would have me purchase books written by those guest speakers; she and I would enjoy reading, discussing and recalling the people she had encountered.

Mom also liked to go to various cultural events on a regular basis. There was the Greek Festival at the Church in Elkins Park during Memorial Day weekend, the Cherokee Festival during the same weekend on the Ambler Campus of Temple University, the Japanese Drummers at the Mann Center and the Chinese Cultural Center in Philadelphia where for several years they had brought chiefs from China to serve a wonderful meal and tell the guests about the provinces where they came from. There were Ukrainian, Japanese and Irish Festivals to go to. While at these events,

Mom would talk to everyone she met. She wanted to know as much as she could about everyone and their culture.

Shirley Schriftman wanted to know all she could about the world around her. She would want to meet people of various nations and learn all they had to share. She also would share information about her culture and religion with them.

Her years in the State Department during World War II might have been an early stimulus of that interest, though I suspect my mother was born with a natural curiosity. Besides, it was probably more elemental in that she just loved people.

Mom, Shamrock and guests from Japan.

Barry, Mom, Shamrock and guest from Japan.

Japanese restaurant with Toru, Yamamoto and Tsumeyo.

K.C. and Mom at Cherokee Festival, Temple Ambler Campus.

Cherokee friend, Germaine "Gem Penele Kaiulani"
Cherokee Festival, Temple Ambler Campus.

Cherokee Festival, Temple Ambler Campus.

Holding Indian child dress from Cherokee Festival.

Holidays

Family celebrations were very important to my mom. Holidays, birthdays, and other occasions became major projects. "When are you going to help me?" Mom would ask. "Passover is only three weeks away and we don't have anything ready. You promised me you would help."

I was Mom's everything assistant when it came to preparing for these events. There was cleaning, food shopping, gift buying and decorations that she organized and put me in charge of helping her with. I would have to juggle work with helping her get everything ready.

I knew, however, how much she enjoyed doing this. Each year, there would be something new and special she would want to do. It might be a special new dish. It might be something she read to add to a prayer. It might be preparing some special decoration we had to buy.

Once she made a Passover dinner with an Italian theme. We went and bought various special vegetables. She even made a carrot soup, which, of course, my brothers thought was funny. But she wanted to try to make it a unique experience for everyone. She also liked compliments. "Isn't this good?" she would ask about her own cooking. Mom was always proud of her efforts.

Passover Seder services always followed the same pattern with the same Haggada (Prayer book). The prayers before dinner followed the book and were read with some speed without interruptions because everyone wanted to get through and start eating. The same songs were sung and prayers recited. We would have our first laugh when we sang "Behold It is the Spring Time of the Year." By the second verse we never had learned the melody. After dinner and by the third glass of wine everyone was giddy. We did "Who Knows One" and "Had Gadyo." These are two cadence poems talking about the ultimate judge and ruler—God. The children would look for the Afekomen (the half of the Matzo). We would open the door for the Prophet Elijah (kind of like Santa Claus visiting the homes at Christmas). This door-opening was done by the youngest child. Someone would drink the wine from Elijah's cup, and when the child returned, we would also know that Elijah had been here. Of course, even the child caught on to this little joke.

One Passover Mom invited everyone from Parents without Partners. I really mean everyone. As many as 90 parents and children showed up for an event that lasted from 6:00 p.m. to 3:00 a.m. the next morning. A full description is in the chapter on "Parents without Partners."

The last two Passovers of her life were at our home. My friend Nan came over in 2008, and we sat at the kitchen table with my mom. That year Mom participated in the service singing the songs and holding her book. In 2009 Nora and I had to help her down the stairs. She sat and listened but couldn't participate in the service. She did eat the food my friend and I made. Nan was so sweet to cook and participate in our home service.

Thanksgiving was a very special holiday. Sometimes we would travel to Boston to spend the day with Aunt Bettie. Other times my mother would host the dinner. A couple times we went out to dinner. Then in later years there were trips to Deena and Dan's home in Pittsburgh. The last time I took Mom to Deena's was for Thanksgiving in 2006. Roy, Lera and Sasha had gone out together and Sasha came back with us. On the way back we stopped to eat at a rest stop on the Pennsylvania Turnpike. Mom went inside to the ladies' room. About 10 minutes later a woman came out of the ladies' room and asked if there was someone named Ross around. She said that Mom was stuck in one of the stalls. The door would not unlock. A repairman was sent to get Mom out of the stall. Sasha turned to me and said, "Only your Mom could have something like this happened." Mom came out and was laughing about getting stuck in the toilet. In hindsight, that episode might have been just simply early memory loss of how to unlock the door. It was a wonderful little trip, though, as the weather was warm for late November, and we all had such a good time.

For Hanukah we would make latkes (potato pancakes) with apple sauce or sour cream (your choice). Mom would hang holiday cards from one end of the living room to the other. She would have a long string. The cards were from all over the world, from men who had rented rooms from her in the past, or exchange students who took her English and American History classes. The cards were from Japan, Taiwan, Sweden, France, Germany, Italy, Czechoslovakia and Iran. We would sing songs and play dreidel games. Sometimes as children we would get our presents at Hanukah. If the holiday fell around Christmas we would open our presents on Christmas morning, just like many of our Christian neighbors and friends. As a child we would have a tree. We didn't call it a Hanukah Bush as some Jewish people do. It simply was for decoration. Mom had a "Shirley" tree that was planted in the backyard of 236 Winchester Street in Boston. It was still there in 2005 when Lee and Mom stopped by while I was running the Marathon. As a child I wanted a Ross tree which was planted in the backyard at our house in Baltimore. I don't know if that tree is still there.

When I became an adult, Christmas was spent celebrating with our friends. We would be invited to a church gathering or to a friend's home. Other times Mom and I would visit hospitals or nursing homes to relieve staff, deliver meals to people who were shut in, or help cook a festive meal at a homeless shelter. We would later go out to a Chinese restaurant for our dinner. The joy of this day was that Mom and I were doing something important together and enjoying each other's company.

Mother's Day and Father's Day: These were always special holidays for our families. We would travel to see grandparents; get dressed up and go to Longwood Gardens in Kennett Square, Pennsylvania; have dinners at home; or go out to eat. The sense of a close family spending time together will be my fondest memory of these two holidays.

Memorial Day was almost always begun with a parade and memorial ceremony in whatever community we lived in. We would follow this with a barbeque or go to the pool. As an adult I would take Mom to the Devon Horse Show, or in later years, we would go to the local Greek Church in Elkins Park for their festival of food and music on Sunday and the Cherokee Festival at Temple University on Memorial Day. Mom loved to learn about different cultures. We would leave these events with musical recordings on tape, dresses, ethnic accessories or other items. A program booklet was always purchased and a donation made. Food was consumed and purchased to eat later.

Labor Day sometimes involved a trip to Ludwig's Corner for the Horse Show. This was followed with my volunteering for the Jerry Lewis Muscular Dystrophy Association Telethon. Since 1979 when the Montgomery County Young Democrats took on this charity as a project until now I still help in the mailroom every year. Mom would watch and donate what she could. Of course, she kept looking for me. In telethons you never see the people in the back room stuffing and sorting the mail. You see the stars, the guests and the volunteers manning the phone. "I didn't see you," Mom would say when I got home. "I watched all day." We would then have dinner and talk about the success of the fund raiser and what Mom had seen on television. After the long summer and the long weekend, that next day which is always Tuesday was a busy work day trying to catch up with clients that were away or handling service problems that hadn't been resolved the week before. Mom and I always felt a little sad that the summer was coming to an end and that we both had work to do.

Mom and K.C. at Ludwig's Corner.

New Year's Day is very special in the Philadelphia area with the Mummers' Parade. When we were young we had gone to the parade several times. In later years Mom would tape the entire parade, catalog it and save it. There are probably 30 hours of cataloged Mummers viewing in the TV room. On New Year's Eve we would go to Parents without Partners or to our Russian friends' home. Sometimes Mom and I would just stay home and watch TV. We would toast each other and go to bed. Twice we spent New Year's morning at the 5K Run for the Hatboro YMCA in Carpenter Park in Horsham. Mom brought K.C. and the two of them were wrapped up quite warmly to watch me run this winter event. This race always intrigued me because while other people were still in bed recovering from New Years' eve revelry, there were always a handful of healthy runners ready to run a race.

July Fourth was a very special holiday for Mom. Growing up she and her family would go down to the Charles River in Boston and sit on the Promenade on blankets while listening to Arthur Fiedler and the Boston Pops Orchestra. The highlight would be the cannon fire to the "1812 Overture" and then the fireworks. Almost to the end of her life every Independence Day we would close out our day watching the Boston Pops concert on television and lately with Keith Lockhart conducting.

When we lived in Springfield, Delaware County, the parade would pass right by our house along Powell Avenue. When we moved to Maple Glen we were fortunate for several years to have a July 4th Parade pass right down our street. Featured in the parade were old (vintage) cars and modern cars (Corvettes at the time) and fire engines. All the kids in the neighborhood rode their bicycles in the parade. The parade ended in the Maple Manor Swim Club parking lot. The whole neighborhood would then spend the day at the pool.

During other years Mom and I would go down to Independence Mall and attend the Liberty Medal Ceremony to see award winners such as the High Commissioner for Refugees for the United Nations Sadako Ogata, Nelson Mandela and the former South African President F.W. De Klerk who ended Apartheid. After those Independence Day ceremonies Mom and I would go all around Olde City to Penn's Landing and enjoy the food festival on Chestnut Street. Just being there with her and enjoying our love for our country was something special.

We would also go to many of the local parades. There were parades in Fort Washington, Glenside and Oreland. We Americans have a curious practice on this holiday. People who you have never met sit next to you on lawn chairs along the street and watch other people walk down the middle of the street. After they've all passed, we all pick up our chairs and say, "See you next year" and leave. Sure enough, the next year, we all do it again sitting on the same sidewalk in the same location watching the same people and vehicles pass us by. What brings us back every year?—a sense of community and a love for our country.

I will always remember the joy my mother got out of each holiday and each season. Without her it is so different, but I am working to continue our celebrations as each holiday arrives and each season changes as life continues without her.

Conducting Hanukah services.

Mom, Lee, Ilana and Nanette. Holiday meal.

Letters to Aunt Bettie

Mom and Bettie, Brookline house

One day after Mom died, Nora came for a visit. I was going through some boxes and had found a small metal box. I had not been able to open it. At Nora's suggestion we got a screwdriver and the two of us pried open the box. What we found inside was amazing.

This must have been a box that had been at Aunt Bettie's home in Boston. My brother Roy and I had brought it back to our home when Bettie moved in with us way back in 1980. It had never been opened since then.

Inside were more than 30 letters Mom had written to Bettie between 1977 and 1980. Bettie had kept every one of them and had carefully folded and put them in this little metal box. Since she was all alone in Boston before she moved to our home Bettie must have sat and read them for hours. She was in her early 90's at the time and reading them must have given her comfort; she must have appreciated them so much.

In Mom's typical fashion the letters were long, detailing what each member of the family was doing, how Mom felt about all kinds of things, and how much she loved her Aunt Bettie. My Mom's thoughtfulness for other people is so apparent as expressed in these letters. She had taken the time in her busy life never to forget the aunt who sheltered the entire family during the depression and who had been so good to her growing up. Bettie's real name was Bessie but, she was also known as Bettie, and Mom would write her name as Bette.

As always my Mom was meticulous in putting a date on each letter. The cost of making long-distance phone calls would have been a financial burden for my mother during the late 1970s. An eight-cent stamp with a lengthy typed or handwritten letter was the cost efficient way to go. (It's a shame my Mom isn't running the Federal Office of Management and Budget. Even though she was mathematically challenged she never wasted money.)

Here are excerpts from Mother's letters to Aunt Bettie.

March 21, 1977- Monday

Dear Bette:

I have a few moments before I go to lunch, so I thought I would drop you a line. I will try to call you later this week if I get a chance. How are you feeling? Signs of spring are starting to appear around here, although the weatherman is still predicting more snow this week. I hope not. It's been so cold and miserable all winter. Besides, we are asked to keep our thermostats down so it is cold at work.

Lisa called me yesterday. I had written her inviting Doug and her to come for Passover since it falls on a weekend this year. She said they will come after work on Friday, April 1st. I haven't seen her since her wedding, so it should be fun.

Tobey, Roy and Deena came over yesterday and had dinner with us. Nan also came over. It was a lot of fun. My dog Mollie, who is a Labrador retriever and quite big, kept kissing Deena. She would giggle and put her face forward for Mollie to do it again. The dog is bigger than she is and would lean down to lick Deena's face. Deena would say "Oof, oof," and when she would pat the dog, she would say "Ni—Ni" meaning Nice, Nice. She is such a little doll. I know you would love her. I hope you will be coming to Lee and Nan's wedding as then you will get a chance to know and love your little grand niece. She is so affectionate.

I spent two hours with my lawyer Saturday. The roller skating rink where I broke my back will not settle, so I guess we will have to go to court. I don't know if I'll get anything anyway, but I do know that I have had severe pains ever since the accident and probably always will. Also, I lost a year's pay and a year and a half of salary increases which puts me behind in my yearly increases. Oh well, what will be will be, I guess.

I got a letter from Miriam this week. I haven't heard from her in quite a while. She wrote that she hadn't heard from me in a long time. I guess she did call me last. I never call her as it is too expensive to call Florida, but I did think that I had written her. Maybe not.

Well, Lee will be graduating college the end of May. He has been accepted to dental school for the fall and is graduating with high honors. On April 15th he will be receiving an award from the President of Temple University for his constantly high grades.

While I was taking Fortran IV (a computer language) here at work, Lee has been taking it at Temple, so we were able to work together on the homework. I don't think I could have passed it without him. Since I came to work here almost 5 years ago, I have taken 15 courses. Still, I am just a secretary and can't break into the computer field. Maybe my broken back has had something to do with their not wanting me to take on too much responsibility. I guess because of sick leave, etc. It's such a shame and so hard to live on so little–as you well know.

Well, I better end this letter now. Take care of yourself, Bette, and have a good Passover. I'll probably talk to you before then, but just in case I get tied up at work and can't stop to call, may this year be a healthy, happy one for your and let's hope I'll be seeing you soon.

Love,

Shirley

April 19, 1977

Dear Bette:

After I spoke to you the last time and I went home from work, I found a letter waiting for me. Also, last week I got a letter, so I guess it's my turn again. I hope you are feeling well and enjoying this gorgeous weather. It is just too nice to work. On my lunch hour, I go outside and sit on the grass and enjoy the lovely breeze. Next door to the company for which I work is a farm and I love to watch the horses. They seem so serene.

Last Sunday, Barry, Lee, Roy, Tobey, Deena and I took a drive to New Hope just to enjoy the atmosphere and take the barge ride on the canal. It is a barge drawn by two mules, like the Erie Canal.

We went into one art gallery and they had some pictures etched by someone by the name of Icart. Well, the picture over my bed at home is an Icart. We asked them what it was worth and they said $450 to $500. Boy, do I sleep in class! It used to be Miriam's painting dating way back to the 1940s.

Well, it's getting closer and closer to the wedding. I believe Nan is sending out the invitations around the first of May. The wedding is June 18. Last week, Lee received an award from the President of Temple University for scholastic achievement. After the ceremony, we attended a reception and I saw a lot of the people I used to work with five years ago when I was a secretary at Temple University. Then Lee, Nan and I went out to the Middle East Restaurant for a special dinner, complete with a belly dancing show. We were home by 9:00 p.m. but we really had a wonderful evening, just the three of us. One of the belly dancers kept poking Lee's shoulder with her hip. It was so funny. He tried to look very nonchalant but he was embarrassed. Nan and I had a good laugh about that. The rest of the family did not go, as I couldn't afford to take everyone out, but I am so proud of Lee's achievements; and Nan will soon be his wife so this was the graduation celebration. Nan is also graduating next month. Next fall Lee has been accepted at Temple University Dental School. I wish he were a dentist already as I need plenty of work, but I don't have the money to pay for it.

Last week, my dog, Molly, accidentally bumped into my jaw and one of my lower teeth is now loose. I hope it doesn't fall out. The gum is really sore. Then about a half hour later, I bent down to pat her just as she decided to jump up and lick my face and darned if she didn't hit me right in the eye and broke my eyeglass frames. I am wearing eight-year-old glasses now because I can't afford to go to the eye doctor. He will insist upon my getting a new prescription along with new frames. My last prescription is about four years old. Oh well. Such is life, I guess.

Well Bette, I better end this letter now and get down to the cafeteria or I will use up my whole lunch hour. Take care of yourself. I will call you whenever I have an opportunity. Meanwhile stay well and enjoy the sunshine.

Love,

Shirley

May 25 (Wednesday), 1977

Dear Bette:

Lee tells me that the invitation for his wedding came back [indicating] that you will not be coming. Of course, I am very disappointed as it has been so long since I have seen you. Besides, I wanted to show off your great grand niece Deena. However, I can understand if you feel that you better not do any traveling, and I only hope that you are well.

He received answers from Lisa and Doug and also Miriam and Heb. Both families will be here. We haven't heard from Deedee and Gene yet, but last month Deedee did write that she was going to try to come even if Gene couldn't make it. His two little daughters are so adorable, Bette. You would absolutely love them.

Saturday Tobey and Roy held a surprise wedding shower for Nan and Lee. It really was lovely. Tobey is quite a hostess. Since it was a hot day, she made a Jell-O mold, a whipped cream and pistachio mold, a tuna fish salad, all kinds of relishes and to top it off, she made a delicious lukshun koogle (noodle pudding). Her parents air-mailed the tea rolls and cakes from their bakery in Chicago, and they were delicious. Nan was really surprised. Lee told her that they had a lot of shopping to do and she didn't feel like it. He insisted they had to go shopping as before they would realize it they would be married and on their honeymoon so that they had to go out no matter how hot it was. So she put on some jeans and reluctantly prepared for a day of running in and out of stores. Then he told her that they had to stop by Roy's first since Tobey's mother had mailed the wedding gift there, not knowing Nan's address (this part was true but, of course, they didn't have to pick it up that day except for the fact that he had to have an excuse to get her to the shower). When she walked in the door, her face went white and then flushed bright red. She got some lovely gifts. Since they bought themselves a king-size mattress, she received 4 king size sheets and pillowcases, she also got a king-size quilt. I bought them a crock pot (electric slow cooker). She also got a cheese tray, and a lox and bagel tray, three cookbooks, some pots and pans, a bridal book, flatware settings for eight, etc. Well, it won't be long now (less than a month).

I think I wrote you that they are going to Israel on their honeymoon. She has a large family living there (half of her family came to the U.S. to escape the Nazis, while the other half went to Israel), so her cousin found them an apartment for the month. Lee is so excited. He has been taking courses in Yiddish and also in Hebrew as he wants to talk in those languages. Her parents gave him a beautiful camera.

I think I wrote you that he received a Phi Beta Kappa and a University Presidential award. Well, tomorrow he gets his degree. He graduated Summa Cum Laude which is about the highest honor a college can give. Not to be outdone, Nan is getting Magna Cum Laude (which is the next highest honor). In August, he will start dental school. God willing, in four more years he will be a dentist. I hope my teeth hold out as I need plenty of dental work and can't afford to have it done. She doesn't have a job yet, but will start looking in August. I worry plenty about how they are going to be able to manage. They rented an apartment starting July 15, but God only knows how they will be able to pay the rent, buy food, etc. He won't be able to work while he is going to dental school. But they are so in love and so excited about getting married, they don't worry at all.

Now for the Roy Schriftman family – Roy has been very busy—what with doing double work (one of the men in his office has been ill so Roy is doing his work as well as his own) working Saturday and Sunday as well as week days. He gave up his night job as a teacher at the Community College since he is going to school two nights a week. Tobey is feeling O.K. since she had the thyroid operation. Poor kid.

She has had a baby, gall bladder operation, and a thyroid operation—all in one year. But she is a sweetheart and I truly love her. As for Deena, you would absolutely eat her up. I just wish you would come and spend some time with us. You would enjoy it so much. Deena is 16 months old now. She calls Barry "Baddy"; I'm "AMA"; Tobey is Mommee; Roy is Dadee. Lee is "EE"; Ross is "OSS." At the shower, Tobey said, "Wait a minute; I want to get paper and pencil to make a list," so Deena got the paper and said, "Make listee." Lee's future mother-in-law is also named Shirley, so Deena calls her "Shirdee". About half-way through the shower, Tobey decided Deena had to take her nap or she would be thrown off schedule, so she picked her up and started upstairs with her. Deena looked down at everyone and said as sweet as she could, "Nappy time for Deena." What a little pumpkin she is!

Well, Bette, as I said, I can understand if you cannot come to the wedding, but you can well imagine how very disappointed I am. I so hoped that in the end you would decide to attend. Anyway, I'll write you all about it. Meanwhile, take care of yourself. Enjoy the beautiful weather. All the flowers are in bloom and it is such a lovely time of the year. Write when you can.

Love,

Shirley

Wednesday, June 15, 1977

Dear Bette:

This is the first chance I have had to answer your letter of June second. Things have been very hectic here, as you can imagine. It's funny! You think I write nice letters. Well,

I think the same of you and always look forward to receiving yours.

Yes, Lee and Nan are really going all out on their honeymoon. I do worry that there won't be anything for them to live on when they get back. He starts dental school in the fall. But in a way, I can understand his feelings. All my married life I waited until we had money in order to take any really wonderful trips. Well, Herb was always sick and the money always went to doctor bills. If my parents hadn't helped us out, we wouldn't have even gone to the Catskills or Florida on vacations. At least Lee and Nan will have this wonderful trip to Israel to look back upon—just as you do for your trips to Europe.

They already have an apartment about ten minutes away from Roy and Tobey in Northeast Philadelphia. I haven't seen the inside, but Lee did drive me around the neighborhood.

Well, in only a few days they will be married. Her cousin from Cambridge called me last night. He was willing to drive you to Philadelphia for the wedding. I am disappointed that you aren't going to be here, but I can understand your feelings about travelling. I just wish we lived closer.

Last Thursday, I finished the class I took here at work on the EXEC 8 computer equipment. That makes 15 courses I have taken since I started working at Univac almost five years ago. I have the same salary classification as I did when I started to work here. I guess my age is against me.

I rented the spare bedroom for the month to a fellow who is here from California to attend classes. He is a customer engineer (fixes computers) and was here four years ago when he rented the room for seven months. This time it is only for four weeks, but thank God because I sure need the money. Also he is a very pleasant person and [he] already fixed my dryer. He is working on my stereo and the refrigerator now. Both are acting wacky.

I am expecting Deedee to arrive A.M. by plane on Saturday. Miriam, Herb, Lisa and Doug will be driving in from

Washington by 2:00 in the afternoon. I am having a luncheon at my house for any relatives from out of town and anyone in the wedding processions. I bought two turkey breasts and a large brisket. The wedding reception is at 9:00 p.m., the wedding is scheduled for ten and we will probably not have dinner until eleven. That's why such a big luncheon, in the middle of the afternoon.

Deena will be at the luncheon but they have a sitter for her for the evening. That little one is a real doll. She calls me AMA and whenever she sees me she asks, "Berry?" (Barry). If you ask her a question she usually answers "Kay," meaning O.K. Tobey dresses her so cute. I took care of her one Saturday a few weeks ago.

Barry finishes school this week and already has a summer job lined up in a print shop. It is such a hot place to work in the summer but he loves it. He is getting an A from the vocational technical school as he has done a wonderful job there. Thank God he passed all his regular courses and will be a senior in high school next fall.

Ross continues to be very busy with his daytime and evening jobs, as well as all his Democratic tasks. I don't know how he keeps up with it all, but it doesn't seem to trouble him. He is such a good kid and is slowly paying back all his campaign debts from the last campaign. It is such a pity that he came so close but did not win. Someday, I hope, he will have what he wants so badly.

As for me, I just keep plugging along. My back has been giving me a lot of trouble lately. I guess when it is rainy, I will always have trouble. In good weather, I feel pretty good.

The organization I belong to just had its Regional Council Conference. I am Public Relations Director, so I was plenty busy getting publicity in advertising and articles in the paper and also on TV and radio. We had about 130 members from all over the State of PA. They had some good speakers in the daytime and in the evening we had a dinner/dance. It was most successful. During the past year I have been on four different TV shows talking up the group. I also gave a seminar at a college on Saturday and conducted a panel discussion at a private Catholic school. All of this is volunteer work and the only money is for expenses.

Well, Bette, I better bring this letter to a close now as I have just been given some typing to do here at the office. Take care of yourself and write when you can. I look forward to mail from you.

Love,

Shirley

June 30, 1977

Dear Bette:

I was happy to have the chance to talk with you on the phone when Miriam and Herb were visiting you and then again when I called to let you know about Lisa. It's too bad the second call had to be to report on her operation, but I am glad that I was able to report good news.

I spoke to Lisa yesterday. Although she sounded very weak, she had no complications and is doing well, thank God.

We are still waiting to hear from Lee and Nan. They are still on their honeymoon. The wedding was absolutely beautiful. The two of them looked like wedding dolls on top of a wedding cake. She wore a gown with a hoop (like Scarlett O'Hara); he wore a white tuxedo. He has a mustache now but he still smiles like a teenager.

I made a luncheon the day of the wedding for all the relatives from her side of the family and my side of the family, so there were about 36 people at the house. In the evening the Nirenbergs had quite a spread of food. There were about 250 people at the catering hall. They served hors d'ourves before the wedding. It's a good thing they did since the ceremony wasn't until 10:00 p.m. Then after the wedding they served kosher Rock Cornish hens with wild rice, string beans with almonds, soup, salad and pastry desserts. At 1:30 a.m. they cut the wedding cake and wrapped slices for everyone to take home. Shirley Nirenberg looked beautiful in a lovely pink gown. I wore a blue one that Tobey picked out for me when we went shopping. The orchestra was terrific and I did plenty of dancing. At one point they played some Jewish music and put Lee on one chair and Nan on another chair and lifted them up to the ceiling. We all danced around them. Ross caught the bride's garter and had to put it on the girl who caught Nan's bouquet. That was funny as the emcee teased them both.

Things have quieted down quite a bit since everyone left. This Monday night, Ross and I are singing with the Upper Dublin Family Chorus at the July 4th celebration. We did it last year, too. However, this year, we haven't been to any of the earlier rehearsals so neither of us know[s] the music. Monday night is the performance. It's a lot of fun but neither of us [is] prepared, so I guess we won't sing too loudly.

Barry has a job now. He is working in a print shop. He hopes that one day he will be able to own his own shop. I guess his hands will be full of ink for the rest of his life. He is such a good kid though. I really love him. This week he is taking care of the dog next door while they are on vacation.

I guess I better get back to work now, Bette. I'm sorry I couldn't talk longer on the phone. Why don't you come and pay me a visit? I do miss you. It's been so many years already since we have had a good visit together and I love you. Incidentally, today is Tobey's birthday, so I will go see her tonight after work.

Love,

Shirley

July 11, 1977

Dear Bette:

I am absolutely sure that I will hear from you this week. Do you know why? It's because every time I write to you there is a letter in the mail on its way from you to me. How are you feeling, anyway? Up until this morning we went through about five very miserably hot, humid, sticky days. Thank heavens it cooled off during the night last night and this morning I wore a jacket to work.

Since you have never seen Lee's Nan, I am enclosing a copy of the newspaper article concerning their wedding. She is much tinier-framed than the picture indicates. I am also enclosing a picture of Ross (Barry has his back to the camera; he's wearing checkered shorts). They made over $200 for Easter Seals. They would have done better but there was a storm watch that night and I guess a lot of people were afraid they would be caught in a cloudburst. It never happened. It was just hot and close. The WIP Metromediocres are the announcers for that radio station and very popular in and around the Philadelphia area. The radio announcers won 22 to 9. Ross brought in 4 of the 9 runs. Barry was the pitcher. It really was a lot of fun to watch and not a very seriously played game at all. The Young Democrats really don't have a softball team, but they wanted to raise some money so they got together for three practices and played the Metromediocres who play about three nights a week. After the game Ross invited the teams back to our house for hotdogs, soda and beer.

I spoke to Lisa Friday. She is recuperating well. She has turned out to be such a sweet little thing. I wish we all lived closer so we could see each other more often.

I have received two letters from Lee and Nan from Israel. In the last letter they wrote that they were planning to spend a couple of days in Jerusalem, so I guess they will write again when they get back to the Tel Aviv area. Meanwhile, as soon as the apartment they rented in Philadelphia is ready, I am supposed to pick up the key from the real estate office.

Tobey and Deena are supposed to drop by tomorrow, but Roy goes to school three nights a week so I guess I'll have to wait a little longer before seeing him again. Deena is so adorable, Bette. They took her to Valley Forge Park on July 4th weekend and she saw a Conestoga wagon. She looked at this covered wagon with two people sitting and holding the reins and thought about it. Then she said, "Look. Big Stroller." I guess that was the closest thing she could associate it with.

Well, Bette, I guess I better get to work now but I just wanted to let you know I was thinking of you. I still wish you would come for a visit, but I know that in the summer nothing in the world would keep you away from baseball.

Say "hello" to your neighbors for me and be well, Bette. I love you.

Love,

Shirley

July 22, 1977 – Friday

Dear Bette:

I have a few minutes while I am waiting for the time cards from my boss so I thought I would drop you a line. Isn't it funny the way we keep writing to each other at the same time and our letters always cross in the mail? It shows that even the miles do not keep us apart, at least in thought.

How did you survive the heat spell? It has been absolutely terrible here. Over 100 degrees and sometimes I have seen thermometers along the highway reading 103 to 105. The nights were unbearable between 93 and 95. There are times I wish I had air conditioning.

Poor Tobey has been sick again. She has been in the hospital since a week ago today. It's been one thing or another for her ever since I have known her. I hope this is the end of it now and she will be well and strong again soon.

I took off three days from work to take care of Deena. That baby is an absolute doll. She is just like Roy when he was a baby. She is lovable and sweet and no trouble at all. On top of that, she is so bright. Tobey and Roy have a little 5 x 5 vegetable garden. They grow cucumbers on it. Deena calls them "cupacumbers."

One day when Tobey was really feeling depressed, the doctor said she had special permission to see Deena as he felt it might perk her up. Lo and behold, I put the baby in the car and we went off to the hospital. When Deena saw her mother in the wheel chair, she thought for a moment and looked at the big wheels and said, "Mommy in bike." Her little mind is always working and thinking and trying to associate new things with things she already knows about.

Tobey's mother came yesterday and this is why I am back to work today. Anyway, Evelyn asked Deena, "Who do you love most in the whole wide world?" and Deena responded without any hesitation, "Molly." Molly is my dog. When I asked Deena, "What does Molly do to Deena?" she said, "Eats me." What she means is licks me but since Molly is a big Labrador retriever, when her tongue licks Deena's face, her entire face gets wet with one sweep of the tongue; so I guess Deena's interpretation of that is that she eats her.

Well, my roomer left yesterday. He was here for two months but his training course is over now, and he is on his way back to California. Tonight, another man is moving into that room. He is here for ten months from Japan for training. He doesn't speak much English, so I don't know how we will communicate. I guess I'll have to learn Japanese. (Author's note. Notice that my Mother will try to learn Japanese rather than trying to make this man understand her English. This is the way my Mother thought of understanding others.)

Thank God the company I work for is big and keeps bringing in personnel for training. Without these roomers I couldn't possibly hold on to the house or pay very many bills. My salary doesn't even cover one month's gas and electric bills, let alone house payments, water, telephone, food, dry cleaning, etc.

Well, all the time cards are on my desk now, so I better process them and get them down to payroll so we will all be paid. Take care, Bette, and don't worry about Tobey. She is on her way to being well again now. May this be an end to her medical problems. She is a wonderful girl and like my own daughter. You had a lot of the same medical problems when you were in your 20s. I remember your telling me about them. Meanwhile, I hope you are O.K. and I wish you could come and visit with me. I do miss you and haven't seen you in about 3 years now.

Love,

Shirley

August 2, 1977

Dear Bette:

As usual, our letters crossed in the mail again. Isn't it funny how we always do that? It shows we are always thinking of each other around the same times, I guess.

I was sorry to see that you were thinking back to last winter again, though, Bette. What's past is past and you shouldn't keep thinking about it as it can only upset you and make you sick. This is the best time of the year. Try to think of baseball and beautiful skies and lovely flowers. This is the time of year when God puts on his best displays and we are lucky to be alive and able to enjoy it. I know your front porch is situated in such a way that you can enjoy that tree and the gentle breezes that flow through it. I always have loved sitting out there. I can remember when I was a little girl and I took a picture on that porch holding my dog Scrapsy. You remember he was voted the "Dog with the Most Personality" in all of Brookline. The boy two or three doors away had entered him in a contest. We didn't even know about it, but when we saw the local paper, there was Scrapsy's picture with his Blue Ribbon. He was one of a litter of puppies that belonged to Poorvu's dog. Do you remember?

Now the boys and I have a lovely dog. Her name is Molly. She is the largest dog I have ever had. She is a Labrador retriever and when she kisses you, you know it. One lap of her tongue and little Deena falls down. Deena loves the dog, though, and says "Molly eats me." She means licks me.

Tobey has been sick again and was in the hospital for two weeks. The poor girl has had one thing after another. Her mother was here for about eight days but is going home today. I took off a week from work to take care of Deena but that was a pleasure. She is such a little doll.

Ross and Barry were away at a Young Democrats Convention. They got home Sunday night. They were exhausted as five kids shared one hotel room with only two beds and took turns each night sleeping on the floor. However, they had a wonderful time. They haven't stopped talking about it.

Lee and Nan are due back from Israel this Sunday. I will probably drive to New York to pick them up from the airport. They certainly had the dream honeymoon of all. He starts school again in about three weeks and has four more years to go before he becomes a dentist. I picked up the keys for their apartment from the real estate office. It is a nice apartment in a building with about 14 apartments in it.

I have a new roomer in my house. This man is from Japan and works for the same company I do. He will be in Pennsylvania for 10 months, so that will be a help. He doesn't speak much English, but I sent him to an English/Japanese teacher in the neighborhood. I still have Lee's room vacant and I am trying to get that one rented. Meanwhile, anytime you feel you want to come and visit, you can use it. If it gets rented, we can always share the master bedroom where I sleep.

Meanwhile, enjoy the summer. So much of it is hot and humid. It is so nice when it is about 80 and breezy. I love it that way and generally sit out under a tree during my lunch hour to eat my sandwich. Yes, I have gotten much heavier since I last saw you. No one at work believes that I was ever a skinny pickle. I am a heavyweight now.

Well, Bette, I better get back to work now. Remember we all love you.

All my love,

Shirley

Friday, September 23, 1977

Dear Bette:

It was good talking to you on the phone last week. Yesterday was Yom Kippur and, as usual, I fasted. It does me no harm since I am too heavy anyway. (Imagine me every saying that!) Barry, Ross and I went to both Rosh Hashanah and Yom Kippur services.

Tobey has been feeling much better although she still tires very quickly. Unfortunately, a week ago Sunday Tobey's grandfather was rushed to the hospital because of cancer. The decision was not to operate. Tobey took Deena and flew to Chicago to be with her family for the week.

I have some good news, job-wise. Last Wednesday my boss called me into the office to talk with me. He told me that starting October 1st I will no longer be a secretary. For six months I am on probation as a programmer/technician. If I do well, it will mean a good raise for me at the end of the probation period. I guess all the years that I have been taking computer classes and studies are finally going to pay off. I only hope that I will succeed as it is not an easy job and semi-professional. Of course, I have nothing to lose because if I find that I cannot do the new job, there is always secretarial work to fall back on.

Also, on September 25th I will be celebrating my fifth year with Univac. My boss and his wife are taking me out to celebrate on Monday. I enjoy the people I work with very much. Only the salary has been a terrible draw-back, and it has been very bad, financially, especially the year I broke my back and had to go on welfare. I still have to pay the government back for the money they gave me during that time.

I spoke to Lisa last week. I called her to wish her a Happy New Year. She is feeling fine now and the boys and I are hoping to go to Washington in a few weeks and spend the weekend with Lisa and Doug. Barry and I are also hoping to take a vacation between Xmas and New Year's this year and go down to Florida. It has been a long time since we have done anything. He has worked so hard at the print shop this summer and now, after school, he deserves some time to play and relax. We will probably stay at the Blue Horizon where we stayed years ago. Even in season it is only $11 a night per person and is right on the ocean. It isn't very fancy but I don't care. It will be nice to get away.

Meanwhile, I am looking for a night job so I can put the money aside for the trip. The air tickets cost plenty. Maybe I'll see Deedee and gang then as they usually visit with Miriam and Herb at Xmas time.

Well, Bette, I guess I better sign off for now and get down to work. Since I was out yesterday, there is plenty of work waiting for me and I better get to it before they change their minds about giving me a better job on October 1st.

Take care of yourself Bette. May the coming year be a good one for you with good health, good weather and may it be a time of enjoyment and no problems.

Love,

Shirley

Thursday, November 17, 1977

Dear Bette;

I received your letter of November 10 but this is the first chance I have had to answer it. Ever since I started on my new job I have been sitting at a computer terminal putting information into the computer. This morning, the system is having some kind of special run and I can't use it, so I am taking advantage of some free time and writing you a letter.

Tobey, Roy and Deena came over again last Saturday. Her doctor has his office near me so when she goes for her appointment, she drops Deena off and I have fun with her while she and Roy sit in the doctor's waiting room. Deena gets more adorable all the time. We took Molly for a walk and Deena kept saying, "I'm having fun with Ama" (I am Ama to her). Then I got a coloring book for her which she used three weeks earlier. It is a coloring book about "Over the Rainbow." Last time I told her the little girl's name in the coloring book was Dorothy. This time when I got out the book, Deena said, "Me wanna draw Dorothy." She never forgets anything. When Tobey and Roy came back from the doctor's office, I took them down to the brand new shopping center in our neighborhood for lunch. There is a Brooklyn Bagel and Noshery there, so we ate there and Deena had fun playing with a pole that was next to our table.

Ross continues to work for the Pennsylvania State Auditor General's office and presently is going over the books of one of the prisons. I'll be glad when he is finished working there. In the evening he is still working very hard in the insurance business, but things are very bad and he is not doing much in the way of sales. Naturally, his love of politics continues and he is always busy with that. Tonight, he is taking the evening off and going to a B'nai Brith dinner. He is active in that organization also.

Barry continues his love of cars; he is forever working on the car that was handed down to him (first it was Ross'; he gave it to Lee and when Lee got married he shared Nan's car and gave the Datsun to Barry). It is a run-down, beat-up old car, but Barry loves it and is forever working on it. He still works at the print shop and loves that also.

Our real estate taxes are going up by 12%, which is another 3- or 4-hundred a year. Including my mortgage, taxes and insurance, I shell out $290 a week now and gas and electric on the budget is $98 a month, plus a settle amount on the 12th bill each year. Now they want to up it 15%. My salary went up $7 a week on the new job. Big deal!

I am sorry you have so much trouble with pain in your hands. It must be arthritis. I wish there was something the doctor could do to relieve the pain for you. Yes, I do love you very much and feel sorry that we live so far apart. I am hoping that next May when I have a four-day holiday, I can put together some money and come and see you. Of course, that is a long way off.

As for now, I better go see if the computer has been fixed so I can get back to work. I enjoy your letters, so write.

Love,

Shirley

Tuesday, March 28, 1978

Dear Bette:

I don't have your letter with me, but since I have some free time and I am thinking of you, I decided to write.

Well, after three days of heavy rain, the snow is all washed away. Of course it is very muddy and plenty of puddles, but today is sunny and clear at long last. I hope the state will soon get to work on the potholes. The roads are in terrible condition and very hard on the cars. I have to buy 4 new tires and have all the rust holes fixed on my car, but it won't pass state inspection unless I do so. I have no choice. Barry's car had to be junked so he can't go to work as there is no public transportation. I may get a loan so I can get him a 1974 Vega.

Meanwhile, I have been having a lot of dental problems. I had teeth pulled 9 days ago. I only have five teeth on the bottom now and my upper teeth are all gone on the side. Right now I look like the 122-year-old woman from Russia in the yogurt commercial. Have you seen it on television? I am ashamed to go to work, but I can't afford to stay home.

Yesterday Tobey and Deena took a plane to Skokie, Illinois, to visit her parents for two weeks. I know Roy will miss them as he likes only to be with them. He has made a wonderful husband and father, but that is easy with a sweetheart like Tobey and a honey bun like Deena. Tobey's sister-in-law just had her second baby daughter so Deena is all excited at the prospects of seeing the new baby. She told Tobey, "We have an extra bedroom. Why don't we buy a baby, too?"

The Sunday after my birthday, Ross, Barry, Lee, Nan, Roy, Tobey and Deena took me to the Chinese restaurant to celebrate my 53rd birthday. We had a great time even though I had to gum down my food and keep my mouth covered. I'll be glad when the partials are done.

Barry is almost done with high school and vocational/technical school. He will graduate in June. I hope he will go to community college. He's already been accepted but isn't sure he wants to go. He is a good kid though and very good at fixing things around the house. He painted and wallpapered my kitchen, the fifth bedroom, the laundry room and the powder room. Last year he painted the outside of the house.

Ross is still working for the State Auditor General's Department in the daytime and sells insurance in the evening. He is planning to come to Boston on the weekend of April 15 and April 16. On April 17 he plans on running in the Marathon again. (Author's note, this turned out to be my fastest marathon race at 2:57.) If you would like company, I'll take the time off and ride up with him so we can visit you. We'll get in late Saturday night, sleep at your house, and spend Sunday with you doing whatever you want. He'll have his car. Then on Monday, you and I can watch him run past Coolidge Corner before he finishes. Ross and I will then come back to Pennsylvania. In fact, if you would like to come back with us and spend some time vacationing with us, we have plenty of room. Although I work in the daytime, I could come home at lunchtime some days and take you out to eat. Then when you are ready to return to Boston, Barry and I would drive you back on a weekend. The weather should be nicer in a few weeks and there is a lot to see. Besides, you would enjoy Deena and could meet Nan. Also, the next weekend is Passover, so you would be here for the Seder. I think Lisa and Doug are coming from Washington, so you'd have a chance to see them also. Please think about it. We all want you.

At any rate, if it's OK, I'll definitely see you late at night April 15th with Ross. Take care and write. I'll try to telephone you from my work before the 15th.

Love,

Shirley

Thursday, July 6, 1978

Dearest Aunt Bette:

Well, I am well settled back into my work routine after a most wonderful 2 and ½ days visiting you. The time went altogether too fast, however, and I wish we lived closer so we could see each other all the time. I do wish you would have come back with Barry and me for a visit to my house, but I know you are concerned about getting your roof and gutter fixed and also get the newspaper bill straightened out so I am taking a rain check on a future visit by you. Perhaps, Mrs. Dougherty, the lady who visits you on Friday, can be some help in getting both these matters straighten out. From what you told me she sounds like a very fine person.

It is a good thing we left Brookline for Pennsylvania when we did because by the time we approached New York it was pouring, windy with lightning and thunder. It took hours to get through New York, New Jersey and Pennsylvania. Barry and I want to thank you for a wonderful time. We enjoyed every minute of it. Barry thinks you are great and wants to come back the first chance he can. We enjoyed eating at Premier II on Harvard Street, seeing the Kennedy House again, seeing the new downtown Boston around Faneuil Hall, having the Greek pastry, Baklava, having ice cream sundaes at Brighams and enjoying the chicken dinner with potato pancakes and apple sauce at your house. You have always been fun to be with.

Whenever you decide you want to come to our house, just call or write me, and we will come and get you. You can stay as long as you like, and when you are ready to go back we will drive you.

I hope you are having less trouble with your hands. It sounds like it might be poor circulation. I love you very much and will try to visit you again soon.

Love,

Your niece, Shirley

Friday, July 14, 1978

Dear Bette:

When I got home last night your lovely letter of July 11 was waiting for me. You always make me feel so good with all your flattery. Everyone needs a boost now and then and you sure raise my ego.

That is funny about your clock starting to work again after all this time. The only clock in my home that works is on my oven. I haven't even had a working watch for about seven years. I usually call on the phone or turn on the radio to get the time.

Both Ross and Barry love you too, Bette, and were happy to have paid you a visit. Maybe after the Young Democrats election in August is over we'll be able to come again. Ross is running for State President of the Young Democrats and between his two jobs, his volunteer work and his campaign, I don't know how he ever finds time to sleep, let alone find time for social activities.

This Monday evening he is in charge of a baseball game between the radio station WFIL and the Montgomery County Young Democrats. The proceeds will go to Easter Seals. Barry is also playing in the game.

Tonight my department at work is playing another department in a softball game. Since I'm too old to play, I volunteered Barry and Ross and I'll serve as spectator. They plan on hotdogs, hamburgers, soda, beer, potato chips and pretzels. It was fun last year but it is threatening to rain, so the whole thing might be cancelled.

Did you finally pick up your pills at Coolidge Corner? Sometimes I go to the grocery store to pick up something special and then spend all my money buying things I see and come home without the item I went in for. So I know the feeling.

I don't have any help house cleaning or gardening, but my place is falling apart. When something breaks it stays broken as I haven't the money to fix or replace things. Your place looks beautiful and makes me feel ashamed. If you can keep your place so nice, why is mine such a mess?

I'm glad Mrs. Dougherty stops by every two weeks. Be sure, though, when she does you let her do your arguing with newspaper circulation departments, insurance claims departments, etc. (Author's note: Mrs. Dougherty worked for the Department of Public Welfare in Boston and would look in on my aunt.) This is what she was trained for and she can help in that way. She sounds like a nice person. My social worker is trying to get me a roomer. She got me one man. He paid for two weeks, then went to Massachusetts to visit his married son and decided to remain there, so I'm still without a roomer and the needed income. I put my name on a list at a local college. Maybe a student might be interested in renting one of the spare rooms.

Bette, I love you, too. You've always been a wonderful aunt and I always think about all my summer vacations with you. Remember when we used to go horseback riding at Owasco Lake? Remember the trouble I had with my braces when I ate roast beef at the Home Dairy Cafeteria? Remember when you and Uncle Harry took me on the rides at Emma Jettick Park or to the summer playhouse in Skaneateles? Those were wonderful, wonderful years. I wish you would come here so I could show you Pennsylvania and take you to all the nice inns and restaurants around here. Although I work five days a week, we could go out on weekends and evenings and you could take it easy during the daytime. Why do we all live so far apart?

Well, I better get back to work now. Tuesday I am being moved to another aisle, so I have to start packing. They are always moving personnel around where I work. It is a pain in the neck.

Love,

Shirley Ruth

Tuesday, July 25, 1978

Dear Bette:

I hope this letter finds you enjoying pleasant weather. For four days we have sweltered in hot, humid weather varying between 94 and 101 degrees. Today, it has cooled down, but it is raining. Saturday a friend came over and we went swimming at the pool four houses away. Then in the evening Barry, Ross and I went to the Valley Forge Music Fair to watch and listen to Seals and Croft. They are composers, musicians and singers. It was really a great evening. Then Sunday a friend picked me up and we drove to Ocean City, New Jersey. It was very hot and sticky driving there, and I felt as though I would pass out. The first thing I did when we got there was buy a tall glass of orange-aid. My lips were dry and salty. After that we sat in the sand near the Boardwalk so we could be shaded. The ocean water was delightful. The ride back was not as hot but traffic was horrible. All of Philadelphia must have been at the shore.

Then last night my friend and I met after dinner and we went to the new Robin Hood Dell West. It is like the Shell in Boston. The concerts are free and the place is beautiful. We saw and heard Eugene Ormandy and the Philadelphia Symphony Orchestra and van Cliburn in piano concert. It was a really lovely experience.

Meanwhile, I continue to run back and forth to the dentist. This week my partial plate was finally ready. I already have a lower partial. Now I have a matching upper. I feel so uncomfortable.

Roy, Tobey and Deena got back from Chicago yesterday. I guess I'll see them this weekend. Hope you can read this chicken scratch.

Love,

Shirley

Thursday, September 28, 1978

Dearest Bette:

We were happy to talk to you on the phone last Sunday. Wasn't that surprising news about Nan? She is 10 weeks pregnant now. They are very happy about it.

Lee still has 2 years more of dental school and then it takes four or five years to establish a good practice. He is very smart and has a business in their apartment. He builds integrated circuit boards for computers and studies hard to be a dentist. Nan is a good girl and is fixing up their apartment with very little money, but it is a warm, cozy place.

I saw Roy, Tobey and Deena Tuesday night. Tobey is five months pregnant now and feeling a lot better than she did the first time. Deena gets smarter every time I see her. She watches the news on TV and told me all about the plane collision in San Diego. Roy just got back from his business trip to Brussels, Belgium, and London. He bought me a Wedgewood pendant from London and a hand-made lace table setting from Belgium.

Love,

Shirley

Wednesday, October 18, 1978

Dearest Bette:

I haven't heard from you since I called you on Rosh Hashanah, but this is my third letter to you since then. I hope everything is O.K. and that your hand is not bothering you.

The weather has turned cold now, but the trees are so beautiful in their fall foliage. I love the lovely reds and oranges and yellows on the trees as the green gives way to the autumn tones. Each morning when I drive to work, it is a real feast for the eyes.

Last Sunday I really had you on my mind all day. The first thing in the morning Ross and I drove down into Philadelphia where he ran the Provident Insurance Marathon. Do you remember how we watched him run in Boston last spring? Of course the weather was a lot chillier and I wore a sweater, a jacket, and then I put his track jacket on while I stood outside waiting for him to pass. Somehow, I found myself serving glasses of water to the runners as they passed. There were two tables set up and both had Gatorade and several runners asked for water. So I grabbed a bunch of empty bottles and ran across to the nearby boathouse where I filled them with water. This kept up for about an hour.

After Ross passed I walked over to the Art Museum. Again, you were on my mind. They are having a special exhibit this month on French Art from Napoleon's time. It is called the Second Empire. Anyway, I kept thinking of all the stories you used to tell me of your trip to Europe. They even transported furniture from the French palaces and I saw the cradle the Empress Eugenie was given upon the birth of her first baby. You really would have enjoyed the exhibit, Bette, and I kept wishing you were here so I could take you to see it. We had such a good time sightseeing in Boston last summer.

Anyway, after I saw the exhibit, I came down the steps of the art museum just in time to join in on the First Annual Restaurant Fair. Can you imagine 60 restaurants from the Philadelphia area participated? It went from in front of the Art Museum for five blocks toward Center City and was two blocks wide. Each restaurant had a booth and temporary kitchen and prepared its best menus for visitors to sample. The newspaper report said that 500,000 people visited the fair in the one day. I had crab gumbo from Old Original Bookbinders. Then I went to the Phoenix Korean Restaurant for honey chicken on a bed of rice. From there I wandered over to another booth where I had scallops wrapped in bacon. At the Japanese booth, I had a steak concoction. From there I wandered over to a restaurant called Monk's Inn where I had 20 steamed mussels. At another booth I had quiche Lorraine and I finished up my meal at still another restaurant called The Fisherman where I had the most delicious pie I ever tasted. It was called Chocolate Chess Pie. It was yummy.

By that time it was 2:30, so I got back in the car and drove to where I was to pick up Ross after his race. We got home about 3:30 and I got down to doing my housework and back to reality once more. It was such a beautiful day though.

I am having trouble with my typewriter. Every time I hit the letter "I," it falls off and a "K" is typed. Please excuse it.

This Sunday I am expecting a visit from Deedee and family as well as from Lisa and Doug. They will spend the whole day and we will all celebrate Barry, Ross and Lisa's birthdays together.

Meanwhile, Bette, keep warm and write me when you can. K love you and miss you and K wksh I could see you more often. (Author's comment: I left the K in instead of the I as described by Mom with her typewriter problem.)

Love,

Shirley

Tuesday, November 14, 1978

Dear Bette:

I have a few minutes between phases of jobs I am working on to be completed by other departments and so will take advantage of the free time to write to you.

I hope this letter finds you well and that the weather in Boston hasn't turned too cold yet. The sun is shining here, but it is finally cold enough for me to wear my winter coat for the first time this year.

Finally, I got my dryer fixed. It broke down last March and for a while I was hanging the family wash all over the house. During the summer I hung it outdoors, but now that it is getting cold I decided to see how much it would cost and get it fixed. Hopefully, it will work through the winter.

Gradually, I am also replacing my venetian blinds. Most of them have been broken for years. I went to K-Mart and got some cheap plastic window shades. It's better than having to undress in the dark. Ross put them up for me, and it makes quite a difference!

Sunday, I got to see Lee, Nan, Roy, Tobey and Deena. They joined Ross, Barry and me for dinner. Deena gets cuter all the time. She goes to nursery school at a synagogue close to their home and loves it. She knows the prayers for the bread (Ha Motzi) and for lighting the candles (Baruch Atah Adonai) and tells me Good Shabbat when I call on the phone on a Friday. She will be three years old in January. Time goes by so fast.

This Thursday I will complete my latest lunchtime course here at work. It was called "Product Line Survey" and each marketing department sent representatives to tell the class all about the particular Univac product they sell. I'll get another certificate; that makes 17 courses I've taken in six years. They ought to give me a diploma.

Barry is very happy with his new car. It's a Datsun 200SX (a tiny sports coupe). He has 1,200 miles on it in 14 days and had a tune up last night. I hardly ever see him since he got the car.

Well, the phone just rang. One of the jobs is ready so I have to go get it and get to work myself.

Love and kisses,

Shirley Ruth

Thursday, December 7, 1978

Dear Bette:

As usual, our letters crossed in the mail again. It sounds as though you also are having a lot of problems these days.

Did the roofer fix your roof? Where did you get him from? How did he get hold of the watch in the first place? Did the policy finally show up? It sounds terrible. Are you positive that he took anything? It would be terrible to accuse him and have him arrested and then later find the missing things in a drawer somewhere. (Author's Comment: My Aunt was developing dementia and was either being taken advantage of by contractors or imagining things.)

Well, Barry moved out last week and now I have three spare bedrooms. Only Ross and I are left in this big house. I wish you would consider selling your house and coming to live with me. Although I have to work, I get home by 5:30 each night and am home on weekends. We could be company for each other and go places and do things together. You wouldn't have to worry about roofers, insurance, taxes and could enjoy life a little.

Thanksgiving Day, Roy and I took Deena to the parade. She loved it. She looked at the girls in the parade in their brief costumes and said, "They must be very cold." She is so smart, God bless her. My mother and father would have eaten her up. She is so excited about becoming a big sister in March. Roy and Tobey took Deena shopping to see Santa Claus. He asked her what she wanted for Xmas and she replied, "Chanukah presents." What a sweetheart she is.

Bette, I don't want to promise but if the weather is OK and it is not snowing on Friday, December 15th, Ross and I will drive to Brookline in his car after work and get in about

10 at night. We'll stay until Sunday, December 17 and have a good weekend with you. I'll write or call you next week to let you know for sure after I hear the five-day weather forecast for that weekend. So pray for good weather.

Meanwhile, you should get in touch with Mrs. Doherty to see if there is anything she can do to help you with the roofing, insurance, theft and dental problems. I do love you very much, Bette. You are a wonderful person and I don't know of anyone who doesn't agree with me.

Love,

Shirley Ruth

Saturday, January 20, 1979

Dear Bette:

I received your letter early in the week. Yes, I too love our dog Molly. You are right. She is a girl dog and very, very lovable and affectionate. I think she loved her visit to Brookline. (Author's Note: I am amazed we took the dog all the way to Boston, but it was probably my Mother's idea so that Bette could see her.) I still think of how she kissed you and when we said, "Wag your tail, Molly," she began wagging it so hard it kept hitting the bed. She is the biggest dog we have ever had, but she is so very affectionate and well-behaved.

Last Thursday Barry left for Washington, D.C. He starts school there next Monday. He will be staying with Lisa and Doug until he finds a place of his own. Don't ask me why he doesn't go to school right here in Pennsylvania. It will cost more to live away from home and be harder for him, but he made all his own arrangements. I hope it works out well for him and I hope he does well in school. Basically, he is a good kid but he is pushing himself into adulthood too fast. I just hope I can hold on to the house so if he decides to come back, I will still have a room for him.

I have rented two rooms now—one to a man who works where I do and is originally from Jamaica and one to a lady from a club I belong to. Now I have Barry's room, so I'll put a notice on the bulletin board to see if I can get that one rented also. I need the money badly. Everything is so costly.

Last week I had car problems. It took two days to get it fixed and it cost $74. The car is eight years old and I have 110,000 miles on it, so it is to be expected, I guess.

Ross continues to work very hard at two jobs and with all his volunteer projects.

Well, take care, Bette. I watch for mail from you and wish we weren't so far away from each other.

Love and kisses,

Shirley Ruth

Friday, June 29, 1979

Dearest Aunt Bette:

I received your short letter yesterday, along with the picture from the newspaper. I think the girl in the picture looks more like Miriam did back in the days when she was in college than it looks like I did. However, Ross looked at it and agreed with you that it resembled me. Anyway, thanks for the compliment. According to the article the girl in the picture makes $1,250 a day to model for magazines. I wish I could make even ¼ that amount each day. I don't make that a week and in fact, I don't make that much a month.

From the fact that your letter was so short, I realize that your hands must really be giving you a lot of trouble. A neighbor of mine recently had a stroke and she lost the ability to work with her hands. The doctors and nurses have been giving her physical therapy and last week they told her to go to the toy department in the local store and buy a package of Play Dough. It is a kind of clay. They told her to work with it, squeezing it and shaping it. They claim, the more she works with it, the less pain she should have. You should ask your doctor if he thinks that might be helpful.

As for me, I am still at home sick with back and stomach problems. I saw an orthopedic man since my last letter to you. He thinks I have degenerative arthritis in the spine. The family doctor diagnosed it as a pinched nerve. I don't know what it is, but I still can't go back to work. Meanwhile, I am taking the medicines that both doctors prescribed. Maybe in another two weeks or so they'll let me go back to work.

Meanwhile, I am waiting for my paycheck. Since I have been out sick beyond my sick leave, I have to wait for my paycheck to come from the insurance company and the bookkeeping departments in insurance companies are never in a hurry. Meanwhile, I can't send Ross out shopping since I have nothing to pay for groceries with. I have plenty on my shelves but can't replenish it as I use it until the money comes in, so don't worry.

Well, Pennsylvania finally started gas rationing. Wednesday, before the gas rationing law went into effect, Ross waited 3½ hours in line and they would only sell him $5 worth of gas so it didn't fill his tank. Now, the lines are much shorter and he can buy gas on odd numbered dates. The gas stations promise to stay open six hours a day until they run out, so things are somewhat better along those lines.

The truckers are still striking, however, to try to get the price of diesel oil down. So the grocery shelves are getting sparse and according to the TV news, the warehouses can only hold so much produce, so the farmers are beginning to plow under a lot of items like tomatoes and cantaloupe since they can't get them to the market. It is a shame the world is so full of greed. Most of our problems economically are caused by greed and power-plays and meanwhile it's the everyday person who must suffer the consequences.

Even though your letter was short, I am glad you wrote to me as I think of you all the time and worry when I don't receive at least one letter each week. Your handwriting is as clear as ever so don't worry that I can't read it.

Once I am back on my feet and back to work, Ross and I will arrange to come to Brookline to visit you. We'll come to see you provided we can get the gas to travel so far. That's another problem we would have to solve.

Well, take care of yourself. We love you very much and only wish we were closer. You know you are always welcome here and if you ever decide to come, we'll come and get you. All you have to do is let us know.

Love,

Shirley Ruth

July 18, 1979

Dearest Aunt Bette:

I still haven't heard from you and this is my fourth letter. Perhaps today's letter will bring word from you. I hope you are O.K.

I wrote you that Miriam's youngest daughter Lisa had her baby. I am not sure but I think the bris for Brian Edward Jones is this coming Sunday. I guess my four sons, Roy, Ross, Lee and Barry will go up to help form the minion. I doubt very much if I will go as the jouncing of the car would be very hard on me at this time.

As for my own granddaughter and grandson, I think Roy and Tobey are going to bring them over for a visit this Saturday. They are so much fun to be with. Tobey told me that Roy taught Micah how to make a clicking sound by hitting his tongue on the roof of his mouth and now when the baby sees Roy, he clicks his tongue. They put the phone to Micah's ear and I talk to him and he makes goo sounds at me.

As for Deena, she is having a great time this summer. Roy and Tobey sent her to day camp three mornings a week and she loves it. She is almost 3½ now and very precious and affectionate. I know you would love her. When she starts laughing I laugh so much I cry and wet my pants. You know me and my weak bladder!! Those two little ones are the joy of my life and I know now how Nana (Freda) used to feel about my four boys when they were little. No wonder she and Dad used to come and visit me so often back in those days.

Barry has been home quite a bit this summer. He works for Lee, helping him with his electronic business. Lee makes integrated circuit boards as a living while going to dental school. This summer he has started practicing dentistry at the clinic and really loves it. In addition to helping Lee, Barry is also doing some heavy gardening work for Lee's father-in-law and is getting paid fairly well. He has to make plenty of money in order to make the car payments, but he loves the car and feels it is worth it.

Meanwhile, my 1971 Galaxie has been sitting in the garage for about six weeks now ever since I got sick. I guess it is just as well since whenever I drove it, something would go wrong and I owe $300 in repairs. Besides with gas being over $1 a gallon now, it cost over $22 to fill the tank, and I don't make that kind of money; so in a way it is just as well that I haven't been working as I wouldn't be able to afford the gas and repairs anyhow. Of course, a lot of the same money is presently going for medicine and doctor bills so you can't win for losing.

Ross continues to be very busy with his two jobs and all his political and charity work. This Saturday he has to go to Harrisburg for a meeting. He rarely takes it easy but seems like a happy person. Last Saturday he ran in a charity race for the American Cancer Crusade and came in 52 out of 2,000 runners. However, there was a tragedy connected with the event. The helicopter covering the event for TV news crashed and the photographer and sound men were both drowned in the river right beside where Ross was running. Ross said when they were filming his running a few minutes before, they were flying so low and close to him, he had to hold on to the number on his chest for fear it would blow away. He had a sudden intuitive feeling that something was about to happen. Suddenly the helicopter's rotary blades stopped turning and it fell right into the river next to the bridge where Ross had just been. I guess it is something Ross will never forget.

Barry just came home from his friend's house. His friend got a guitar as a gift. He is very excited about it and wants to play it for me.

Write to me Bette as I get worried about you when I don't hear from you. You know how much I love you. If I don't hear from you soon, I will call you in a few days.

Your ever-lovin' niece,

Shirley Ruth

Tuesday, July 24, 1979

Dearest Bette:

I am really getting worried about you. This is my fourth letter to you in three weeks and I have not heard from you once in all that time. I know you have a great deal of trouble with your hands and I hope that there is nothing else wrong and it is just that it is difficult for you to hold a pen and write me. If I don't hear from you by the weekend, I will call you.

I am still not back to work since the back pains flared up again and the doctor does not want me returning to work until I can go a full day without pains. I am a lot better than I was two months ago, but I still have to stop every couple of hours and lie down and take the pressure off my back.

Barry and Ross went to Washington last weekend to visit Lisa and Doug and see the new baby. It was Brian Edward's bris and so Deedee, Gene, Julie and Debbie were there also. Gene's mother was also there as were some friends and Doug's brother. Barry and Ross had a wonderful time, and it was a good weekend especially for Ross since he works so hard as a general rule.

Before they left on Saturday, Barry drove me over to Roy and Tobey's house and I spent the afternoon and evening playing with Deena and Micah. The baby can sit up now and can roll over from his stomach to his back.

Today Barry decided to take a day off from work and go to the shore with some friends of his. So Ross and I will have supper alone together for a change. Ross is still working very hard at his two jobs but hasn't had an insurance sale in months, so it is really getting rough for him economically. He is such a good person and does so much charity and volunteer work in addition to all the work hours he puts in. I hope God will be good to him and soon things will turn around for the best for him soon. (Author's comment: I only wish Mom would have known that I am doing OK financially now.)

As for Lee and Nan, they are very happy. He is working at the dental clinic over the summer and Nan is always busy needle-pointing something. Her walls are covered with things she has made.

I saw a picture of Rose Kennedy in the paper last Sunday. She is 89 years old now. Do you remember when we went to see their old house near the Devotion School off Harvard Street? It was a very interesting tour and the recordings of her voice explaining about each room really made it very interesting.

Well, I want to get this into the mail box before the mail man arrives, so I better bring this letter to a close now. Please let me hear from you. Remember, I love you very much. You have always been like a mother to me, and I worry when so much time passes without any word.

Love and kisses,

Shirley Ruth

Sunday, September 23, 1979

Dear Bette:

It was very good talking to you on the phone on Saturday. Ross, Barry and I wanted to wish you a good New Year (Rosh Hashanah) and we were glad to hear your voice, although I am worried about you and can't help that.

We worry because when Ross and I were in Boston we saw how you had lost some teeth from the front of your mouth and have not gone to a dentist to have new teeth made. We worry because no matter how you say you have plenty of food, we know that it must be very difficult to eat with your teeth in their present condition. You must go to the dentist. You must go to the doctor for a check-up. He might be able to relieve some of the pressure you are suffering in your hands. Please let Mrs. Doherty take you to both your doctor and your dentist as soon as possible. This is very, very important.

As far as you staying in the house all the time, Bette, that just isn't good for you. I wish you would agree to come and stay here for awhile. It isn't good for anyone to be alone day after day the way you are. I know you love your home, and I can well understand that. It is a beautiful home and you keep it lovely and clean. We will come and get you. If you agree to this and you can come and stay with us all winter then in the spring you can go back to Boston if that is what you want to do and enjoy your own porch again. On the other hand, if you decided in the spring that you wanted to stay here, I have a beautiful front porch and back patio and the flowers and sunshine and the neighborhood is lovely and I know you would enjoy it. Besides, I could take you places, and we could enjoy each other's company.

I know Miriam also wants you to come and stay with her. If that is what you want, then please do it. I wouldn't be angry. Rather, I would be happy that at least you would not be alone. It's whatever you want as long as you are with someone.

The point is that if you insist you want to stay in Brookline all by yourself, then you need some outside help because you are having too many medical problems to take care of yourself alone and are lonely. I know there is an organization called Meals on Wheels. They bring cooked food everyday to elderly people or people who are sick. They clean up afterwards and that way you get well-balanced meals everyday. Maybe Mrs. Doherty can make arrangements for you to have this kind of daily help. While you would still be alone, at least you would get hot meals.

Please Bette, take care of yourself. We love you and want you to come and visit. Just remember you have a family that wants to be with you.

Love and kisses,

Shirley Ruth

Thursday, October 11, 1979

Dearest Aunt Bette:

I hope you are feeling O.K. Did you get snow in Brookline this week? Yesterday, quite to everyone's surprise the cold rain that was coming down all the night before turned to snow around 9:00 a.m. and continued snowing until about 3:00 in the afternoon. When I got out of work, the car had snow all over it. The green grass and flowers all had a thick coating of the fluffy stuff. No one was dressed for it.

The worst of it is I had all my old rain gutters and spouts taken down over last weekend in preparation for putting up new ones. The new ones are lying in the back yard and the workman hasn't been able to put them up all week because of the crazy weather. Meanwhile, it sounds like a waterfall in the house since the rain and snow are all coming down against the side of the house and into the basement. I hope we have a good weekend so he can get the job done.

Tonight Ross and Barry went to the Montgomery County Democratic Dinner. Moe Udall was the guest speaker. I didn't have the $17.50 for the dinner ticket and besides I am teaching a class at work and spend every evening working on the class assignment for the next day. I teach two days a week on my lunch hour and for 20 lessons I will get $350, but it takes hours to plan the sessions, to try out the assignments on the computer, debug them and get them perfect for the class so they can try their hand at it. It is interesting, though, and I like it better than the work I do all day.

This weekend, Tobey's mother is coming from Chicago and will meet Tobey in New York. Tobey is very excited since her mother and she have not taken a trip together since she and Roy got married and they are looking forward to a great weekend in New York. Then Evelyn will have a good time with her grandchildren for a couple of days before going home.

Barry went to his dentist this week. He had x-rays taken and was told he has one cavity. Do you know who his dentist is? It's Lee. Lee works at the clinic at Temple University three days a week and has had almost 100 cases already in the six months since he has been training. If you were here, he would take care of your teeth. Lee will finish dental school in another year and a half and then we can call him Dr. Schriftman. How about that? My son, the dentist!

Barry is still working second shift for Smith Kline Medical Laboratories. He is a pill inspector and makes sure all the pills go out in good shape. He likes the job and the money but I don't like the hours since he goes to work in the afternoon while I am at work and comes home after I am asleep, so I only see him on weekends.

Ross is very busy with his campaign for Montgomery County Controller. I don't think he has a ghost of a chance to win the election in this Republican stronghold, but that doesn't stop him. He puts his whole heart into it.

Roy is working on his second master's degree. He hopes to get it in the spring. This one is for Business Administration. (The Author's comment: It was an MBA.) The first one he got in theoretical math. He is some smart guy.

Meanwhile, Bette, I hate to think of you alone in your house all winter. I'm glad you saw the doctor. When are you going to see the dentist? Remember, Medicare and whatever

Massachusetts calls Medicaid will take care of it. You don't have to pay for dental expenses.

My nice roomer left two weeks ago. He only planned to stay until he bought a house in Pennsylvania and then his wife and children would come from Indiana. Now the young kid who rents Lee's old room gave me notice that he is leaving October 27th.

This would be a good time for you to come and visit me or stay with me for as long as you like. I have a five-bedroom house and it looks as though only two bedrooms will be used within another few weeks.

I used to be able to work with the Family Services here in Montgomery County to get older citizens who wish companionship and family life but then that part of Family Service's activities was turned over to the Welfare Department of Pennsylvania, and that agency won't let any family take an elderly person unless at least one member of that family is home all the time; so that let me out.

Give my love to Bertha Freed when you talk to her and also to Selma downstairs. I'll write you again in a few days. If you feel like calling, please do so.

Love,

Shirley

Saturday, November 3, 1979

Dearest Aunt Bette:

I hope everything is OK. I haven't heard from you since before Ross and I visited you way back the last weekend in August.

I went over to visit Roy and Tobey and the children on Halloween night. Tobey made Deena a witch costume out of black cotton muslin. It was a cute little dress with raglan sleeves and a full cape in the back. She put plenty of make-up on Deena's face and she looked adorable. She didn't want to look cute and when we went door to door and people would say, "Oh, look at Deena. She is a cute little witch," she would say, "Oh no. I'm not supposed to be cute. I'm an ucky witch, listen" and then she would go, "Heh, heh, heh," in a witch voice and everyone would laugh and want to hug her. This she could not understand. "Why aren't they afraid?" she would say. God, what an adorable little three-year-old she is.

As for Micah, this is his first Halloween so they didn't dress him up, but either Roy or Tobey would sit on the stairs with him and hand out the Trick-or-Treats to the children who came to the door and he was very interested. He was given his first lollipop. He was adorable with it. He put the ball of candy in his mouth and showed surprise when he began to salivate a sweet taste. Then he tried putting the stick end in his mouth and saw that it didn't have any taste, so he carefully turned it around and put the candy ball back in his mouth. It was so funny to watch him. He is 8 months old already. Can you imagine that?

I spoke to Miriam long distance last week. I also got a letter from Deedee and one from Lisa, so I heard from the whole Kandall family this week. Lisa, Doug and their little baby Brian are going to visit Deena for Thanksgiving weekend, so Deedee invited us to come also for that Saturday after Thanksgiving. I'll have my family here for Thanksgiving Day, but I guess we will visit Deedee that Saturday. Her little daughters are also very sweet—Julie and Debbie.

I continue to be very busy at work. Every night I come home and spend about two hours preparing the class plans for the next day's class I am teaching. I have three more weeks before the class finishes. However, since I have taught it completely, the next time around will be easier since I kept all my notes and references. Out of 16 students when I started only three dropped out, so I guess I have maintained their interest. As far as my regular work is concerned, I have been working about 9 hours a day just to try to keep up with it.

On top of all that, Ross' campaign takes a lot of time. Just as soon as I finish this letter and drop it in the mail, I have to go door-to-door campaigning for him. I have scheduled for myself 100 houses today. Next Tuesday is Election Day. Although he campaigns very hard and is definitely the better candidate for County Controller, it is very doubtful that he will win since there are about 65% Republicans in this county, about 28% Democrats and the rest are non-partisan. A friend of his came in for four days to help him campaign. They left at 10:00 a.m. this morning. They want to cover 2,000 homes today, tomorrow and Monday. Tuesday, he will spend the day visiting the various polling areas and Tuesday night we will know the results.

Then the following weekend, he is running in another marathon. He never stops to rest. I don't know where he gets all that energy. Tomorrow night we are going to a wine and cheese party that the candidate for Township Commissioner is giving. Ed Heller and his wife Sheila are originally from Boston and it seems like home when I am with them because not only do they talk about Boston a lot, but they both have the Boston English way of talking like you do. He was the first Democrat to ever win in our town. Ross and I were very proud because we worked very hard to get him in the first time. I hope he gets re-elected as he is a very nice person and takes the job of township commissioner very seriously.

My back is still giving me a lot of pain and stiffness, but I am determined not to let it get me down. I hardly sleep at night because as soon as I wind down and get into bed, the pain sets in and keeps me up all night. The other night I didn't fall asleep until 4:30 a.m. Then I woke up and didn't look at the clock and hurried to work one hour early. I was dumbfounded when I pulled into the parking lot and no one was there.

Stay well, Bette. We all love you and wish we could be together.

Love,

Shirley Ruth

Tuesday, November 27, 1979

Dear Aunt Bette:

This is the first chance I have had to write to you since I wrote to you just one week ago. On Wednesday, I left work a couple of hours early so I could get home and clean the house before Thanksgiving. On Thursday I cooked the traditional Thanksgiving turkey with walnut stuffing, made candied sweet potatoes, orange cranberry relish, turkey and chicken chopped liver on celery sticks, turkey and chicken soup with matzo balls, green beans and Sara Lee black forest cake. Tobey made a pumpkin pie with a whipped cream topping. I also had sherbet and candied dates. Roy, Tobey, Deena, Micah, Ross, Barry, my friends Gladys and Sam, and I ate until we were so stuffed we couldn't move. We took a lot of pictures and when I get them developed, I will send them to you.

On Friday, I did more housecleaning. I was too tired to do the dishes on Thanksgiving, and lo and behold they were waiting for me on Friday. I have a dishwasher but it took three loads to get all the dishes in. We are still eating turkey. I also managed to do a little Xmas and Chanukah shopping.

Then on Saturday morning, Ross, Barry and I went over to pick up Deena, and we took her with us on our day trip to Deedee and Gene's new house in New Jersey. It is really a lovely colonial home set back on a quiet street with other similar houses and a wooded backyard with lovely shade trees in the front. Her children are adorable. Debbie and Julie both have big round eyes. They are sweet little girls and very generous and loving. They played so nicely with little Deena and let her play with all their toys and dolls. Lisa and Doug were also there with their new addition, little Brian. He is a cuddly little baby and didn't cry once the entire 12 hours we spent there. Deedee has a French poodle miniature (silver fur) that is called Princess. Lisa and Doug brought their cat, Sot. So it was a full and lovely day and I enjoyed every minute of it. When we arrived, Deedee had made cheese blintzes and turkey salad for lunch. In the evening she made a pot roast brisket. She also made a yummy chocolate dessert with candy shavings for a top and covered the whole thing with a hot fudge sauce. I'll bet I gained 10 pounds over the holidays.

Then on Sunday I made a second big dinner for Lee and Nan. They came over Sunday since they spent Thanksgiving with her parents. Rather than give them leftover turkey, I made a leg of lamb with mint jelly, roasted potatoes, a green been and French fried onion casserole, the last of the turkey matzo ball soup, a cheese cake and Nan brought a banana cake. So it was another day of feasting. I am bursting with all this food.

Last night I made turkey chow mein. Tonight we had turkey salad. Tomorrow night we'll finish the leg of lamb and then Thursday night we will have hot turkey with gravy. Meanwhile, we will take turkey sandwiches to work tomorrow. (Author's note: Mom always figured how to make different dishes out of leftovers from a major holiday like Thanksgiving.)

Well, that about brings everything up to date, Bette. How are you feeling? Are you eating the food that is brought by Meals on Wheels? You'll really appreciate it once the icy cold weather comes and you won't be able to get out because of snow and ice. How are your lamps working? Does the light in the kitchen pantry work O.K.? If not, don't forget I put a new switch I bought in the top drawer of the breakfast room. Someone can put it in for you if the other one doesn't work properly.

We all miss you and anytime you want to come here, please just call and we will come and get you. Meanwhile, take care of yourself and stay warm. I'll write again next week.

Love,

Shirley Ruth

Monday, December 3, 1979

Dearest Aunt Bette:

Well, here I am again with my weekly letter to you. Saturday Roy called me and asked if I could come and baby-sit since they wanted to do some shopping. I was so happy that I had made no plans for the day. I got right in the car and drove over there. Micah looked so cute in a little knit suit. They told me he could stand up and hold on to the crib or playpen. Well, he wanted to show off for me so he let go and made "pat-a-cake" and "so BIG!" for me and wasn't holding on at all. He was very proud of himself and sat down and applauded himself. Deena and I laughed at that one.

This Wednesday night I am going to baby-sit again. Roy's office is giving another man and Roy a dinner. It's because Roy did such a wonderful job in that department and has worked overtime so much and always got them out of any computer problems. Now he is transferring to the International Division and will be working on cost comparisons of drugs. It's a wonderful opportunity for him, and I hope he enjoys it and makes a success there just as he did in the computer center.

I only wish the world news was better, but things in the Arab world never seem to change; and it's a terrible thing that our Americans got caught up in this terrible situation. I hope they can bring the hostages back but I am afraid all 50 may never get back. (Author's comments: She must have been talking about the hostage taking in Iran which, of course, is not an Arab country. She was probably simplifying the situation for Bettie.)

Well, Bette, Ross is going out to see a customer now, so if I finish this letter now, he'll be able to mail it for me. Take care of yourself. Write me if you feel up to it, but if you are having difficulty with your hands, I understand. I'll write to you anyway.

Love and kisses,

Shirley Ruth

Saturday, January 26, 1980

Dearest Aunt Bette:

Here I am again. I hope this letter finds you feeling O.K. and that the weather is not too bitter or snowy. It is supposed to snow again tomorrow or Monday, but so far we have been lucky this winter. The only time we had driving problems was when the trucks waited too long before going out to salt. That morning rush hour was a terror of sliding and slipping and I never did make it in to work that day.

This week, I lost a day of work also. However, it was not because of weather. It is just that my car is so old and in such poor condition, it doesn't always run. I can't buy another car because I owe too much on the repairs on this one; and besides, I don't have the down payment. Cars are about $6,000 nowadays. It's a terrible bind.

On Tuesday night, Ross took me to the opening of the headquarters for a candidate running for the State Legislature over in Plymouth Meeting. It was a very nice evening. The candidate is a lovely woman and I hope she wins. After the meeting, we all went to Friendly's for a bite to eat. I enjoy being with these people.

In March, we are planning to have a fundraiser. We are going to have a Sunday morning brunch in honor of the two men we got in for Township Commissioner—Ed Heller (originally from Brookline; in fact, his mother lives on St. Paul Street) and Norton Freedman. They are the first Democrats to ever win office in this township in 80 years. I am co-chairing the brunch, so I guess I'll have plenty to do for the next month and a half.

Molly, the dog, is begging to go outside now, so I guess this is a good time to bring this letter to a close. Please take good care of yourself, eat well, take care of your teeth and your eyes and I hope the arthritis in your hands is letting up so you feel better.

With love and kisses,

Shirley Ruth

Sunday, February 24, 1980

Dear Bette:

I am in the middle of cooking a pot roast but I thought I would sit down for a few minutes and write to you. I hope that you are O.K. It's terrible not knowing how you are doing.

Yesterday Ross, Barry and I went over to Roy and Tobey's for Micah's first birthday celebration. Poor little thing! He had a terrible cold and didn't quite know what to make of all the fuss and excitement. We put his presents on the floor next to him. He didn't notice them and cried for someone to pick him up. Then Roy started to open the first present. Micah stopped crying and looked to see what was in the box. Then he realized that all the presents were for him and he was delighted. Between coughing and getting his nose wiped, he kept reaching for the presents to see what each thing was. Just like Roy when he was one year old, he loved the little cloth books and kept bringing them to us to read. But most of all he liked the stuffed toy his Mommee and Daddee gave him. It has a string on it and when you pull the string, it says different things. One of the things it says is, "I really love you." When Micah heard that he pulled the stuffed animal close to him and hugged it, saying. "AHHHH, AHHHH." It was so adorable.

Deena is so good with him. She kept giving him his toys and wiping his nose. She is like a little mother.

The time goes by so fast. Lee's wife, Nan, is due on March 7, so she could have the baby anytime now. Wouldn't it be strange if she had the baby on March 14, my birthday?

I think I wrote you that I bought a new car, finally. I should have bought it a long time ago since I spent so much on repairs for the old car. But I kept hoping that each repair would finally get the old Ford in working shape once more. It never did. Now I am trying to sell it but the biggest offer I got was only $50. I owe $400 in the last few repairs so I am trying to find someone that will pay me at least $150.

Meanwhile, the new little car seems to be O.K. Unfortunately, they are digging up my street right now in order to put in township sewers so the car is covered with mud. It doesn't look new and shiny because of all the mess, and I can't wash it every day. I hope they get done soon.

Maybe after the spring elections are over, I can get Ross to come with me to visit you for a weekend. Right now, he is very busy campaigning. He is the campaign manager in Montgomery County for Craig Lewis who is running for U.S. Senate. He skips dinner half the time because he works two full-time jobs and campaigns all the rest of his waking hours.

Remember, we love you and think of you all the time. I know we are very close in love for one another but I want to do more and feel very frustrated that while you stay where you are I can't do much more than write to you and think about you.

Love and kisses,

Shirley Ruth

Monday, April 14, 1980

Dearest Aunt Bette:

I have been so busy at work these days; I just haven't had a moment to myself. That's why I am writing this letter this evening right after supper, before I do the dishes. This way I will get it mailed on my way in to work in the morning. I am enclosing a few snapshots I took at Deena's birthday party and at Micah's birthday party. I wrote on the back of them so I won't repeat myself now. I hope you like them.

Next week I'll send you some pictures of little Seth, Lee and Nan's baby. I got the originals back from the camera store and have requested that copies be made. I know you will like them. Imagine—Seth is almost 5 weeks old already.

Is the weather starting to get warmer in Brookline? This weekend was absolutely beautiful here in Pennsylvania. On Saturday Roy and Tobey took me with Deena and Micah to Independence Hall, the Liberty Bell, Ben Franklin's grave, out to lunch and to a shopping mall. We had a wonderful time. All the trees were blossoming. I love the early spring time.

Yesterday was so warm; I didn't even wear a sweater when I went crusading for the American Cancer Society. I did five streets and took in about $55. Ross did five other streets and brought in $98. However, overall the crusade has not been as good this year as last year. Last year we won the award for bringing in 150% of the goal. This year we will be lucky to bring in 75% of what was requested. Ross was Crusade Chairman again this year for the Wissahickon District, and I was one of his polling district chairmen. Anyway, it was such a lovely day. Everyone was outside planting or cutting the grass. Our place is a mess. We never have any time to take care of our personal projects because of all the volunteer work, politics, jobs, etc.

Well, I guess I better sign off now and get the heating pad on my back. It's raining today and the dampness hurts my back. I twisted it yesterday when I leaned over in my bed to turn off the lamp. Take care of yourself, Bette. We love you.

Love and kisses,

Shirley Ruth

Thursday, April 24, 1980

Dearest Aunt Bette:

As I promised you last week, I am sending you some additional pictures of Deena and Micah as well as some pictures of new little Seth. I hope you like them. The pictures were taken the day of Seth's bris at Lee and Nan's apartment. Deena and Micah were all dressed up for the big event and look so cute in the bird cage chair in Lee and Nan's living room.

Saturday and Sunday, Ross and I were busy from noon until dark going door to door canvassing our neighborhood for the Democratic state primary. It really paid off in our district as everyone we recommended won. However, statewide they didn't do so good. In fact, the man Ross worked so hard for U.S. Senate came in 5th out of eight candidates.

Well, I signed a contract to have someone connect the sewer line from the street to my house. It will be done early in May. I have to pay the township $210 for permission. That really is funny since they demand that you hook up and then charge you an arm and a leg for permission. The contractor is charging $350 for his part of the job, providing he doesn't hit rock or other obstacles. Keep your fingers crossed. Then I have to wait to get my bill from the township for the cost of the sewer line in the road from one end of the property to the other—approximately 150 feet. That may be as much as $3,000, but we can make term payments. Lots of luck! I can't manage another penny of monthly payments for everything. You can't get blood from a stone. (Author's comment: I am not sure how we ended up managing to pay for the sewer installation, but we must have.)

I hope you are well and that the weather is nice and you are enjoying a pleasant springtime. Don't forget to take your eye medicine. Have you been to the dentist yet?

Love and kisses,

Shirley Ruth

May 1, 1980

Dearest Aunt Bette:
I hope you enjoy the pictures I sent you both last week and a few weeks ago. I know I love looking at them. Deena is getting to be a little lady and holds long conversations on the phone with me. Micah, of course, can only say a few words so when he gets on the phone, he says, "Hi, Ama" about 10 times and then hands the phone back to Tobey.

I heard from Grandma Schriftman today. It seems Grandpa Al was having trouble with his eyes. So about eight weeks ago, he had one eye operated on and then next Tuesday he will have the other one operated on. They live in Miami Beach now all year round. I saw Bea and Paul Weissler and Edie at Passover time. They are the same as ever. Rona is married now and a teacher in West Chester County, New York. Edie is a fashion designer. God, how the years go by. I still conjure up memories of them as little children.

This Saturday, I am going to a graduation party of a friend of mine from PWP (Parents without Partners); she is getting her MSW (Masters in Social Work). I am so proud of her. She is about 30 now. She had a terribly hard life. She married too young, about 17 and was stuck with a dope-addict. He beat her so badly once she was in the hospital. Anyway to make a long story short, she lived on welfare for years while she raised her son. She went to high school and graduated. Then she went to Temple University and graduated from there. Now she will get her master's degree. She is specializing in working with the deaf and blind. She is such a sweet young woman and full of fun—always singing and laughing. Her twin sister is surprising her with this party. Ross and Barry are also invited.

Barry's friend, Roger, is living with us right now. His mother and father are both in convalescent homes, and it is doubtful that they will ever come home. They are selling their house down the street in order to pay for the rest home. Roger stayed with his married sister in Detroit for about six months but really wanted to come back to Pennsylvania. So last Friday, Barry called me at work to say that Roger was flying in from Detroit and could he stay with us for awhile. He had nowhere to go. He is only 18 so since I have no boarders at the present time, I said O.K. So now I have both Barry and his friend Roger home—neither one is working as yet—so I really have to stretch an already meager income even more. But Roger is a good kid and needs a start. I am heartbroken for his mother and father. His mother was my first friend when I moved here almost 17 years ago. She was always so active in community activities and school-related projects. It is such a shame.

Well, how are you doing this week? I just wish you would come here for a visit or to live. You have no idea how much we love and want you to come. We could help you if you were here and you would be good company for me. The other day I was telling people at work how we used to go horseback riding when I was about 16. You rode Jennie and I rode Queenie. I used to have so much fun at Owasco Park with you and Uncle Harry.

Well, now I am a grandmother of three grandchildren and you have not only two nieces, but two grand nieces, four grand nephews, three great grand nephews and three great grand nieces. But you live so far away you are not getting to enjoy them.

The sun finally came out today for the first time in over a week. I'll write you again next week.

Love and kisses,

Shirley Ruth

Soon after this letter, Mom and I went to Boston and brought Bette back to our home. For the last two years of Aunt Bette's life my mother gave her loving aunt as good a life as she could. Aunt Bette was now safe, as healthy as possible for someone in her 90's and had lots of happiness. We enjoyed all the wonderful times my mother had promised in her letters. Bette died one afternoon eating ice cream, one of her favorite activities.

Bettie on our front porch, Maple Glen.

Tolerant Mom

Mom was a very tolerant person. She showed this by her actions, not her words. She didn't teach tolerance. She taught love for all people. My mother could strike up a conversation with a complete stranger and talk with them about all kinds of things. She never saw color, religion or other difference as a hindrance. In fact, she thrived in wanting to know more about other people.

The only story about race that she ever told me years later was about an incident in Washington in the 1940s while escorting her mother to the theatre. She claimed it was the Ford Theatre, but I don't know if that is true. She told the story of standing in line for tickets to a performance at Ford Theatre and the couple in front of them was denied admission because they were black. My Grandmother said to the teller, "This is the nation's Capital. If only certain citizens can get in this theatre, then you will no longer get my business." My grandmother took my mom by the hand and they left.

Throughout my life I never heard either of my parents or any of my grandparents make a disparaging remark about any person's race, religion or background. It seemed this was just not in their nature.

When she first got married and my Dad and Mom lived at the Lock Raven Boulevard Apartments in Baltimore, there were two young men that lived together in one of the apartments. Mom would tell me years later how she hated the fact that the neighbors called them names assuming that the men were gay. It really bothered her and she would tell the neighbors how she didn't appreciate their comments. She said the two men were very nice to her and were respectful and quiet.

I remember the lesson my mother gave to me and my brother Roy in Baltimore about children calling someone a bad name at a snow sledding hill. When we got back to the house she told us that colored people (the polite word in the 1950s) were no different than anyone else. They just have a darker skin color. I didn't know what she meant so I kept looking to see if there were any green or purple people because I was curious to see what colored people might look like.

With her sons, my mom never prejudged any of our girlfriends. She just wanted us to be happy. I had a serious relationship with two Catholic women during my young years. Marie was Eastern Orthodox and Dorothy was Roman Catholic. I came within days of marrying Dorothy, a sweet girl who got cold feet. My mother was always supportive and felt terrible for me when the wedding was called off.

Things sometimes turn out for a reason. When he heard that my wedding wasn't going to take place, Henry Miller, a good friend with whom I once worked, said, "It was just not in the cards." The fact that I didn't marry and raise a family at that time in 1985 made it easier to care for Mom at the end of her life. With a family of my own, it would have been much more difficult.

When my brother Roy married Lera, a Russian girl from the Ukraine, Mom couldn't wait to meet her. Mom made a special effort and she brought a dozen roses to present to Lera on their first meeting. On the day my mother died, Lera confided to me that Shirley was the nicest person she met in America.

Mom loved Tobey, Roy's first wife, and Nan, Lee's wife. She wanted all her children to be happy and whatever decisions we made over the years Mom was our staunchest supporter. Mom had a love for people and liked being with everyone.

Tobey and Roy's wedding.

Lee and Nanette's wedding.

KC attacking Roy with her tongue. Mom and Lera laughing.

Uncle Eddie and Sister Rose

In 1985, I had moved to the Kingswood Apartments in King of Prussia in anticipation of my wedding with Dorothy. She and I had decided that this would be a good location for our first home together since her family lived in West Chester and my business travel and commute to my office in Feasterville would be a halfway point. Mom would be all alone in the house in Maple Glen for the first time in her life. Moving day was very hard for her when I left in August. Mom did understand, though, that the time had come. She was now an "empty nester"—without a companion other than her dog.

As it turned out Dorothy had gotten cold feet three days before the wedding and I was now alone in the apartment. I decided to stay. I also decided to become active in the Democratic Committee in Upper Merion. I became the committeeman. One day while campaigning I knocked on the door of another apartment in the complex. An elderly gentleman answered the door and quickly became my friend. His name was Eddie. He was in his 90s. He introduced me to his kid sister who was living with him. Her name was Rose and she was in her 80s. Eddie and Rose were Brooklyn, New Yorkers. They also were lots of fun.

Eddie was a feisty, independent spirit. He was tall and lanky with a shock of grey hair. Rose was a quiet, but still spunky, tiny lady.

Eddie found out I was an insurance agent and decided to do business with me to help one of his family members. He also liked to hang out with me. "When are you coming over? We gotta get out of here and go somewhere," he would say during his phone call. We would go out to restaurants. If it was a weekend, many times Mom would come along.

One time Eddie wanted to go to Atlantic City, so Mom, Eddie, Rose and I spent two nights at a hotel near the casinos right on the Boardwalk. We got a wheelchair and trucked all over town. On the first slot machine Eddie played, he won $200 in about 10 minutes. "That's amazing," I said. "Ah! That's nothing," was his response. "We need to win some real money." Mom and I couldn't help but laugh.

He also decided to visit his nephew Bernie and his wife Linda and their children way out at Sag Harbor on Long Island. Eddie traveled light. He had just a little bag when we went to pick up him and Rose. "Is that all you are taking?" I asked. "Yeah. I got everything." When we arrived he opened his bag. All that was inside were a toothbrush and a shirt. "Damn!" he said. "I forgot my shoe horn." All of us broke out in laughter.

He took all of us to a seafood restaurant on Montague Point. We had a wonderful time. Mom and I enjoyed spending time with fun-loving people, regardless of their age or their physical condition. Eddie and Rose eventually died, but I have great memories of the four of us hitting the road on some adventure.

Gladys and Mom

On a Saturday sometime in the 1970's Mom met Gladys at a Bar Mitzvah. Mom had been invited by a friend to attend his son's big event. Gladys was a relative. Gladys and her husband Sam were seated at the same table as Mom, and their friendship was sealed right away.

Gladys was a wonderful, friendly lady. She also would be the life of any party and full of fun. That was a commonality the two women held. Gladys was also blind and deaf. Those qualities never seemed to stop her, though.

To communicate with Gladys you would take your finger and write out the letters on the palm of her hand. Although her blindness wasn't total, she had never learned sign language. It was just extremely difficult for her to see what someone was doing. As you would write on her hand, Gladys would be thinking and shaking her head in acknowledgement. Then a big smile would come across her broad face and she would say, "Ah!" She could talk as most hearing-impaired people do, and her words were understandable. You could have a pretty good conversation with her, in fact.

Mom and I would take Gladys to many events. She would come to our house. We would go to lunch with her and Sam. Once we took her to Sea Isle City for the Island Run. Although she couldn't see or hear, Gladys could smell the ocean and feel the breeze. We went to dinner after the run with my friends Bill and Trish. The restaurant was very crowded and it was late. We were tired, but we were all having a good time. Suddenly, a waitress accidentally spilled an entire pitcher of ice water on Gladys' head. Most people would have been furious about this. Not Gladys. She shouted out with surprise, "What happened?" We wrote on her hand. She started laughing hysterically. After getting her dried off and listening to an embarrassed waitress apologize, we all were talking about Gladys' drenching and laughing about the incident.

Eventually, Gladys lost her beloved Sam. Their son lived in Canada, which made it difficult for him to help his mother who was now living alone. I would stop by to check on Gladys when I was in the Northeast section of Philadelphia where she lived in a row house. Mom and I would still take her to lunch. Her health and her ability to care for herself diminished. Eventually, Gladys went to a nursing home. She was very unhappy there, as they didn't communicate with her that much because the staff was busy with other residents. Mom and I would visit, but Gladys became increasingly depressed. She had lost the sparkle that she formerly had. Gladys died unhappy. Mom was heartbroken. "Don't you ever put me in a nursing home," Shirley demanded again. "I promise," was my response. I miss Gladys and the fun the three of us used to have.

Gladys and Mom at Sea Isle.

Trish, me, Gladys and Mom at the restaurant at Somers Point.

Ross, Gladys and Mom at Sea Isle.

Gladys and Mom, good friends.

Friendly, Helpful Mom

My mother was a friend and help to many people during her life. I believe she received great joy out of these relationships.

The men who rented rooms became her friends, and she would cook for them. There was Kathy, a young woman she worked with who became her friend. Giving advice, Mom would help Kathy through her problems.

There were members of Parents without Partners that would talk to my mom about problems with their relationships. Mom was their "big sister," especially for the men. This was disappointing to her, as they never looked at her as a love interest but merely a good friend. Mom never had that kind of relationship after my parents divorced. She tried to make up for that loss by fostering closeness with family and friends.

She helped Eileen, one of the members, by talking with her about her problems. Eileen went on to obtain a master's degree. Mom helped Sofia and Michael Vicksman who had immigrated to the United States from the Soviet Union. Not only did she help get furniture together for the family, but during the birth of their daughter the Vicksmans did not have a car. Mother would drive Sofia to doctor appointments.

Mom did what she could to help Roy's wife Tobey when she was diagnosed with cancer. She would pick up medicine or stay with the children when Tobey had to go for treatments.

There was also the day that my friends the Hershgordons suddenly lost their dad, Morris, who had been our office manager at our insurance agency. Mom came to the office and handled the phone calls the day after he died.

Mom became friends with Denise; a high school classmate of mine. They would go to lunch or shopping together or just talk.

Mom's kindness to others extended to people outside her family. There were the visits to the homeless shelters and to the Jewish Congregation at Graterford Prison for Friday night prayers. There were the visits to nursing homes and to sick friends. Even when she herself had Alzheimer's Mom always insisted on visiting sick neighbors or attending a Shiva House after someone died.

Vince Phillips' long-time friend Tyrone always liked to tell the story of the time when he met my mom at Vince's daughter Adrienne's confirmation party. "Do you have a ride home?" my mother asked Tyrone. "My son can drive you home if you need a ride." He would laugh about this and tell others about my mom's kindness long after this event, as she hadn't asked me if I would drive him. Of course I would have done so. (Tyrone died suddenly and is missed. He had come to my mom's funeral only months before his own death.)

It is no wonder so many people came to Shirley's funeral. Many of them appreciated the kindness and friendship my mother had shown to them over her lifetime.

Giving and Receiving

My mother was a very giving person. Not only did she love and care for her family and friends, she helped others whenever she could. Mom and I would visit nursing homes, deliver meals to people who were homebound on Christmas Day, cook dinners at various shelters, and work at hospitals on Christian holidays so that the staff could take time off.

For many years Mom and I would serve breakfast to formerly homeless residents of the Bethesda Project in Philadelphia. Every year during the holidays we would do a special Hanukah brunch. Mom would conduct a service explaining each candle of the Menorah and have the residents read the prayers describing the meanings. I would make latkes (potato pancakes). We would then stay for an hour or two playing the Dreidel (spinning top) game with the men and women.

Mom loved going to these gatherings and the residents liked our visits. We all became good friends. As the years went by, these visits became more difficult for her. She would sit with the residents and be served the breakfast while I would conduct the service.

The last time I took her on one of these outings was December of 2008 to the Bethesda Bainbridge Home. This was a residence for about 20 men. They had come to know her over the years, but her visits were infrequent. The previous visit had been in December of 2007 while she was still active but with Alzheimer's and under care already.

During that visit she went back and forth to the kitchen. Her last visit was much more difficult. She became agitated. However, the men took good care of her. "Someone get Ross' Mom a plate of food," someone shouted out. "Have her sit over here on the couch." While the rest of the volunteer crew of Natalie, Leon, John and I worked on making breakfast, the men watched over Mom as if she were their own mother.

This is what I call giving and receiving. For years Mom and I had a relationship with the residents and staff of both Bethesda Broad and Bethesda Bainbridge. We gave and they received. But we also received. We received their friendship and love. And they gave back to Mom just as much. I will always be grateful to them for being blessed with their caring as we cared for them.

At their annual volunteers appreciation evening the Bethesda Project gives out medals to everyone in attendance who has been a help to the program and to the residence. The medal is stamped with the image of a homeless man in a blanket sleeping on a street vent to stay warm. The inscription reads, "Through the darkest night. I am with you." I put my medal on my mother's pillow for two reasons. First, she was always there for others in their darkest night. Second, I was there for her in the darkness and fear of her illness at the end of her life.

Arnold and Mom, smiles at Bethesda Bainbridge.

Hanukah brunch at Bethesda Bainbridge.

Hanukah service at Bethesda North Broad.

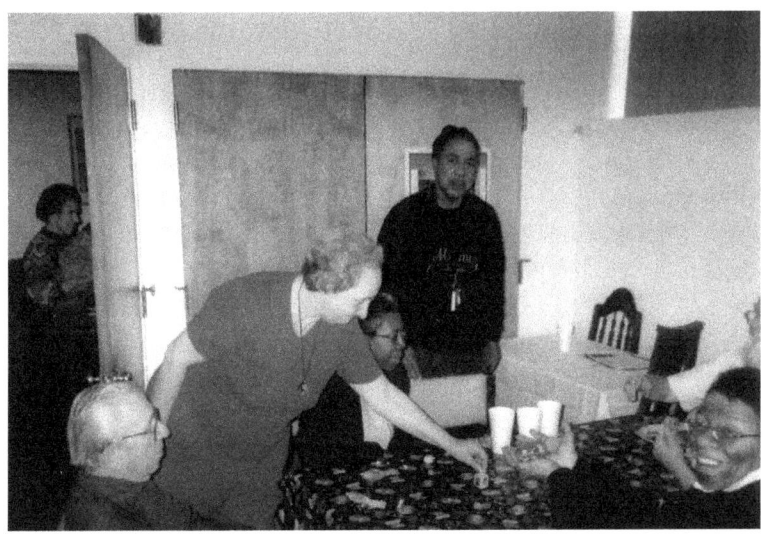

Mom spins dreidel at Bethesda North Broad

The Russians Are Coming

One day my mom came downstairs as I arrived home from work. "The Russians are coming," she shouted. "We have to get ready." Mom was head of the Soviet Jewry Committee at Congregation Rodeph Shalom. The Vicksman Family was arriving from Georgia in the Soviet Union. They would be coming to Philadelphia and the Congregation was sponsoring them. Mom started making calls to as many congregants as she could, asking for donations of furniture and appliances. There would be several apartments in Northeast Philadelphia that this large, extended family would be living in. The family included Michael and Sofia, parents of both, Raisa and her daughter Aileen and Zina and Vova, Victor and Sabina and their children Lisa and Illya. This would be quite a major undertaking. My mother, as always, was up to the task.

Mom instructed me to rent a U-Haul truck to help with the move. With the help of my friend Emilio Garcia driving, we went around picking up the furniture. Other friends and my brothers helped as well. We then delivered the furniture and set up each apartment. The family worked very hard alongside the volunteers Mom had organized and we had everything done in one day.

A few weeks later Mom invited everyone to our home for a big "Welcome to America Celebration." Their family bought all kinds of Russian food and we sang and danced.

At New Year's, the Vicksmans invited us to their home to celebrate the New Year. There was so much food and drink we were stuffed. When the ball went down on Time Square in New York striking the Happy New Year sign, the ladies brought out another chicken dinner and we toasted the New Year.

Michael Vicksman became a doctor and moved out of the Philadelphia area. Some of the family members moved to

Connecticut, but some are still in the Philadelphia area. For my mother's 80th birthday they came to celebrate with a lady that had helped them years earlier when they first arrived in America.

As chair of the Soviet Jewry Committee one of the projects my mother organized was a letter-writing campaign to Jews in the Soviet Union who wished to come to America. The Soviet government called them Refusniks since they refused to remain part of the grand communist ideology of the time. The letter-writing campaign was designed to let the Soviet authorities know that people around the world were aware of these people and their plight. The more letters (which the KGB would open and read first), the more the communist regime would know that people were watching. The letters could talk about everything about yourself and your family, but specifically could not address politics or efforts to leave the Soviet Union. Mom would write all about her family, her sons, her animals, her vacations, the books she read and a myriad of other topics.

Valery and Lydia Pevzner and their son Gregory lived in Odessa. They were one of the families we wrote to. When they finally were able to leave the Soviet Union and come to America, they settled in New York City. They were very excited about being there. Mom and I went to visit them. We met in Central Park and they took us on a carriage ride as a gift to Mom for all she had done for them.

Valery told us that one day while still in the Soviet Union the KGB called them in for an interrogation. "Who is this Shirley Schriftman?" the KGB agent demanded. "We are too busy to read her long letters." Valery said that he thought that the reason they were finally allowed to leave was that the authorities got tired of reading my mom's long letters.

Years later Mom would write to her new daughter-in-law Lera's mother Valya who lives in Sevastopol. Valya told me recently how much she enjoyed e-mailing back and forth with my mom. An interpreter would spend hours translating their letters back and forth.

Once Mom went to a meeting of the Philadelphia Area Soviet Jewry Committee. The speaker was Natan Sharansky, probably the most famous Refusnik. She got to talk with him and get advice about the best way to communicate with Refusniks and help them when they got to the United States.

One of my mom's greatest attributes was her willingness to get involved and effectively advocate for others. She was also an internationalist as she wanted to know so much about so many other peoples and cultures and wanted to truly understand them and be their friend. There is not a continent on this earth (except for Antarctica) where Mom did not have a friend.

Welcome Party

Victor, Ross, Sabina, Mom and Lisa.

Ross, Mom, Sabina, Ilya and Lisa.

Parents Without Partners

AMBLER, PA., JUNE 30, 1977 Page 13

Single Parents

Hospitality chairman for the Pennsylvania Eastern Regional Council, Maxine Rose, left, Lafayette Hill; and Organizer of the Buxmont chapter Shirley Schriftman, Maple Glen, discuss the activities their chapter hosted for children the recent Parents Without Partners (PWP) regional summer conference in Willow Grove. The "Getting to Know You" conference featured workshops for PWP's board of directors, activities for children and seminars for single parents.

Soon after my parents' divorce my mom joined the Northeast Philadelphia Chapter of Parents without Partners. Shirley Schriftman was not a person who would ever isolate herself from others, especially after a traumatic event like a divorce. She would be a participant and a leader working with others who had the same experience.

The members of Parents without Partners are dedicated to the well-being of their children and support one another. The organization advocates for the needs of single-parent families. Mom's caring for others and for her own children made this the perfect organization for her during the 1970s and 1980s.

As expected Shirley Schriftman quickly became a participant and an organizer. She also made many friends. There were Micky, Eileen, Marlene, Florence, Al, George, Chris, Fred and dozens of others who became her friends.

Besides supporting their children and having family events such as picnics and trips, the chapter gave these single adults a chance to socialize and maybe meet a new mate. Mom had several male friends within the group and had several dates but never developed a deep personal relationship. She was usually the "big sister" to both the guys and the women. When they had problems with an ex-spouse or a new relationship they would come to Shirley for advice and a shoulder to cry on. Even though she didn't find a new "special someone" everyone loved her.

Various club members would plan and host holiday events. Micky, who lived in the Frankfort section of Philadelphia, hosted a Christmas Party. (My GTO got stolen off the street that night, but was found in Germantown a week later in still good shape.) Eileen and Marlene would invite everyone to their church in King of Prussia. There would be a summer picnic at Neshaminy Park.

Mom helped organize a new chapter soon after joining the Northeast Chapter. It was the Bucks/Mont Chapter for Bucks and Montgomery County.

The biggest and most challenging event, though, was at our home in Maple Glen. Mom and I hosted a Passover Seder for the membership of both chapters. 90 parents and children came for the evening. We rented chairs from a local funeral home. We conducted two Seder services. One was in the family room and one was in the living room and dining room. People brought food and our little kitchen was cooking central. Later in the evening many of the smaller children were asleep all over the beds upstairs and the parents were singing, laughing and enjoying themselves downstairs. Some people stayed until 3:00 a.m.

I have many good memories from the events with Mom and the things we did with our friends who were in the PWP Chapters. Unknown to us at the time, Dad had become active in a PWP Chapter in Palm Springs where we lived.

Dad was proud of his four "boys" and I am certain he talked about us to his friends in PWP. This organization helps many people just from the sharing itself. I still remain in touch with some of Mom's friends.

Flowers

Mom had a green thumb and loved flowers and plants. Both inside and outside our home there would be her work on display. Hanging plants, vegetable gardens, flower gardens, shrubs and trees were major projects of hers during the spring, summer, and fall. I, of course, was her assistant. "You have to make the circle bigger!" she would shout out the back door when I was preparing a new garden area for her. She had a garden on her back porch. One year there was mint that we planted under the kitchen window. It spread so fast that the entire kitchen smelled of it.

In the back corner of the yard was a vegetable garden we grew in the late 1960s. We planted corn, radishes, cucumbers, watermelons and carrots. At one point it seemed we could have started our own produce market.

Spring and fall weather changes resulted in a day on the weekend where I would miss a lot of work helping bring in or set out the big planters Mom kept as well as all the hanging plants. It was a major project as some of the planters became quite heavy to lift.

Even movable tree went in and out of the house with the change of seasons. They still do today.

More recently, one year Mom decided to create a whole area of a garden just past the driveway in the backyard. We put down bricks and concrete trim. On top there were all kinds of planting pots and birdbaths which she filled with petunias and other flowers. It took the two of us weeks of work, but she created a beautiful garden. Here are pictures of her work. Recently I tried to duplicate her efforts. See page 234 for the results. Not as spectacular as her efforts.

My mother was one to appreciate the beauty of nature and to honor it by cultivating and caring for her flowers, plants and trees. She created a piece of the Garden of Eden in and around our home. When we first moved in, the ground was very hard and dry with lots of rocks in the soil. Over the years we changed it into a green lawn with bushes, trees, flowers, plants and gardens. As we soon discovered, the builders had simply piled dirt and rocks over a backyard that had been a meadow and stream for the grazing cows of the original Dillon Farm. As the years went by and the rains and snows came, the land began to settle. Now during certain times of the year, "Lake Shirley" fills in with water and there are ducks and other animals floating in the little pond in the backyard. It is a beautiful sight.

When we went to Roy's house to meet his future bride Lera for the first time, Mom insisted on stopping at a flower shop to buy long-stem roses to welcome Lera. Red roses show love, and Mom was so excited about meeting Roy's new love.

Toward the end of her life, I would bring home flowers for Mom. It might be Sunday morning after shopping or a holiday. It might be Valentine's Day, Christmas time, Halloween or Mother's Day. I would bring her flowers. Although she couldn't get up from her bed, she would reach out and touch the flowers. "They're beautiful," she would whisper. She had a calm look on her face. She would stare at them after I placed them on her table or by the window. I know it brought back to her whatever she could still remember of her days as a gardener making her own patch of heaven.

Our front lawn.

Mom at work.

Mom's completed work.

My lame attempt to duplicate Mom's work.

Shirley the Patriot

My mother loved her country. She believed in the American dream and she lived it. Her parents were grateful for having the opportunity to come to America and to live free and work hard to raise and support their family here.

Growing up, my mother saw many of her classmates go off to fight in World War II. She did her part in the work she did for the State Department and her voluntary work with the USO visiting the wounded soldiers at Walter Reed Hospital.

Later in life she became very active in politics running for office herself. She was also very involved in her community.

On July 4th Mom and I would go to Independence Mall for the Liberty Medal Ceremony. We would attend parades and memorials, including the September 11th remembrances. We would hang not one flag but two out the window of her bedroom and bathroom upstairs. One would be a 50-star current flag. The other would be either a 13-star of the original colonies or a 48-star flag of her childhood before Alaska and Hawaii became states.

Mom would go to legislative meetings with me or to township or school board meetings. She traveled to Washington to lobby for incentives for long-term care insurance during the Mother's Day rally. Here is a picture from that trip with Congressman Phil English of Erie who held that seat at the time.

No better example of how Mom felt about her country exists than the letter she wrote to the *Ambler Gazette* in July 1976 at the nation's 200th anniversary. I am grateful to the Old York Road Historical Society for finding this document for me. Here is what she wrote.

Titled by the *Ambler Gazette*: "A Mother's View of the Bicentennial Celebration"

"Dear Editor:

With the end of the inspiring days of the Fourth of July Bicentennial celebration, I want to share my emotions of gratitude.

It began for me on Friday, July 2 with attendance at the Willow Grove Naval Air Station air show. No matter how many times I have seen the Blue Angels, chills go through me as I see their maneuvers. This year, it was even more inspirational as I also saw the Canadian Snowbirds in their salute to our nation. To sit on the grass near the runway and watch the first plane to open this special show go taxiing past me, its red, white and blue stripes gleaming in the sun set my heart palpitating and my mind filled with nostalgia (nostalgia that would repeatedly flicker through my mind's eye during the next four days).

I thought back to the days when, as a teenager, I saw the newsreels and read the papers concerning World War II. I could see my bedroom in Washington, D.C., with the flannel flag hanging opposite my bed. That flag was to be handed down (with its 48 stars) to my sons, each in his own turn.

I thought of my diary which started in 1939 at the World's Fair in New York and of the girl in Holland (Anne Frank) whose diary was to be so different.

As I saw the planes take flight I thought of my sons Roy, Ross, Barry and Lee who were in the Civil Air Patrol, particularly of Ross who has put so many years into his training there and the many Search and Rescue Missions in which he was involved, his dedication. No wonder at the age of 18 he received a scholarship for the International Air Cadet Exchange which was to fly him to Germany, Italy and Israel for one month.

On Saturday, the Schriftman family went to Springfield to observe and participate in the Bicentennial parade and activities.

Sunday was not a time for lying lazily in bed. At 8:00 a.m. we watched on television the services throughout our land in honor of Our Birthday. Then we drove over to Valley Forge National Park where we could talk with more people. This time it was people from all over the United States who had made treks across our country in Conestoga wagons, sometimes in wagon trains and sometimes, as with one 70-year-old woman from the State of Washington all by herself—all yearning to return to the part of the nation where it all began.

No words can fully portray my emotions as my family and I came to the crest of one hill and started across an expanse to see all the wagons in a half-circle stretched out in the distance. As we came close, we could read the names of the states on the canvasses. Over 2,500 Americans had made that trip, some from as far as Alaska, others from across the Pacific in Hawaii, some of our own state of Pennsylvania.

Monday, we were up by 7:00 a.m. anxious not to miss a moment at the Festival grounds. Ross and Barry helped to set up the Democratic Committee, then joined me in the dress rehearsal of the Upper Dublin Family Chorus.

After the rehearsal we watched the parade in Maple Glen which passed in front of our home.

All afternoon we visited various booths at the Festival set up by organizations in and around the community. One of the first people I saw was a very fine gentle lady of about 75, dressed in a colonial dress complete with bonnet and purse which she had so lovingly sewn with the help of her daughter almost 14 years ago. I remembered back when, for the first time, I got off the train in Ambler to look for a place for my family to live and my eyes feasted on this gentle soul wearing this same outfit proudly taking part in a birthday celebration for Ambler. As I gazed down Butler Pike that day I knew this was the place for our family to take part in America.

Again in the present, my family and friends watched a marvelous Upper Dublin High School pipe and drum corps, a contingent of Scotch bagpipes, a homespun play about George Washington, a group of American folk dancers, a most wonderful pianist from Upper Dublin, Duane Quenzel, a rock group followed by a charming hour of dancers from the Philippine Islands. As they traced their history through the invasions of different Asiatic backgrounds and their colonial immigrations up until the present. I thought how all these people have brought their cultures to our United States. Nowhere else in the world do people maintain love of their former heritages and yet blend into the culture of this new breed of people. Even where I work, there are people from Poland, Scotland, Israel, Ireland, India, Iran, Africa, etc. Then it came to our turn to perform for the celebration—The Upper Dublin Band and the Upper Dublin Family Chorus. We were an hour late and some of us were fearful that we would miss the fireworks. Others spoke of the late hour and the workday ahead. We were all tired, yet we filed in and stood behind the band which had already been playing many stirring numbers. We wondered if any audience was left to hear us. Our smaller children gathered on the stands.

As I heard my sons' voices, I thought of the many acts of kindness performed by them without any fanfare—collecting for charities, working for hours on TV telethons. I thought of the girls in our community who work as volunteers at hospitals. I remember the battle Ross fought for a track team at Montgomery County Community College and the voter registration drives, the panel discussions he organized to bring candidates to the people. I felt so happy that we live in the United States where all things are possible.

The song finished with a standing ovation from the audience. My eyes filled with tears. At the grand finale, the high school band struck up a rousing offering of "Yankee Doodle Dandy" as flag-waving batonists marched down the aisles. I was glad that we went out into the darkness and down onto the field to see the fireworks.

All of the events of these four days brought back memories of my years in Washington, D.C., when I graduated high school and then went on to work for my government while attending American University at night. It was my great privilege to work for Nelson Rockefeller in the Office of Inter-American Affairs. I thought of the day President Roosevelt died and we worked until 3:00 a.m. getting the press releases ready for the other American Republics.

How close we were in common sorrow that night. How close we have been as Americans during these four magical days of anniversary.

Don't let us ever lose this closeness for together we can proceed to unheard of majesty. We can be one family if we but put in the effort.

Democracy and freedom are not to be taken for granted. We must always continue to work together. It is worth the struggle.

I thank you God for making this country not only a dream but a reality. Give us the guidance and strength to take care of what we have. Cause us to prosper as a people. Let not only the ears and eyes of our officials be open but may their hearts and minds ever work with the deepest of understanding when called upon to make decisions. Let us as citizens remember our obligations to remain always aware of what is happening and what needs to happen.

I love you, America.

May each generation work for the good of all and proudly pass its heritage down to the next generation.

Shirley R. Schriftman
Dillon Road
Maple Glen"

My feelings about what America stands for and what it can become were instilled in me by my mother, Shirley Schriftman.

Shirley Loved All God's Animals

"Some day they'll pass a bill that will speak in the cause of all God's loving creatures who cannot speak for themselves . . ." "Yes, Pop, some day man will face His Maker out there—and beside him will be standing the dog he kicked down here in the world below." St. Peter will say, "Can't let this man in." And the dog will say, "Then I'm not coming in either!" "It won't be the man taking the dog into Heaven. Yes, more likely, the dog will be taking the man!"
Mr. Jolly's Hotel for Dogs ~ Beth Brown

This passage from my mom's favorite childhood book tells me that if there is a heaven, many grateful animals will be lining the road welcoming my mom into the gates. There will be many dogs, cats, horses and even chickens. She loved her pets and all animals so much. They were her companions and her friends. She was their protector and provider.

Throughout her life she would donate money to various charities that help animals. There is DELTA Rescue in California run by former Actor Leo Grillo, Wild Horses in the West or local SPCAs that she gave to or the Popcorn Zoo in New Jersey where we once took her dog K.C. for a Halloween Party. When she didn't feel she could contribute, she would write long letters to the charity explaining why and how she feels strongly in support but just can't contribute now. Here is one example:

> "I sold my car for $500 and now Ross shops for me and works 16 hours daily. The house is falling apart, the driveway is 50 years old and I have flooding in the basement, garage, etc. So much for old age.
> Sincerely, Shirley Schriftman."

I tried to explain to her that she costs the organization money by sending them a letter in a business reply envelope. Sometimes I would put the stamp on and mail it back. Sometimes I would keep the letters as remembrances of her kindness and love for animals.

Besides all her own animals, she loved horses. We would visit Chincoteague Island for the pony swim in the summer, the Devon Horse Show on Memorial Weekend, Ludwig's Corner Horse Show on Labor Day and Winterthur in Delaware for the cross-country races. Of course, our dog would have to go with us as well.

During her childhood Mom had several dogs. There was Jigsy, Rexy Bozo and Scrapsy. They were mutts, usually with Boston Terror and Beagle in them, the little roly-poly types from "Our Gang." Her family loved these dogs as well. These animals were inside dogs, part of the family, participating at the dinner table by getting scraps of the leftovers.

When I was a small boy we got Princess; another mutt. She was black and white with floppy ears and a round belly. Our home movies in Springfield, Delaware County, Pennsylvania, are filled with Princess running around with me and my brothers. She met her end many years later crossing the street at our home in Maple Glen. The attraction of a bone or other treat across the street at a neighbor's home resulted in her demise.

In Springfield we also had a canary named Tweety. He had a little cage and Mom would sing to him and he would chirp. Back in the 1960s Springfield Township had a truck that would come by every couple of weeks and spray insecticide. Unfortunately, the spray killed our bird. I buried him in a little box in the woods behind the Township Building.

We had a puppy named Scrapsy (a beagle) and there was Teddy (a black mix) and Snoopy (a beagle). Sadly, each of these dogs died on Dillon Road by being hit by cars or trucks. We took in a brother and sister puppy from Catherine Barone, Mom's attorney, whose dog had a litter. My mom named them Bucky and Senator after Hubert Humphrey and his wife Muriel whom Humphrey had called Bucky. They were collies.

We played guest host for Tex, a dog my brother Lee and sister-in-law Nan had found abandoned on the road in Texas when Lee was in the Air Force down there. Tex was a nice collie. When they had returned to Philadelphia they needed a place for the dog to stay until they got their home situated. Mom gladly took in this lovable dog.

We then got Ragsby (another beagle mix) from a family who had put their dog up for adoption. They said the name came from the first letter of each member of their family. However, this dog loved to pull on rags and other items, so Mom thought the name came from this behavior. On a vacation in Boston there was an unfortunate incident on the

Concord Bridge. Two other dogs running across the bridge attacked Ragsby. My dad held the dog up by her leash and pushed the other dogs away. Ragsby was never the same again and began to have lashing out, biting episodes. Eventually, we had to have the vet put her down. It is terribly painful for a loving family to have to euthanize their pet and we mourned Ragsby.

Our next dog was Molly, a black Labrador. She was a wonderful dog. She went everywhere with Mom. She got a special treat one Sunday morning. Relatives had come in for a birthday and my mom had driven over to the Broad Axe Deli near Ambler to pick up some lox. Mom put the bag in the back of the station wagon and started to drive back home when she realized she hadn't gotten the cream cheese. She went back in the Deli and when she came back out to the car, Molly was licking her lips. She had polished off 10 pounds of lox.

Molly got old and sick, and again Mom and I went to the vet for that terrible time to say goodbye to a friend. Mom always would regret these trips and feel terribly guilty. "They wanted to live," she would cry.

After Molly we got Shamrock, another black Labrador. He was a very smart dog and could actually play the piano. No, really. One day, Mom and I were sitting in the kitchen and we heard chords being played on the piano. We went into the living room and no one was in there except for the dog. Another day we saw Shamrock actually playing. We were pleasantly shocked. He would take his snout and put it on the keys, turn his head and make the chords. He also figured out if he put his paw on the pedal it would make the sound last. He would also sing to my mother's playing, "Take Me out to the Ball Game." His singing was more of a howl. One year Mom purchased a musical tape of a flutist at the Cherokee Festival. Shamrock loved the music and would sing to it. When he would go somewhere in my mom's small station wagon he would bark as she drove. You would hear the barking either getting fainter as my mother drove away or louder as they pulled up into the driveway.

Shamrock was a strong dog and hard for my mother to walk. Mom tied a rope to the back door and the dog would have free reign of the yard for 50 feet. However, one time while I was at work, Mom was letting Shamrock out when he saw a rabbit and took off at top speed. Mom was pulling the rope out and was standing next to the door. As Shamrock got to the end the rope, it went taut and slammed the door closed. Her head was in the way. Mike, our neighbor took Mom to the emergency room. She was bruised and bloody, but as always, she healed quickly.

Shamrock was a water dog. He loved to swim. Mom and I would take him to the Loch Alsh Avenue Reservoir near Ambler. We would tie a long rope to his harness. He would wade out into the middle of the small lake and swim around with the ducks. It was really funny seeing this big black dog with yellow and green ducks surrounding him. He never bothered them. He just enjoyed being out there in the middle of the lake with them.

Shamrock was a very smart dog. One time Mom said she was watching a movie in her TV room. The film was "Places in The Heart" with Sally Field. At one point in the movie a tornado was approaching the farm. Shamrock was watching. He jumped up, grabbed my mom by the arm and pulled her into the other room. He thought what he saw on TV was real and wanted to protect my mom.

When Shamrock was seven he began to have health problems. He had a narrow chest and the vet said his organs were sideways. He had a series of operations and then got cancer. I used to call him, "Mr. Bones." He was getting thinner and weaker. He still would sing to the piano being played, but would do so from a lying position. Finally, his day for the final visit to the vet came. Mom sat with him till the end. She was heart-broken and kept saying, "I shouldn't have done it. He wanted to live." But the truth was Shamrock was in pain and had lost his ability to maintain continence. It would have been cruel to allow him to suffer further.

About two months after Shamrock's death, a contractor named Gary Bunch came to the house to give Mom estimates for some repair work. Mom was still crying about Shamrock. Gary told her that his wife had asked him to find another home for their puppy. The Bunches had a new baby and the puppy was nipping at the baby. We took in this little dog they had named "K.C." Gary said the name came from their baby who would look at the dog and say "Ksee, Ksee, Ksee." So they named her "K.C."; she was a Boston terrier and beagle mix. As she grew, K.C. got to be another roundish dog similar to the ones seen in the pictures from my mother's childhood. She was a sweet dog and Mom called her "My nurse." K.C. could sense where my mother's legs would hurt from past bruises or arthritis. While my mother would watch television, K.C. would lie on the bed for hours with my mom and lick her legs at the very spot where they hurt. Some nights I would come home from work and there would be Mom and K.C. sound asleep next to each other on the bed in the TV room with the television running. They were very close.

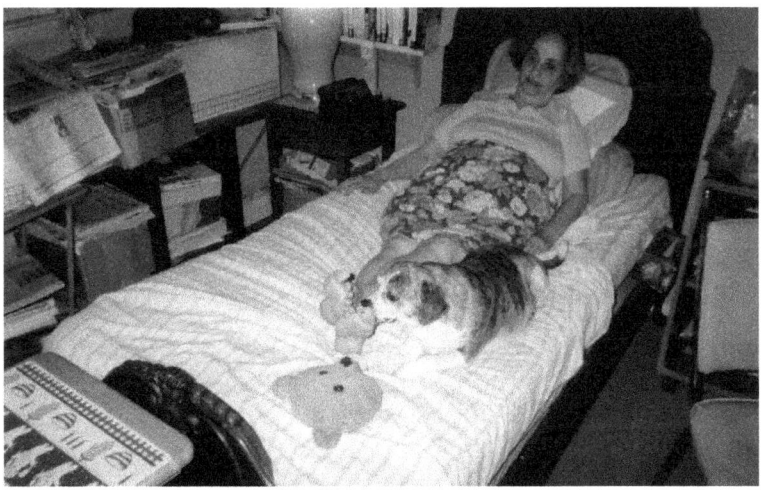

K.C. Mom's nurse.

Mom and K.C. would go for long walks through the neighborhood. I would get a call from Mom after she returned. "We walked all the way to Welsh Road and back. It took us three hours," she would report. That was because she talked to all the neighbors she saw along the way over this two mile round trip trek. She would chat with everyone. Sometimes she would see the Wydan children across the street. She would stop to talk with Theresa Wydan, and just to be silly, she would take her false teeth out and smile at the kids. They thought it was very funny. Mom would then go in the house and lie down. She would fall asleep. Of course, the dog would be sleeping with her. I used to tease her, "When people say to me, ah, your Mother sleeps with dogs; I tell them it is true." When Mom awakened when I came home from work she would think it was the next day. "You didn't come home last night," she would say. "Mom, it's the same day." She would laugh about being confused.

"Ya mother sleeps with dogs!"

As Mom got older, it became increasingly hard for her to manage caring for the animals, so more of the responsibility fell on me. Mom's concern for her animals was still strong and she was still in charge. When it would snow, not only did I have to shovel the driveway, I had to shovel the backyard so there would be an area where the dogs could "make." "Make the area bigger," she would demand. How many people shovel their lawn for their animals?

K.C. probably had the longest life of any of Mom's dogs. At 14 she developed a tumor. Mom and I took her to the animal hospital for her surgery. Mom did not want to put her down like she had done with Ragsby, Molly and Shamrock. It was already March of 2007 and my mother's illness was beginning to show itself. All the way over to the Metropolitan Animal Hospital near Norristown Mom kept saying, "If anything happens to this dog, I'm through. I won't go on living. I will not put this dog to sleep." Dr. Simpson was the surgeon and the kind of doctor I would want to have if I was a dog. She explained everything to Mom. She had an assistant come out and let us know when the operation was starting. The assistant came out after the operation to let us know they were finished. Then Dr. Simpson came back out and let us know that things went well. She even allowed us to come back and see K.C. We picked her up a few days later and she lived another two years. At the end the tumor had gotten bigger. However, I was fortunate that K.C. died at home in May of 2009. Nora said she just keeled over, twitched a little, and then passed away. I decided to tell Mom that evening. "Mom, I have some sad news," I said to her while she was sitting on her recliner in the TV room. "You know that K.C. was very old and that she was sick. Well, she died today." Mom looked at me and said, "No she didn't." "Mom, she did die," I said. Mom cried a little. I gave her a hug and then she seemed O.K. It would be hard to know, as Mom's illness had progressed to the point that the memory cells would come and go.

After K.C.'s death, I wrote this poem:

She handed me back my dog in a little box—the nice girl at the vet. Sixteen years of life, just a little box. I said thank you and took my little dog in the little box back home. "Come on," I said to the box, "We are going home."

My mother's dog. Fourteen years of long walks with Mom all through the neighborhood. Sniffing, wagging her tail and loving the petting she received from children along the way. "Can I pet your dog?" the children used to say. "She is so cute!"

Now Mom can't walk because her head doesn't tell her feet how to walk. I ask my mom, "Is your head working good today?" Her inseparable friend, the dog, she got old and sick. Two years of life added at the end through my mom's love and caring for her little dog.

Now I take her home. I will open the little box and our little dog will dance on the wind. Sixteen years of companionship. Good friend. I thank you and love you. Farewell.

K.C. and Mom, our front porch.

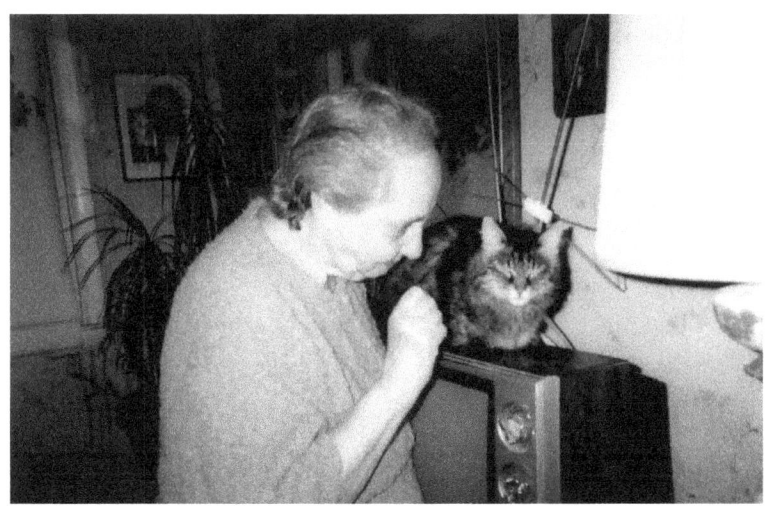

Mom and Bright Eyes.

We also became cat people—by default. First, there was Peewee who was my Cousin Lisa's cat. After her divorce Lisa had to move to an apartment that did not allow animals. Peewee was an indoor and outdoor cat. He would sit on the porch with the neighbor's cat that would come visiting. Sometimes the two cats would look at each other and meow through the screen door. Peewee had some kind of heart attack or stroke, as we heard him screaming one morning. He was lying under a dresser in one of the bedrooms. I gingerly got him out from under the furniture and into the cat carrier. The vet had to put him down.

Then there was Bright Eyes. He was one of many cats of my friend Ed Davenport. Ed lived in Norristown. I had met him during the 1979 municipal elections. I was running for County Controller and Ed was running for Register of Wills. Ed had developed polio at five years old and was an advocate for the disabled. He loved cats and Bright Eyes was the king of Norristown's cat community. Ed's brother Tony asked Mom and I if we would take in this cat when Ed died. Mom, of course, said yes. Bright Eyes was about 16 years old at the time and lived another three years with the excellent care that Mom gave him. Here is a picture of Bright Eyes and K.C. sitting on the bed in the TV room.

K.C. and Bright Eyes, stare down.

In late August 2005, a major hurricane hit the Gulf Coast. It was the Katrina disaster. My mother watched reports on Animal Planet about the devastation and the number of pets that had been separated or lost from their families in the storm. Not one to just simply sit and say "what a shame," my mother sprang into action. She called the numbers on the screen and researched where animals were being shipped to. She kept telling me that we needed to save these animals. She also wanted to help people and had volunteered to take in entire families. She corresponded with a family who finally settled in Atlanta.

I was against taking in more animals. "Mom, how are you going to handle them?" I asked. "I'm at work all day. You already have a dog to take care of and it costs money." "You're being cruel," she would state, trying to lay on the guilt. "These animals need our help. I never knew you were like this!" I finally relented and said, "O.K. One dog and one cat."

It took until Christmas Eve 2005 before we went to meet with Lori at Last Chance Ranch outside of Quakertown. Lori who lives and works at this equine retirement farm had been taking in cats and dogs from Katrina. Mom and I went up to pick up our animals that afternoon. Of course, K.C. went with us. There was a fox terrier named "Monkee" in one of the cages. She was long and lively. She had white fur with big black spots and a white and brown head. With her whole backside wagging along with her tail, it was evident that she was very happy to see us. There was a cat named Helen who had no eyeballs. Helen had a brother. Mom insisted we not split up Helen from her brother. "She will need him to help her," she insisted. We ended up taking both cats and the dog. After signing all the papers, the six of us (Mom, Me, two dogs and two cats) piled into the car and started to drive home. Mom immediately renamed Monkee. "I don't like that name," she said. "Let's name her Happy because she is so happy. Let's name her Happy Girl. The female cat's name got changed too. Instead of just Helen, she became Helen Keller; named after the famous deaf and blind girl. Later on during my mother's illness she started calling the cat "Fisty". I would ask her, "Why do you call her Fisty?" "Because her name is Fisty?" she would respond.

I think Happy Girl was called Monkee (yes, not spelled M-O-N-K-E-Y) because she sounds like a Monkee when she gets excited. She was a bundle of energy. She was also a big shock at first to K.C. who was now 13 years old. It would be like a spinster aunt who always lived alone having her punk rock niece suddenly living with her. Happy would charge around the family room knocking K.C. over and then nip at her ears. Happy Girl was destructive. She chewed up three pairs of my mother's eyeglasses. Mom would leave them on her desk. The dog would grab them and I would find them chewed up on the floor under the bed. Also, Happy was not house-broken. A good dog trainer-coach taught me how to train her and now she is a very well behaved dog with a special spot she picked out to make in the backyard.

As Mom developed Alzheimer's disease, she started to tell people that Happy Girl had been tied to the porch of a house in New Orleans and that she was found in a crate upside-down in the flood. They were great stories, but we really never found out how Happy Girl and Helen Keller were rescued, just that they were shipped up North from the Louisiana Humane Society. The story of Happy Girl, Helen Keller and Mom made it into the local Progress Newspaper as a Valentine's day feature.

Two days after we got the animals, the male cat died. It could have been the shock of the changes or maybe a change in diet. Mom came down that morning and said she thought the female cat had died. When I looked I realized that it was the male.

Three days after we got the animals, we couldn't find Helen Keller. Mom and I spent two hours looking for her all over the house and the garage. Then Happy Girl found her in the garage and cornered her. I was able to pick her up and bring her back inside.

We now settled down to more work with more animals. It wasn't easy, though, as Happy was constantly getting out the door when my mother, whose reflexes were slow, did not close the door quickly enough. Eventually, I had a fence installed in the backyard covering about a third of the lawn. We could now just open the door and Happy could run from corner to corner and not escape.

There were funny incidents as well concerning our new pets. One day after returning from appointments to my office, I had received five messages from my mom concerning Helen Keller. The first message: "I have looked everywhere and I can't find the cat." The second message: "I am really getting concerned. I looked in the garage. Happy Girl looked too. We can't find her." Third message: "I went next door and asked Mike Healy if he has seen the cat. I'm really concerned." Fourth message: "I called the police. No one has reported a missing cat." Fifth message: "Guess who is sitting next to me." Not only is Helen Keller a blind cat, sometimes she is an invisible cat.

Our Happy Girl was awarded the most energetic dogs in the Ambler Pet Parade in 2007. It was her sniffing and greeting each and every dog and human in attendance that got the judges' attention.

In February 2009 while having a little Valentine's Day dinner in the kitchen with Mom and Nora, I put Happy Girl in the living room so she wouldn't grab Mom's food. Unfortunately, she went upstairs and swallowed the pom-pom off my mother's slipper. I didn't know at the time what was wrong with her, but after dinner I noticed she was shaking and then vomiting. I rushed her to Bucks County Animal Hospital. The x-ray showed a round white object in her abdomen. It took two days for her to pass it. When she recovered and I went to pick her up, the staff member handed me two items. First was a bill for $900. The second was the digested remains of the pom-pom in a little plastic bag. It had passed through Happy Girl, from her mouth out the other end. I still have the pom-pom, which is the most expensive one I have ever seen. Fortunately, Happy Girl fully recovered.

It was a lot of work taking care of these additional animals, especially as my mom sank more deeply into her illness. But in the long run, I am so glad I lost the argument to Mom about taking in these Katrina survivors. I still have Happy Girl and Helen Keller to come home to. I look forward to their companionship and their love. They are the gifts my mother left behind. Mom would be pleased to know that all three of us are doing well and that her little friends are well cared for. She rescued them and cared for them as she did for all God's animals that she tried to help.

Me and Happy Girl

The very last book Mom read before Alzheimer's clouded her mind was *Marley and Me*; the loving story written by John Grogan about his dog. She laughed and cried when she read it. She loved animals so much. Nora would tell me that Mom would look at her dog and say, "I love you more than anyone." "Even more than your son?" Nora would inquire in jest. "Yes, more than anyone," Mom would say.

At the end of her life, the animals were a great comfort to her and to me as well. Mom's agitation seemed to diminish when they were around. Also, petting the dogs gave me some relief from the stress of caring for Mom. I believe God created this match of humans with their pets to create more peace and joy in the world. My mother certainly recognized that truth.

Animal Planet visit to Fort Washington Park.
Mom with Dr. Kevin Fitzgerald.

Mom's 80th Birthday Party

In late 2004 my brothers and I met to begin planning a surprise party for Mom's 80th birthday. Dancing, food, memories, friends and family would be a big part of this event. We hired a band and rented a party room at a local Holiday Inn. Roy and Lera took Mom to the movies one day and I quickly spent two hours pulling out pictures from her albums showing her with various family members and friends. These pictures would be displayed on several picture boards at the party.

As her birthday approached no one said anything. I could tell she was wondering if anything was planned. I told her that my brothers and I were going to take her out to lunch, but I wanted to stop by the Bensalem Democrats fundraiser. They had invited Joe Lieberman as their speaker and since she didn't get a chance to meet him the year before when I was running for office, we would stop by there on the way. I wanted to make sure she would dress up nicely. Of course, this was all a ploy.

Barry would let everyone know when we were close so that they would get quiet and surprise her. I called Barry across the street from the Holiday Inn. "Frank," I said, pretending he was the Democratic leader, "which Holiday Inn is it in Bensalem?" That was the signal that we would arrive in a few minutes. As Mom opened the door to the room, she saw everyone and her mouth opened wide and she had a broad smile on her face.

Everyone came over to her and hugged her. She was so happy and kept telling everyone the joke we played on her, which she thought was so funny. Family came from far and wide. Besides her immediate family, Deedee and Gene from North Carolina and their children Debbie and Julie and grandchildren were there, cousin Lisa and her daughter Lauren attended. Bea, Paul, Rona and Edye came from New York. Dad's cousins and their wives, the Gitmans, came. The Russian families and Mom's friends from Parents Without Partners were there. Her friends Kathy and Bill were there.

Julie, Connor and Mom.

Friends from the Democrats attended and Larry Curry presented Mom with a commendation from the Pennsylvania State House of Representatives. It read:

> Whereas Shirley R. Schriftman of Maple Glen, Montgomery County in the Commonwealth of Pennsylvania is celebrating her 80th Birthday,
>
> And whereas she is a proud member of the "Greatest Generation" which saved the world for democracy,
>
> And Whereas Shirley Schriftman served with distinction on the staff of the Office of Inter-American Affairs in the U.S. Department of State during World War II and helped to keep our Latin American allies informed of our nation's efforts through her effective Spanish language translations,
>
> And Whereas Shirley Schriftman raised four sons, who through her inspiration and teaching have become credits to their communities,
>
> And Whereas Shirley Schriftman has been an active participant in her community serving as an Inspector of Elections, Democratic Committee Person and candidate for District Justice,
>
> And Whereas Shirley Schriftman has been an adult education instructor at the Upper Dublin School District, instructor of English language for newly arrived immigrants, instructor to middle school students in the Abington School District and special education aide,
>
> And Whereas Shirley Schriftman organized and helped to create the BuxMont Chapter of Parents without Partners and provided her friendship and mentorship to her fellow single parents,
>
> And Whereas Shirley Schriftman worked as a documentation specialist for the UNYSIS Corporation and was an active member of the UNYSIS chapter of International Training in Communications,

And Whereas Shirley Schriftman chaired the Soviet Jewry Committee at Congregation Rodeph Shalom and through her constant letter writing campaigns helped pressure Soviet authorities to allow persecuted Jews to leave the Soviet Union and assisted them in resettling in our nation,

Be it resolved that the State House of the General Assembly of Pennsylvania commend Shirley Schriftman for her dedication and years of service and wish her health and happiness and continued contribution to the life of her community.

Then Mom gave a speech about her life which took about 20 minutes. Three years later, with her illness consuming her, she was watching the video that Seth had made of the event. When the video showed her speech Mom commented, "I talked a lot." Then she laughed.

At her 80th birthday party Mom danced, sang with Uncle Paul, laughed at his jokes, ate, and had a wonderful time. After the event, she carefully wrote thank-you notes to all who attended the party. Barry had prepared a memory book

that people wrote notes in. Here is what I wrote on Mom's special day:

March 13, 2005

Dear Mom,

I have had so many wonderful memories with you over the years—the summer vacations, the Cub Scouts, everyone carting stuff to pack the car, the Civil Air Patrol, the Parents Without Partner Passover Seder, the hours you spent helping type up my reports for school, the advocacy work you and I have done together for wonderful causes, all the help you have given me in politics, the way you have reached out to so many people, the way you strike up conversations with complete strangers, the things you have taught me about doing the right thing. My belief in serving others comes from you and the way you were taught by your parents to respect and consider others. Our intellectual conversations on important issues of the day make me a stronger advocate.

I have unending respect and admiration for you and for all you have done for our family. I am privileged to be part of your life.

Love,

Ross

    I am so thankful that we were able to have this celebration for Mom before illness clouded her mind. She got to know how much we appreciated her and how much we all loved her.

The Movie Buff

Family trip to the movies.

My mom loved films. This might have been the result of a childhood where her entertainment consisted of going to the movie house with all her friends and neighbors; the price of admission was one nickel. In Brookline, Massachusetts, you would not only get to see a movie, but there would be highlights of the local high school football game, local news reels, and national and international news reels. This experience was both entertaining and informative.

As a child our family would go to the local theatre. We saw "Lawrence of Arabia" at the Lawrence Park Theatre in Broomall. We saw "PT-109" (the John F. Kennedy World War II story) at the Ambler Theatre. We would go to the drive-in movies in our station wagon. Dad would park with the back of the car facing the movie screen and put down the tailgate of the station wagon. We would wear our pajamas and lie in the back watching the movie. Other times, we would take the train from our home in Springfield, Delaware

County to Center City Philadelphia. We saw "The Ten Commandments" and "The Guns of Navarone" at the big 20th Century Fox Theatre. We would then have lunch at a steakhouse on Market Street (not the fancy kind they have today, but one that was cafeteria style with tables).

In her later years, I would take Mom to the Philadelphia Film Festival. She had a great interest in movies made in foreign countries and those on interesting and different subjects. Mom and I would also go to the movies at our local theatres on a regular basis. Mom insisted on watching the film right to the end including the credits. She wanted to know everything about the people who acted and made the film.

When Gregory Peck received the Marian Anderson Award in Philadelphia, Mom and I got to meet him and watched "To Kill a Mockingbird" at the Prince Theatre. Mr. Peck had a surprise special guest that day. It was Brock Peters who played Tom Robinson, the falsely accused black worker in the movie. It was a very moving experience for both of us to see such famous actors and to hear them discuss the film.

With the invention of videocassette recorders (VCRs) Mom began to collect a wide assortment of movies; she recorded dozens of movies for her personal library. She also would tape major events such as the Olympics, elections, Mummer's parades and documentary programs on films and actors.

She turned her TV room into a library. She would print out dozens of reviews of movies and put them in large binders and catalogue them. She would have me hang shelves all around the room to store the films in alphabetical order. God forbid I put any of her films back in the wrong spot. In her mind that would be a major problem.

As she ran out of space, she had me put up more shelves along the wall in the front bedroom. In this room she built her library of documentary films, including the 500 "Nations History of Native Americans," narrated by Kevin

Costner. There were also many PBS (Public Broadcasting Service) tapes which she purchased.

For the 10 years prior to her illness Mom spent much of her day working on this project. After her death I decided to watch her films in alphabetical order. I have not made much progress. It would take many years of constant watching to view her entire library from start to finish. I started during the time right after Mom's funeral during the Shiva period. The very first film I watched was "An Act of Murder" with Frederic March and Florence Eldridge. It was a story about a judge whose wife was dying from a brain tumor. The other half of the tape had a comedy, "Sitting Pretty," with Robert Young and Maureen O'Hara. I laughed because this was a little twist of the way Mom was. She used to ask me to watch some very intense or sad film and then ask me to watch a comedy with her. I felt like she was sending me a message.

Movies are a great recorded history of our lives and our cultures. Someday I hope to honor Mom by turning her story into a film. She would have loved that.

Vacations—Schriftman Style

Our family vacations were not fancy affairs flying off to some top-rated resort. They usually were driving adventures in the family station wagon with everyone piled in and luggage in the very back and tied down on the roof. Also, viewing our family movies from the 1960's it appears we were a very wet family as there are plenty of scenes in the ocean, lakes or pools of kids swimming around and parents dunking babies.

As the morning of our trip would drag on with all the packing, Mom would begin to get frustrated. It might be 9:30 a.m. already and she wanted to leave right after breakfast. "The whole day is wasted!" she would announce. Eventually, off we would go. Mom would have her arms folded over her chest and not say a word. In her view we got started too late. As we traveled on, her mood would get better with the anticipation we all had for what lay ahead.

These trips were wonderful experiences and involved sightseeing, history and the simple pleasures of six or more individuals plus the family dog on the road for one or two weeks. Motels, beaches, mountains, rivers, roadside picnics and history lessons were combined into the summer days that my dad would have off from work.

Having four boys in a car cramped in together would lead to the occasional argument. "He is touching me. He is crossing onto my side again." My mother's wise psychology would easily end the arguments. "Herb, turn the car around. The vacation is over. If they won't be good we have to take them home," she would announce. My dad, who would be like the fifth child when we were out having fun, wouldn't catch on to the ploy at first. "Shirl?!" he would whine. "Let's keep going." She would wink at him and then he would realize her strategy. He would slow the car down and get off at the next exit. Everyone would get quiet and we would continue on our way. Sometimes he would have to turn the car around and head down the highway toward home. My poor Dad. It always seemed to take twice as long to get anywhere because of the arguments, but the trips were well worth it.

The earliest trip I remember was to Upstate New York in the late 1950's. We visited Fort Ticonderoga, Ausable Chasms, Lake Champlain, Niagara Falls and the Fingerlakes. In Auburn we visited the Policzers. They were cousins of my Uncle Harry Eisner. The couple's father who they called Opah was a survivor of the holocaust. Their son Joel was

Roy's age. We stayed in their house and toured the area, including a day trip to Lake Ontario at Oswego. I remember eating marshmallows which had been toasted on a stick over a fire. Opah wrinkled up his face and said something in German. Joel's mom said he thought it was disgusting that we were eating burnt dirt.

Mom and Dad with the Policzers.

On this trip, my dad had just gotten an 8-millimeter movie camera and many of the family movies from this trip are dizzying to watch. Dad would span the scene quickly not realizing he had to hold the camera still, take a picture, and then turn the camera off before taking the next picture. Still, there were excited boys and a happy mother running and walking through the various scenes. The film my mom took of my dad showed a more steady hand.

One summer we went to the Windsor Hotel in the Catskill Mountains in an area known as the Borscht Belt. This area was a popular vacation spot for Jewish Americans as told in the movie, "Dirty Dancing." I remember swimming and hiking and being with the grownups at the early show in the hotel ballroom. Our vacations were not just sitting around the pool doing nothing all day. They were chocked full of activity. Let's go do something was always my mother's attitude on a vacation.

Between vacations there were many trips as well. We would visit my grandparents in New York and Washington as well as others in my mother's family in Boston. Sometimes these were starting points for other trips. A grandparent would come along with us after we visited them at their home. Sometimes, their hometown was the destination of the trip, such as the World's Fair in New York in 1964. I remember staying with Grandma and Grandpa Schriftman in their apartment in Brooklyn. A few years before the World's Fair, I remember looking out the window of their apartment and seeing the Verrazano Narrows Bridge as it was being built.

I remember Grandpa Schriftman taking me to Shea Stadium, which had just been opened. Years earlier, Grandpa would take Roy and me on the subway to Coney Island, which was only a few miles from their apartment.

One year we celebrated Passover at Grandma and Grandpa's apartment. In attendance were our family, Aunt Bea, Uncle Paul and their daughters Rona and Edye. In a tiny apartment with a small table we didn't have a lot of room for serving plates. Grandma had made lots of different dishes of food. At one point each of us had two serving bowls in our hands. We all started laughing as we had complete dinner-gridlock. No one could pass anything to anyone else and the table was full with other dishes.

For several years we celebrated Passover at Bea and Paul's home in the Flatbush area of Brooklyn. Uncle Paul had a very large family with many brothers and sisters. They were also musicians and entertainers. Between our family and theirs we had musical instruments and singing, magicians and storytellers. It was a wonderful experience.

Trips to Washington would involve sleeping in Nana and Harry's apartment on rollout sofa beds. Their apartment on Massachusetts Avenue in the Northwest section of

Washington, D.C., was fancy to me. It had plush carpeting and fine furniture. My grandfather Harry Goldman drove an Oldsmobile. He instructed us not to "soil" the windows and doors, so we had to be on our best behavior and keep our hands on our laps. (I thought my mother's dad was stern when I was a kid. I learned over the years what a wonderful and loving man he was. He always wanted the best for his family.) He would take the whole family out to dinner at O'Donnell's and my cousin Lisa and I would enjoy having the warm rolls with the warm icing they poured over the bread. This was a specialty of O'Donnell's and Lisa and I still have a tradition of going to the restaurant in the Washington suburbs when I visit her.

Atlantic City was another favorite family vacation spot. My mother used to laugh at how Philadelphians would say, "Gowin donna shore?" Our trips sometimes were one-day excursions. There was no motel that we stayed in. We would go to the beach and then change in the back of the station wagon with towels over the windows. After spending the day on the beach, Dad would scrape the sand off our feet and legs with a towel, which hurt a lot. Then we dressed in nice clothes to stroll down the Boardwalk looking in the various shops until we got very hungry for dinner. My dad always looked for bargains for dinner until out of frustration my mother would lose it and shout, "Herb! Choose somewhere. The kids are hungry. I'm hungry." We would then stop and eat.

One summer we did stay at a motel on the Black Horse Pike about two miles out of town. It had a pool, and at the time the bay was clean looking, and so was the hotel. Now it is pretty rundown.

Nova Scotia (Horse eating pie, Blue Nose boat, Bay of Fundy, Halifax, red snapper, mining for gold, horse track, lobster pot in Maine, seven rivers in Maine, New Brunswick): In 1967 we planned a special vacation to Nova Scotia. I was already 14 years old and Mom let me help with the planning. Since my brother Roy was driving already and had his own car, we decided to make it easier for everyone and take both cars. We first drove to Aunt Bettie's home in Boston and stayed overnight with her. We then drove up through the northern part of Massachusetts through the small part of New Hampshire along the ocean and into Maine. On our first night in Maine we stayed in Bath. In the morning we drove the cars to the top of a hill above the town and had a picnic on an overlook of the seven rivers. Mom had packed a lunch of salmon sandwiches and we sat and looked out over all the rivers, forests and mountains below. There was a cave to explore at the top and my dad took a lot of movie pictures.

From there we went up to Bar Harbor and took the Blue Nose to Yarmouth in Nova Scotia. At the point where the ferry crosses the Bay of Fundy it is very wide and feels like the middle of the ocean. Later I would imagine the amazing impact of nature when we would be farther inland and see the bay's waters reverse. After departing the ferry, we started driving toward Halifax. While driving through the countryside, Mom, who was always perceptive, yelled "Herb, stop the car. Look over there." We all turned our heads and started laughing. There was a farmhouse to the right near the highway. A horse had stuck its head into the kitchen window and was eating a pie that was sitting on the windowsill. Dad pulled out the movie camera and we got a great shot of this scene.

When we arrived at our hotel in Halifax we were up on a hill facing the harbor. We had an excellent view. The next day we went to the Citadel and got a history tour. While there at the fort we ran into a couple touring from the next community from where we live. It is amazing that you can go that far and run into people who live only a mile or two from you.

Our next day in Halifax we took a fishing trip out into the ocean. We all went and together we caught 24 red snappers. The hotel staff took our catch and prepared it as our dinner that evening.

While staying in Halifax we went fishing and digging for gold. Digging for gold was interesting as Mom and Dad kept telling us we were going to be rich if we found enough gold.

We also went to a race track in Truro. The next day we experienced the phenomenon of the Bay of Fundy emptying of water and then the water coming back in from farther out in the bay and filling it up again.

From there we headed out of Nova Scotia and down the coast to St. John and then home. It was a wonderful trip.

Florida: Trips to Florida were a major operation. We drove the whole way down with all six of us piled into the car. There would be a stop in Southern Virginia or North Carolina on the first evening at a motel along Route 301. The next night we would stop somewhere in Georgia. One time my dad was "speeding" and got a ticket for going 45 miles per hour in a 35-mile-per-hour zone. Back then the southern police officer would have you follow him right to the courthouse. You would pay your fine in cash directly to the judge. They would give you a receipt and you would continue on your journey.

After our experience in "The South" we would sometimes stop at St. Augustine, Cocoa Beach or Daytona, Florida.

Finally, exhausted we would arrive in Miami Beach on the third day. One year we stayed for an entire month. I can't imagine today someone taking that long a vacation away from work with no cell phones or internet, just fun and family time together. It was like having a second home—one away from business. We stayed in a motel along Biscayne Bay and we could fish right next to the pool. The following year, we went back to that same motel and discovered the coconut we had left under the bed the year before was still there. It had grown hair. Mom and Dad checked us out that same day as they knew it wasn't sanitary to stay there. Maybe the motel had changed management.

Our days on this vacation were filled with visits to the Tensors, swimming at the pool at Coral Cables, picnicking on Cocoa Beach, going to the movies (Mom took me to see Walt Disney's "Fantasia," which was an amazing movie for its time), swimming in the ocean and fishing off the pier. Mom and Dad looked for every kind of fun thing to do. Roy, Dad and I went deep-sea fishing one day. Dad got a sailfish on his line but turned the rod over to an experienced passenger because he was afraid he would injure himself because of his stomach problems. It was a huge fish, and we took movie pictures of Dad and the other fisherman with the catch. I got a bonito fish on my line, and it was so big that Roy and I had to both hold it up.

Ross and his bonita.

When the vacation was over, we had our long trip back to Pennsylvania. Our home seemed strange after being away for so long, but we were glad to be back.

Hershey Park: Hershey Park was another favorite one-day destination for our family. From our home in Springfield, it was about a two-hour drive through the countryside. We would take Route 322 most of the way through the rolling fields of Chester and Lancaster Counties. Coming into town and smelling the chocolate factory and driving along Chocolate Avenue with its Hershey's Kisses light-posts was an exciting thing for us.

We would spend the day riding in little motorized cars, having a picnic next to the train that went around the park, eat the deviled eggs my mom made and I loved and swim in the huge pool. Driving home all of us boys would fall asleep. Mom would lift and carry Barry out of the car and the rest of us would drag ourselves into the house.

Montreal Expo & Niagara Falls: In 1967 we went to the Expo in Montreal. Grandma Schriftman went with us. We picked her up in New York City. We then went to Lake Champlain, New York, and then up to Montreal. After Montreal we went to Quebec and then over to Niagara Falls. This was another one of the Schriftmans packed-in-the-car-travel-everywhere vacations.

Niagara Falls. Maid of the Mist.

Florida Trip to See Dad: My father had decided to go to Florida and get away by himself in December of 1969. My mother decided it would be nice if she drove down to meet him. On the way down we couldn't find a motel with a vacancy and ended up staying in the Cherry Hotel in Wilson, North Carolina. The hotel manager looked at my mom with four children and said, "Ma'am, do you really want to stay here?" We didn't know why until later when we realized that this was the sleazy place in town. We spent several days with Dad and then turned around and came home.

Quebec, Montreal, Toronto and Niagara Falls: When I was a teenager we took another Canadian vacation to see the sights in Quebec, Montreal again, Toronto and Niagara Falls. This trip involved a lot of driving but a lot of scenic adventures, history and fun just like when we were little kids. Lee's girlfriend and future wife Nan went with us and we had a great time.

Bettie and Wildwood: When Aunt Bettie was living with us in the early 1980's Mom and I decided to take her to

Wildwood, New Jersey, for several days one summer. We stayed at a motel along the beach. Although Bettie was in her 90's and had a mild form of dementia, she was fun to be with. One morning we took her out to breakfast at a diner on the first floor of a motel. She started flirting with the owner who came to the table to ask how everything was. "You are a good looking man," she said to him. "Are you married?" "Yes," he said. "That's my wife over at the cash register." "Too bad," Bettie lamented as she winked at him. Mom and I couldn't help but laugh. According to Mom, Bettie always loved the men and loved a good time.

One evening we were standing outside a bar that was playing music. Bettie was swaying to the music and so was Mom. As people walked by Bettie shouted out, "Dance with you for a nickel!" Even though Bettie was old and difficult to manage, Mom and I wanted to keep her active and involved. We had as much fun on this trip as she did.

Los Angeles, San Diego, Tijuana: In the early 1980s I became active in the Brotherhood at Congregation Rodeph Shalom. I was assigned to head up the efforts to raise funds for the Jewish Chautauqua Society (JCS). JCS promotes understanding through education by providing college-level courses on Judaism for comparative religion classes, donates books to school libraries, and holds Interfaith Institutes. JCS was started by Rabbi Henry Berkowitz at Rodeph Shalom in the late 19th century. I did such a good job at getting contributions from members of my congregation that the Brotherhood decided to send me to the convention of the National Federation of Brotherhoods in Los Angeles. I invited Mom to come along.

The trip involved lots of meetings but also lots of tours with the other attendees. We visited the Tar Pits in the center of town, the Rose Bowl in Pasadena, Hollywood, a tour of the stars and all the wonderful reform congregations in the area. One night at our hotel, there was an event with all the Hollywood stars in attendance. We were staying at the Beverly Hilton. As stars arrived and people were taking pictures, an elderly lady got out of a limousine and grabbed my mom's hand for support. Mom started to usher her in. Her protectors gave Mom a stern look and took the actress' hand. Mom thought the actress was Gloria Swanson.

While in L.A., we went to Universal Studios with Mom's cousin David Goldman and his wife. She hadn't seen them for so many years, and it was nice for her to catch up.

My dad was living in Palm Springs. He came down to L.A. to take me to dinner. We didn't recognize him with his toupee but he looked good for his age. Interestingly, he had also become active in the leadership of his local Parents without Partners group.

After the convention, Mom and I stayed for a few more days. We rented a car and drove down to San Diego and then to Tijuana. We went to the San Diego Zoo and then we drove across the mountains to Palm Springs to see Dad again. Mom and I went to lunch with him and saw his apartment. From his window you could see palm trees and then look up and see a snow-capped mountain. It was quite a contrast. The baseball coach, Leo Durocher, lived in his building and Dad was very interested in showing us the door to Leo's apartment.

Mom and I said goodbye to Dad, and we drove back to L.A. to fly home. It was always great traveling with Mom. She and I have the same view of traveling. We just want to get up and go everywhere. The trip was only one week but we saw so much.

Utah, Montana, Idaho: In 1982, Barry, Mom and I flew out to Salt Lake City for a vacation. We stayed at Mike Roundy's home and then toured around using his beat-up old Volkswagen, which Mike affectionately called the "Time Machine." Mike had rented a room in our house when he was training as a customer engineer at Univac in Blue Bell, PA. He became good friends with all of us, and I still stay in touch with him today.

Mike Roundy and Mom, Utah, State Capitol

Our trip out west was very interesting. I stayed for the first week and we traveled north. Barry and Mom stayed behind for another week and traveled south to the Painted Desert and other sites in Southern Utah.

The Time Machine was a unique vehicle. Old Volkswagens are not very large, but they were great on gas mileage. The front passenger seat would fall back every time we would accelerate or go up a hill. Mom was sitting in that seat with Barry seated behind me as I drove. Mom would laugh each time she would fall back in the seat.

We went to Ogden, Utah, and I ran an 11-mile race at 6,000 feet above sea level in an area called the Garden of Eden. We went to Yellowstone Park and saw the geysers and all the interesting terrain. Then we went to see the Grand Tetons and visited Jackson Hole, Wyoming. From there we went to Montana and visited a lake created by an earthquake.

We drove back to Salt Lake City through Idaho.

There will never be a trip like that again in Mike's old Time Machine. Barry, Mom and I had a great trip.

Hawaii: In early 1984 Mom came to me when I got home and told me that the Univac Retiree Group was planning a trip to Hawaii. She was excited about going and asked me if I would take her. We would spend one week in Oahu and one week in Maui. I agreed, and we started planning this trip. My recollection is that it was only $800 per person plus air fare. This was quite a bargain even in 1984.

After a very long flight we landed in Honolulu. Upon checking into the Waikiki Hilton Hawaiian Village with the other 20 people on our tour, we walked down the street and found a nice restaurant. We each had Mahi-Mahi, a local tasty fish for dinner. The place was so relaxing and beautiful and we looked forward to a wonderful two weeks.

Our room was facing inward toward the island. From our balcony that evening I could see lights going all the way up a mountain. I decided that I would explore running up there to see where it would take me. (One of the things I've always enjoyed doing is going for a run to explore a new place shortly after arriving.) Later I was told the hill is known as St. Louis Heights. It was quite a climb. It was worth the view at the top looking down into a large canyon forest. Looking back you could see Honolulu to the right, Diamond Head to the left and Waikiki and the beach in front. When I returned to the hotel my legs were very stiff. I lay down and fell asleep. The next morning I awoke to the sound of steel drums playing. I got up and went out on the balcony. Looking down from the sixth floor there was Mom in the middle of the pool swimming back and forth in time to the music. She saw me while floating on her back. She stood up and waved. "Ross! Come down and swim with me!" she shouted. I will always remember this as one of the best moments of our trip. Whenever I hear a steel band playing, I think of my mom dancing in the pool in Hawaii.

Mom, the dot in the middle of the pool.

We had left for Hawaii right after Rosh Hashanah, the Jewish New Year. While we were in Oahu, Yom Kippur, the Jewish Day of Atonement, took place. Being religious we found that there was a synagogue in Honolulu. It was located on the Pali Highway just above the downtown section. For the Kol Nidre service, which is held the evening before Yom Kippur day, Mom and I got all dressed up and took the bus to downtown Honolulu. While waiting for the next bus to take us up the Pali Highway to the synagogue there was a sudden downpour of rain. We could see the bus at the next light coming up the hill, but there was nothing we could do as there was no cover. We were soaked. When we got to the synagogue we each went in the restrooms and wrung out our clothing. We were both laughing. Mom said the weather seemed to be just like in South Florida where it could be raining on one side of the street and sunny on the next.

The synagogue sanctuary was beautiful with open sides. The breeze would come through during the service and we felt very close to nature. The next day we were back up for the long Yom Kippur service and fasting. Since we had never fasted on vacation that was a unique experience. Yom Kippur fasting has been given several meanings. The first is that you are so busy praying for forgiveness that you don't take the time to satisfy yourself. Another interpretation is that the small pangs of hunger you feel give you empathy for others who are hungry all the time. In the evening when the sun goes down Jews break the fast with a meal with family and friends. This was the first time I ever broke the fast drinking Mai Tais. The tour had a cruise on a large catamaran that night along the coast. We had a wonderful time dancing and singing. Mom and I arrived back at the hotel and went right to sleep once we reached our rooms.

While we were in Honolulu we got to see a Don Ho presentation at the Waikiki Beach-Comber. It was kind of a great sing-along of women in the audiences, many of whom were my mother's age, singing "Tiny Bubbles" along with Hawaii's superstar. It was a lot of fun.

While in Oahu we traveled to the North Shore and saw the huge waves crashing against the beach. We also went to a Hawaiian cultural center and spent a full day hearing about the history and culture of the Hawaiian Islands.

A few days later, it was time to leave Oahu and fly to Maui. Leaving a city and a hotel-lined beach for an Island with wide fields and beautiful mountain was a contrast that shows the wonderful variety of the Hawaiian Islands.

Behind our hotel you could look up and see the top of Haleakala, Maui's volcano. A few days after arriving Mom and I took a bus ride to the very top at sunrise. The 12,000-foot climb is spectacular. It was very cold up there. When we arrived, Mom looked out the window to the parking lot and started laughing. There were several young Japanese women who were running from a bus into the visitors' center. They were wearing short skirts and were obviously freezing. Maybe their tour guide hadn't warned them to wear warm clothes. The way they were running made my mom laugh.

We got out of the bus and went into the observatory. What a spectacular view. After the sun came up we could clearly see our hotel way down below us.

During the rest of the time in Maui we toured around the island and learned as much as we could. We enjoyed the food and the people. Of course, Mom spoke to everyone she met and asked lots of questions about their lives and what living there was like.

The time to leave came. Mom was not done with her fun though. She had to buy gifts and items to bring home. Boarding the plane in Honolulu I not only had to manage our suitcases and clothing bags, I now had a gift bag, a crate of pineapples and a hanging planter made of sea shells. I was Mom's *schlepper* (a Yiddish word for the guy who picks up after someone and carries everything). The sea shell planter was the most difficult to handle. It could not be folded. It would break. Walking down the aisle in the airplane I must have looked strange to other passengers. However, that is what my mom wanted. She gave the gifts to neighbors and friends. The planter hung in our family room for many years until it broke.

The two weeks Mom and I spent in Hawaii that October is one of my sweetest memories. Recently I was in the Big Island on a trip with Mutual of Omaha. I could see the top of Haleakala 70 miles away across the water from my hotel. Only the top was visible through the clouds. It was a beautiful triangle that seemed to be hanging in mid-air. In my mind I could see my mom waving to me from the top as I sat and had my lunch by the pool. She was waving back at me from our vacation 26 years before and she was smiling knowing I was again having a good time visiting the beautiful Hawaiian Islands.

Florida, Bat Mitzvah, Washington, D.C., North Carolina, Jacksonville, Aunt Frances and Cousin Mark: In 1989 Mom and I took two whirlwind trips. The first trip was to Florida in February. Joel Policzer and his wife were having a Bar Mitzvah for their son and we had received an invitation. We decided to make a lot of stops along the way. First, we went to Washington and met with my clients Ricci and Kathy. We stayed with my Cousin Lisa. The next day we traveled to North Carolina and stayed with my Cousin Deedee and her husband Gene. From there we saw one of my clients in the little town of Rockingham, NC, and then went all the way to South Florida. Along the way, we were always two minutes late at each stop from where we planned. Mom and I laughed about this because those two minutes can be chalked up to time lost when Mom went back into our house because she had forgotten something when we were leaving.

We arrived on Friday night at the synagogue two minutes after the service had started. We stayed in a hotel in Deerfield Beach and spent a wonderful two days with the Policzers. Then we went down to Miami and had dinner with Aunt Frances, my grandfather's sister-in-law and her son Mark.

From there we traveled to Jacksonville and visited my high school friend Joe and his family. Then we drove up the East Coast and went to Chincoteague to see the wild horses. It was cold out on Aceteaque Island as we stood along the sand dunes. We did see some of the horses. This would be a prelude to other visits to the area in the summertime to see the pony swim.

Boston Marathon, New Hampshire, Upstate New York: The second trip began with a drive up to Boston where I ran the Boston Marathon. We then drove up to New Hampshire to meet with my clients, Scott and Carolyn, who had moved from the Philadelphia area to a small town in the New Hampshire woods. From there we drove to Canandaigua to meet with other clients, Glenn and Joan. We visited Auburn, New York and spent time with Johnny and Sydell Eisner, Mom's cousins. As always, we traveled all over.

Trip by Herself—70th vacation cruise When Mom turned 70 we took her to lunch and then gave her a gift. It was a cruise to the Bahamas, Puerto Rico and the Virgin

Islands. She was thrilled and kept saying, "I'm going on a cruise?" She was still healthy enough to travel on her own. This would be her first solo vacation in her life. She told me how she almost missed the boat in San Juan as she went to the fort and other historic sites and was so busy talking with people in Spanish that she almost forgot the time.

"First captain of cruise line and who is that elegant lady?" Shirley said.

After returning home she must have still had her sea legs. Carrying her luggage to her bedroom to unpack, she fell down the stairs and had to go to the emergency room. But she had a wonderful time on her trip.

Gettysburg with K.C.: One time I took Mom and K.C. with me to a State Board meeting of the Pennsylvania Association of Health Underwriters. Kitty Gelinas who was President at the time decided to have a summer meeting at her house in Boiling Springs near Carlisle. She and her husband ran a bed-and-breakfast hotel. Their home was right along the creek. We enjoyed the visit and then drove out to Gettysburg and spent the day touring.

Vince and Claudia (Ocean City and visits to Harrisburg): Many years ago I developed a friendship with

Vince Phillips, the lobbyist for the Pennsylvania Association of Health Underwriters and his wife Claudia. I would travel to their house and stay overnight before a presentation in the State Capital. When I arrived I would always call Mom and let her know I had arrived safely. Vince would stay at our house when he would be in Philadelphia for a presentation to the local agents' association meeting the next day.

Their daughters Elizabeth, Adrienne and Carolyn would tease that they wanted snow to come in the winter and say, "When is Ross coming?" I always would end up at their home during some blizzard that would arrive when we had meetings or presentations in the capital.

The Phillips family was very welcoming to my mom. We visited their home in Harrisburg and went to Gettysburg, taking K.C. the dog with us. We visited them during their summer vacation in Ocean City as well. When Carolyn was small, Mom loved taking her into the water at the beach. Our visits were always relaxing.

Chincoteague Island: In 2003, 2005 and 2007 Mom and I visited Chincoteague Island on the Delmarva Peninsula. Since she loved horses and loved the story of "Misty of Chincoteague," this was a perfect place for a short vacation. We drove down from Philadelphia, which took only four hours. We stayed at the Mariner Motel (now a Quality Inn). Next to the motel was a fenced-in area with a stable for Lightning, a descendant of Misty. Mom loved that horse. When she first contracted Alzheimer's, she would tell people how the horse followed her up the stairs to the second floor of the motel and licked her neck and face. This obviously was not true. However on our 2005 trip, Mom was standing at the fence petting Lightning. The horse suddenly grabbed Mom's blouse. The blouse had a design of leaves on it and the horse must have thought that they were real. Mom laughed and the horse had a surprised look on his face. He thought he would taste oats and all he got was cloth.

One evening we went to the downtown area to visit the little shops. We took the car. When we came out there was a family of ducks quacking at us. Mom said, "I think you took their parking spot." We both laughed because the ducks were adamantly squawking at us.

Next door to the Mariner Motel was a seafood restaurant that specialized in Maryland crabs. It was a very noisy family-style restaurant. The noise was accentuated with all the children pounding mallets on the tables to open the crabs. Mom and I loved going there.

The pony swim was interesting. You could see the "Salt Water" Cowboys off in the distance leading the horses from Asseteague Island to the narrow straights where they would cross. There were boats lined up along the passageway on either side. Also thousands of people watched from the shore.

Then everyone would make a mad dash to the carnival area to see the horses parade into the pens. The carnival was a throw-back to the 1920s and 1930s. You could eat oyster sandwiches, clams and French fries. Kids would ride in the amusement park and the auctioneer would bark out the bids for the ponies. This was all for charity.

Our trip would start on the day before the swim. We would stay the day of the swim and leave the next day after the auction.

In 2007 my nephew Micah went with us. It was July and Mom's Alzheimer's was well into its early stages. I knew this would be her last vacation and Micah agreed to help me take her.

Other than putting on her clothes over her bathing suit and one burst of anger at the auction because she didn't want to leave to go home, Mom was manageable. I would have never suspected that within six more weeks she would have developed the disease full blown and could be unmanageable.

I have wonderful photographic images of the last vacation of Mother's life, especially this one standing next to the Pony Pen with a smile of joy on her face.

Mom and Lightning sharing carrots.

Lightning kissing Mom.

Mom loves Lightning.

She Taught Me How to Be a Caregiver of a Loved One

How we care for those at the beginning of life and how we care for those at the end of life teaches us how we should live our lives. I am blessed that my mother taught me how I should live my life and how to be a caregiver.

The Hebrew word, *Hineni*, is appropriate for caregivers. It means "Here I am." In the Torah there is a line, "Here I am. Send me." I would constantly reassure Mom, "I am right here. I will be right here for you."

Mom taught me how to be a caregiver of a loved one. Her view of caregiving was not simply making sure the patient was fed, bathed and maintained and not to be left at home in a bed. To her it was all about keeping the person involved in the world around them—taking them to events, to the movies, to religious services and family gatherings. That is how Mom took care of her Aunt Bettie. That is how she took care of her father. That is how she taught me to be prepared to take care of her decades later. She never talked about this consciously. It simply was conveyed in my mom's actions.

In 1967 my Grandmother, Freda Goldman, died suddenly. She had a blockage and was afraid to go to the doctor for fear of having cancer. Her system shut down and she died suddenly. My Grandfather, Harry Goldman, was devastated. For a while he had aphasia. He couldn't communicate full sentences. He had been so dedicated to his wife of so many years that he became a lost soul with none of the sparkle and drive that was Harry Goldman. After her death, he moved to an apartment building where my Aunt Miriam lived. Miriam and Harry didn't get along well when Miriam was young and it was hard for them to help each other then. Miriam loved her father, but it was difficult for her to reach him emotionally.

Eventually, Mom convinced my grandfather to come and live with us. When he arrived he was confused and depressed. He would hallucinate as well. He would see Nazis on the front lawn. He would say he saw his mother and father and his brother Bill on the lawn as well, even though they all had died many years earlier. Mom took him to our doctor, Robert Yost, a real *Marcus Welby* of our community. Dr. Yost discontinued 10 of the 13 medicines my grandfather was taking. The result was actually an improved cognitive functionality. Grandpa began to enjoy himself. He was with a daughter he loved who had four sons that he loved as well.

We took him to Atlantic City for a few days one summer. This was the place years earlier he used to take the whole family out to dinner at Hackney's. Now Mom was taking care of him. We have wonderful films of him walking down the street near Jem's Restaurant and on the beach. This was a very different experience for him as people dressed very differently. "Look at those young girls wearing practically nothing!" he said to Mom as he stared at the young women in bikinis. But he kept looking. Mom and I had a laugh about this.

Mom was so grateful for what her dad had done for her so many years earlier. She loved him very much and was a terrific caregiver.

Eventually, he decided he had enough. He missed his Freda so much. He also thought that if he were to die, his death would help my mom financially. He thought he still had a significant amount of money, which he did not. He decided to stop eating. We set up a bed for him in the dining room because he became too weak to move. Despite Mom's best efforts, we finally had to have him transferred to a local nursing home. My mom did not want to have him die there. He was in the nursing home for only five days before he died quietly one evening. He had a peaceful look on his face. His eyes were open and his mouth was slightly open (the same look my mom would have when her time came). She kissed him on his forehead. We then had the funeral in Boston and he was buried next to his beloved Freda.

In the early 1980s my Aunt Bettie began to have difficulty living alone. She was the last living relative in Boston and was all by herself in the house on Winchester Street. The social workers were called in because the butcher and other merchants in the neighborhood would report that Bettie was wandering in and out of their shops and ordering the same items over and over again. She paid a worker thousands of dollars to fix her roof, but no one could verify that any work was actually done.

Finally, the social worker called my mom and said that if she didn't take Bettie, they would have to place her in a state-run nursing home. It would be very difficult to get her to come to our house. Mom had asked her many times. Bettie was a feisty, independent lady. She could have been the model for the old Virginia Slims cigarette company. She had smoked as a young woman and had traveled with her husband Harry all over the world, including trips to Europe on an ocean liner. Her Harry had been about 15 years older than she, and when he died in the 1960's she lived an independent and active life. Her brother Jack lived with her. He had never married. He was one of the nicest men I ever knew. Eventually, Jack died and Bettie was really alone. She would go to Red Sox games, hang out with her friends and flirt with the men. For a while, she did have a "boyfriend," but she outlived him as well. Ripping her out of her life in Brookline would not be easy even though she was now in her 90s.

Mom developed a plan. We would go to Boston for a "visit." We would then take Bettie out to lunch. I would pack up some of her clothing. After lunch we would just drive back to Pennsylvania. My brother Roy and I would come up and get her furniture and other belongings the next week. The attorney who was her conservator would arrange for the sale of her house and those funds would help pay for her care and living expenses.

Our plan worked perfectly for a while. "Let's go for a ride," Mom said to Bettie when we had finished lunch at a restaurant in Brookline. After about an hour of driving Bettie commented on how long this drive was. When she saw the sign "Welcome to Connecticut," she became very frightened. "Where are you taking me?" she screamed. "I'm getting out." She tried to open the car door.

Finally, we calmed her down. Mom convinced her that she would go to our house for a visit. The visit lasted two years until her death. Bettie actually apologized to us after she calmed down. It must have been very frightening to be taken from her home without warning, but we had little choice.

When she arrived at our house my brother Barry and his friend Roger from up the street were sitting in the kitchen smoking. Bettie had been a chain smoker most of her life, lighting one cigarette with another until a doctor told her it was bad for her health. She had quit cold-turkey that day 40 years earlier. Mom said Bettie had thrown out a whole cupboard full of cigarette cartons back then. But this trip to our house had made her very nervous. She sat down at the kitchen table with Barry and his friend and asked for a cigarette and lit up and smoked. I think that was the last time she smoked. My brother also quit smoking a few years later and did it cold-turkey. One thing about my family is that when we make a decision, we see it through.

Now we had Bettie in our house. Roy and I drove to Boston the next week to get her furniture and other items. Roy was a fast driver and not one to take his time on a trip. We had rented a U-Haul, which Roy drove and I tried to follow him in my car. We zipped through New York on the thruway and up to Boston in no time. The hardest part of our trip was carrying Bettie's furniture down the narrow stairway, but we managed to get everything into a rental truck and bring it back to our house. The furniture made Bettie more comfortable because it was familiar; it was hers.

Since Mom and I had to work during the day, we needed someone to be with Bettie until we came home. Other than mild dementia she was easy to manage, not like Mom's Alzheimer's years later. But still we needed good companions to be in the house. We distributed ads and found Florie and Mary Lou. (Florie and Bill are still good friends and visited Mom on her last birthday.) Bettie was a lot of fun, telling her stories and making Florie and Mary Lou laugh. When I got home from my state job with the Auditor General's Department, I would administer Bettie's eye drops. Her companion would leave to go home to her family. When Mom would get home from work, we would have a quick dinner and I would go out on my evening insurance appointments.

Mom with Bettie, Florie and Mary Lou.

Mom and I took Bettie everywhere. We would go to the swim club, an Irish Festival, a Ukrainian Festival, a Democratic Committee picnic, or to the shore. The only problem we would ever have was trying to get Bettie to wear a seatbelt. "Freda, I'm going to tell Momma on you," she would say to my mother Shirley thinking she was her sister. "You can't tie me up like this!" Bettie would shout. But eventually, she would forget about the seatbelt and we would all enjoy the ride.

Bettie had a hiatal hernia. In her second year living with us, the doctor told my mother that Aunt Bettie needed to have an operation to repair it. This would be a difficult operation and a difficult decision considering that she was already 93 years old. Bettie came through the operation all right, but recovery took a while. She was very brave and very tough about it even though she had lost a lot of weight from the stocky, powerful person she had been in her earlier days.

The next year, however, right before her 94th birthday, Bettie died of a heart attack. A temporary aide had taken her out for ice cream. She didn't feel real good that day, but she asked to go. Dying while eating ice cream is one of the better ways to go. The aide felt terrible, but my mother said it was O.K. and that she was so thankful she had her Aunt Bettie with her and was able to help her. Bettie had been very kind to my mom when she was a little girl and Mom was glad she could help.

When my dad's parents grew old and were living alone in Florida, Mom told Bea and Paul that she would love to have them come to our house and she would help take care of them. It was a generous offer. Bea wanted her parents close to her so they went to New York. We visited them several times at the Nursing Home in Coney Island. Grandpa got Alzheimer's. Grandma Schriftman died of cancer. They both were sweethearts and it was sad to see them get sick and then know they were gone.

Visiting Grandma and Grandpa, Coney Island nursing home.

So many years went by after that generation had died. Mom and I continued our busy schedules between work, community, synagogue and family. Then it became my time to be a caregiver. I would be caring for the person who taught me how to care for others. Back when we did it together for others, Mom would constantly say to me, "I never want to go to a nursing home. Promise me that I won't go to a nursing home." I promised and I fulfilled that promise with hard work. The training she gave me allowed me to accomplish this tremendous responsibility.

Caring for a person with Alzheimer's is a continuous learning process for both the caregiver and the patient. Things are constantly changing as the disease progresses. In the beginning of her illness Mom was mobile and getting into everything. I described her as "one hundred miles per hour." She would move boxes around, take china out of the cabinets and bring it upstairs and throw dirt into the dryer and washing machine and turn them on. I would have thought she would be exhausted by the time evening came.

Instead, she was very restless. The relentless activity and agitation took a tremendous toll on me. I lost eight pounds in two months during the summer of 2007. The pressure and stress were unending. There was nowhere to get relief. I would lie on the floor in my office and not answer the phone, which kept ringing. I knew it was Mom calling again and again asking me to come home. I couldn't concentrate. It was very hard to focus on my work.

Mom would do strange things or forget what she wanted to do. Many times she would obsess and do things over and over again. During the early part of 2007, I would have difficulty going to sleep as I would hear Mom walking around upstairs. I described it as sleeping with one ear open. I became a light sleeper. I would hear her walking and get up to check on her. So that she wouldn't see me watching her, I would stand in the kitchen with the light off and peer around the wall to look up the stairs. She kept walking back and forth. I didn't want her to fall. I would just watch her for hours. Finally, she would get tired and go to sleep.

I tried to keep her active by taking her to various events and trying to get home early enough to spend time with her. I used to work until about 9:30 and then we would have dinner together. More and more she would call me and say, "Come home early." There was a sense of urgency in her voice as if she was afraid; 9:30 became 8:30; 8:30 became 7:00. Then it was 6:00. Anything later than 6:00 p.m. threw her into a panic.

I tried to give her good nutrition. I would blend salads for her. I would eat the fresh salad with dressing and take half and put it in the blender. "See Mom, you and I are eating the same thing," I would say. "It just looks different." She would eat it and say she liked it. I would also try to put the Aricept pill in with the salad, but somehow she would always find it and spit it out. I would also blend fresh fruit so she would have a "smoothie" to drink. Despite my best efforts her capacities were still diminishing.

As things got worse, I would fear coming home. I never knew what the condition of the place would be. I would find dishes on the floor in her bedroom. I would find cat food and dog food cans all around with bowls of the pet food all over the floor in the family room. She would open every can of pet food that I had bought. Happy Girl and K.C. were eating and then messing. Since they were dogs they kept eating. Helen Keller (our cat) wasn't getting her food since it was on the floor and she wouldn't navigate around the dogs to get her food.

I needed someone in the home to supervise, but it would be very difficult as Mom would not want anyone there. When I finally did get help, Mom would call me into her bedroom when I would get home from work.

"Why is she still here?" she would question. "I don't want anyone here. You have no right making decisions for me. If she doesn't leave tomorrow, I swear I will leave, and you will never see me again."

I would try and assure her that the aide would leave, which was a lie. "Let me see what I can do," I would answer.

Also, early in her disease Mom would plead with me to get Florie to come and help her. Florie had taken good care of Bettie for us and Mom reasoned that she could do the same for her. Of course over 25 years had gone by and Florie had her own mom to take care of and had her other issues to deal with. Every time we would visit Roy and Lera and pass by Florie's neighborhood Mom would start up again that I should contact Florie and have her come over.

Agnes, our first aide, and I would have to wash dishes quietly. If Mom was sitting in the kitchen, the mere clanging of silverware or plates made her crazy, and she would scream. Noises would cause confusion and panic. In fact, I was concerned as to how she would react when Aunt Bea and Uncle Paul came for a visit in the fall of 2007. Bea is quite reserved in her speech and mannerisms. Uncle Paul is exactly the opposite. He is lively, boisterous and moves very fast for a man in his 80s. When they arrived I was amazed at what happened with my mom. She was laughing at all of Paul's jokes. She was smiling and she was having a good time. Maybe she was remembering all the fun she used to have with our extended family. I took Mom, Bea and Paul to Lancer's for lunch and she had a wonderful time. She didn't get upset until it was time for them to leave after we got back to the house. That announcement put her back into her current condition. She cursed and went up to her bedroom. But while my wonderful aunt and uncle were there, Mother had the best time.

While she was mobile, Mom would follow me out the garage door when I would be leaving for work. From my rearview mirror I would see my mother walking down the street, with Agnes trying to get her back in the house and Happy Girl bolting across Dillon Road. This was not a very good way to start a business day. Besides the difficulty in focusing on work while concerned about what was going on at home, I had a strong feeling of guilt about not being with Mom. I understood this feeling. Family caregivers live with this feeling and they should understand that it is O.K. to feel this way. After all, most of us in this position are trying to do the best we can.

To prevent Mom from opening the garage door and briskly walking out of the house and letting the dog run out in the process, I had the garage door repairman put the button above the door. Now Mom would enter the garage, press the button and nothing would happen. She would look around in the garage and go back into the house. She would say to Agnes, "The machine (meaning the door) doesn't work."

The word "machine" became a word that stuck in her head. "I want to go to the machine," she would say. She could be talking about the dryer, the washer or even the car. She would walk around talking about the "machine."

Mom liked to verbalize during the early time of her illness. "I don't care. Who cares? What do I care? Do you think I care?" she would say on a regular basis. She would also look at me and say, "Did you do it? Just get it done!" This would be something she used to say, but now I don't think she knew what she wanted me to get done. She just wanted to tell me something she wanted to say but couldn't really express anything specific.

Getting out the door to go to work became a project for me. Each step had to be planned out. I would wake up, go upstairs and greet Mom and Nora. I would give Mom her juice with the medicine ground up in it. (She would spit out a pill or tighten her jaws so you couldn't put it in, so putting it in her food or drink was the only way to get the medicine in her.) I would let the dogs out and feed them and the cat. I would wash K.C.'s feet, as she had terribly sore and blistered paws. I would then clean up the bathtub.

When Mom was more mobile she would follow me around when I was doing these chores. Nora would try to distract her by asking her other questions or asking her to help her in another room so that I could get dressed and ready to go to work.

If Mom was downstairs when I was dressing, I would let her sit on my bed and she would watch me get dressed. Sometimes she would lie on the bed. As I got closer to being dressed she would start getting anxious about my leaving. "Do you want to help me in the office today?" I would ask. "Yes, I would. When are you coming to pick me up?" she would ask. "I don't want her to go with us. Just you and me," she whispered, pointing toward the ceiling. Even with her disease she didn't want to make other people feel bad. She didn't want Nora to think she didn't like her.

I would then go back upstairs with her following closely. Once we had her in the bedroom, Nora would try and distract her again with questions or take her into the TV room.

With the dogs and cat fed, my clothes on, the medicine for Mom given, it was time for my escape. "Be ready at 2:00 p.m. for me," I said to Mom and I slowly left the room. Once out of Mom's sight, I quickly went downstairs and out to the car. Once I had backed the car into the driveway and closed the garage door, I could relax knowing that she was in a secure place with a competent caregiver in charge.

The garage door button location change was only half the battle of keeping her from charging out of the house. Soon after I fixed the garage exit, Mom decided to go out the front door. I had Russell put in a double bolt and Nora and I had the key. "Something is wrong with the front door," Mom would tell Nora. But I now felt comfortable going to work.

I would keep my promise and pick up Mom and Nora when I said I would. Mom would whisper, "Does SHE have to go?" "Let's take her out," I would say. Mom would agree. We would go to work and I would give her a magazine to clip articles. Of course, she really couldn't do any competent task. However by flipping the pages, she felt like she was helping me. I did light paper work and talked on the phone with clients while Nora would watch Mom. Usually after 30 minutes to an hour Mom would start walking around and going down the hall. This was the indication that it was time to take her home.

She liked going to my office and also would like to look in on the other places of business in the building. The tile retailer on the first floor had a display that she could look at. They had a full shower on display in their front window. Mom thought this was funny. "Someone can shower in front of the window," she laughed. When we would reach the top of the stairs to the second floor in my building, we would face Kelly who worked for another company in the building. Mom would look in. "She is a hard worker," Mom would say after observing Kelly working on her computer or talking on the phone.

On a Friday evening in January of 2008 I came home from work, entered the laundry room, and heard a whooshing noise coming from the heater. It sounded like the balloon in the *Wizard of Oz* with the fire lifting the balloon. Frightingly, it looked like the same thing. I quickly called my plumber, Dennis Pearsall. He gave me an emergency number for Paul at Delbar. Paul came right out and shut off the system. The old heater had gotten clogged with dirt. It was time for a new heater. That night we had no heat. Nora put extra blankets on Mom. Early the next morning Paul arrived with the new heater and water heater. After then, Mom would go down to the laundry room to look at it. "Buderus. Buderus," she would say as the name of the manufacturer was on the side. "I'm going down to the machine," she would announce to Nora. Mom liked looking at her new blue heater and white water heater. I liked having a new system despite the expense. I am truly grateful to Russell, Paul, Greg, Dennis, Gary, Mike, Pete, the guys at Saw Mill fencing and all the other professional people who helped maintain the equipment and lawn so that I could keep Mom in a comfortable, safe and beautiful home.

Mom liked coming downstairs to look around the family room, the laundry room and the garage. During early mornings when I was getting ready for work I would leave the shaving cream on my face as she came into the laundry room to watch me get ready. "How do I look?" I would say to her. She would laugh and say, "You look great."

One time early in her illness, she was sitting in the kitchen crying when I got home from work. She looked up at me and said, "I'm just a stupid old woman." She must have been thinking about her condition in a moment of clarity in her mind. Realizing that she can't think and do things like she used to upset her and made her cry out of frustration and anguish. "Mom, you are still smart," I reassured her. "Sometimes your head just doesn't work as well as it used to. But you are very smart. You raised four sons. You did many good things." I gave her a hug and she cried. After that, she drifted back into the cloud that is Alzheimer's to return again at a later time to a place of greater clarity.

I know now that she was trying desperately to hold on to who she was by furiously reaching out for attention and involvement in her world. I did my best to keep her at it, but it became increasingly hard to do.

Later in her illness when she was bedridden I would come into her room after I got home from work. I would sit in a chair next to her. "How was your day?" I would ask. "Not good or good" would be the response. "Are you happy or sad?" I would ask. Sometimes she would say "happy". Most times, she would say "sad." "Why are you sad?" I would ask. "Because I am sad!" she would cry. She could no longer even verbalize her feelings about her condition other than "sad." And she was right. It was truly sad for her and for me. So much had changed in our lives.

I bought a chalkboard and wrote the day of the week and the date on it. It read: "Hi Shirley, Thursday, July 10, 2009, 1576 Dillon Road, Maple Glen. Son Ross. Friend Nora." I would show it to her and she would read it. I tried to keep her mind working, but gradually she just read the words without expression or recognition. Slowly, she began to read less of it. "Hi Shirley" might be as far as she would get. Finally, she could only look at it.

Until the last year of her life, Mom still had a lot of strength, especially in her legs. I could sit her in a chair, place her feet on my thighs, hold the side of the chair and she would push as hard as she could to straighten her legs from a bent position, much like a weight-building machine for leg exercises. I used to joke that we would enter her in the next Olympics in the Women's Master Weight Lifting event if we could only move her in the right direction.

As the illness progressed, Mom would reach out to me from her bed when I came home. She would grab my shirt and yell out, "AH! AH! AH!" She would grab my nose or anything she could grab on to. She was reaching out to me as she had for the prior two years. She could no longer talk in sentences. She was trying to hold on to me as tightly as she could for the comfort that a familiar face brought . . . For the feel of having me with her. She needed me. And I needed her.

To communicate with Mom late into her illness, I would say, "Ba, Ba_ _ _ Ba, Ba, Ba!" And she would finish it, "Bum, Bum!" There was no more conversation, just this little back and forth noise making. However, it was reassuring to both of us that we were still responding to each other.

In her clearer moments I would say to my mom, "Remember how you took care of Betty and your Dad? Now it's my time to take care of you. That's all that's happening." I would smile at her. She would just look at me without responding. However, I could tell by the look in her eyes that she knew it was her time to be cared for. It both bothered her and comforted her all at the same time.

Sometimes she would just sit in the bed, look at me and shake her head "No" as if to say, "This isn't right. I'm not right. It just isn't any good anymore." Other times, she would simply look at me and say, "I'm terrible." I would say, "I know. Sometimes your head doesn't work as well as it used to. But, I am right here with you. I am here for you and I love you." I would touch her head and pray that her brain cells would stop dying. I knew the inevitable was coming, but I prayed the process would slow down so that we could still spend happy times together for a little while longer.

Her condition continued to deteriorate. Toward the end Nora and I would have to roll her in the hospital bed to change her. This way we didn't have to lift her or sit her up, which had become very difficult. Nora would change her constantly and move her position to prevent bed sores. She and the hospice staff did a wonderful job keeping Mom from developing sores and preventing the pain that would have been associated with it. She seemed comfortable to the end. Death eventually came, but I believe we were successful in giving her the best care possible. I greatly miss being her caregiver. I want to hold her and kiss and help her again. But my job of caregiver is over and I must go on as she would want me to. Toward the end Mom would look at me as if to say, "I want to stay. But I can't. I have to go." Her time had come and it would have been pointless for her to remain in a state where she could do nothing for herself anymore. I must enjoy the rest of my life without her.

Shirley The Teacher

"The day you stop learning is the day you begin decaying, and then you are no longer a human being"

-- Isaac Asimov

My mom never had formal training as a teacher. However, she enjoyed learning and loved teaching others. She loved reading as well and I have inherited a treasure of books, including a library of American Heritage books and biographies of such famous people as Eleanor Roosevelt, Harry Truman, and historical and cultural books such as those written by James Michener. One of Mom's talents was language. Even at the end of her life, she would correct Nora's pronunciation of words. She had a good ear for language and a sharp mind until disease clouded her brain.

As a young mother she took courses in Russian at the local adult night school in Springfield. She loved to go to lectures by the Rabbis and took many courses in Judaism and comparative religions.

Her first experience teaching was as a language aide at the North Campus of Abington, a local middle school in our area. She would sit with various teenage students and help them get a better grasp of what the teachers were trying to convey. She particularly liked working with students who were known as "slow learners." She was a patient and understanding teacher, and many of the students would confide in her about their personal problems.

She also had been a teacher's aide for a short time for the Montgomery County Intermediate Unit. She helped with special education children. She didn't enjoy this as she felt some of the teachers just wanted to control these disruptive or slow-learning students. She wanted to work with them to help them learn. It was very frustrating for her.

Somehow she got involved with adult education at the high school. She taught English as a Second Language (ESL) to newly arrived immigrants and Spanish to native-born students. She loved it. One time she came home from an ESL class and she was glowing. She said that when she finished the session her students stood up and applauded her.

She was so good at teaching and enjoyed it so much that she decided to start a business teaching people at our home. She ordered textbooks, study guides, historical maps and bought a tape recorder. I kept her financial records, which was not difficult because of the nature of her small operation.

She would have the students speak into the tape recorder and she would play back what they said so they could hear themselves. In her ESL classes the students not only learned English, but she incorporated American History and Civics into the courses. By her efforts, she helped many of them pass the citizenship test.

On several evenings a week her students gathered around our dining room table. There were Koreans, Chinese, Poles, Italians, Germans, Norwegians and Swedes. There were *au pairs* from France and Norway. Between the students and the men renting rooms I often referred to our home as Shirley's International House (not of pancakes).

Her students loved to come to our house. Many times they would stay for hours after class talking and laughing. Some became good friends, like Jessica from China and Jung Yi from Korea. They would visit Mom and take her to lunch.

Mom loved to learn about everything. She could also discuss religion. She had several discussions about the Bible with our neighbor Bob who remarked at how well she knew religion. Mom enjoyed taking classes in Judaism and comparative religions. She never got tired of learning.

Shirley Schriftman loved to give her talented language skills to others and she somehow connected people to one another to make this a better and closer world.

Sayings

Mom loved little sayings. I used to bring some home to her as well. She really was a word-meister; she liked the sounds rolling off her tongue. Even during her illness she could still say, "Fuzzy Wuzzy was a bear. Fuzzy Wuzzy had no hair. Fuzzy Wuzzy wasn't fuzzy. Was he?" Then she would laugh.

The one ditty that gave me trouble sleeping was, "Sleep tight. Don't let the bed bugs bite." As a child all I could think of was bugs crawling over me in my bed.

"My name is Fink. What do you think? I fix pants for nothing?" She would play with this interesting one since it has two meanings. Fink is being facetious or Fink actually doesn't charge to fix pants.

Then there was "I love you. A bushel and a peck. A bushel and a peck and a hug around the neck." Mom used to say this one in a sing-song style and then grab one of us kids around the neck and kiss us. Then I would say, "Stop, Mom" and wipe off the kiss just as little boys do. I still sing this one it to our dog, Happy Girl.

Mom also loved clever stories and poems. Not only would I bring home things I read that were clever or funny, but she would find things and post them.

One of her favorites was something passed around at Univac when she worked there. It was a circle with the word "Tuit" in the middle. "What is that?" people would ask. "It is what everyone needs but never seems to get. It is a round tuit," as in I will do this or that when I get "around tuit."

As Mom got older her mouth and her mind would sometimes get mixed up. She would confuse her granddaughter Deena with her niece Deedee. It would come out Deenee or Deedah. She would then laugh.

Even during her illness she loved to play with words. She would try and repeat the sound exactly. "Can you say, Ahmadinejad?" I would ask her as in the name of the dictator of Iran. She would say, "Amanedijad."

Even in May of her last year, she had a temporary aide named "Aminatu." Can you say it? "Aminatu" was the response.

When we would change Mom, we would say, "Pants." She would repeat, "PAANTS." She would say the word over and over again while we were changing her.

Mom loved the sound of words.

Mom vs. Healthcare

A few years ago, Mom picked up the Dr. Seuss book, *You're Only Old Once.*" In typical Seuss form it goes through the process of the author (Mom and I thought) getting all the various medical tests throughout his visit to a medical center. For all of us who have experienced the probing, the forms and regulations, it is well worth the "visit." By the way, Theodor Seuss Geisel was born in Springfield, Massachusetts, where my mom was born. He died in 1991 and had written this particular book in 1986. He did have a lot of illness in his last few years, so he probably thought it was quite amusing how the health care system works and had decided to write about it.

Mom's experience with our health care system had its good moments and its misdiagnoses. Through it all, she just kept plodding along. At the end of her life I was grateful she wasn't "hooked up" to all kinds of medical equipment. She had a very natural ending. She did have a rocky beginning in her life as far as her health simply because she was thin, which was considered sickly in those days.

Shirley Goldman was a thin child. (She described herself as a skinny pickle.) Her parents were told by their doctor that Shirley would not live past age 14 unless she gained weight. She also needed to rest to prevent a heart attack. (What a different world we live in today with the rise of obesity and the desire for young girls to be thin!)

It wasn't that my mom didn't eat. She enjoyed ice cream, which is very clear from the earliest picture of her sitting on the step of her house in Springfield holding a cone. She looked to be two years old.

Shirley was also an active child who loved to run and play like other children. However, she was not allowed to participate in gym classes. She had to rest. One time she did play baseball. When she hit the ball, everyone said run, and she ran the wrong way. Everyone on her team was mad at her, but she had never played baseball before and didn't know which way to run.

After the lecture my grandparents received from the doctor about Shirley's thinness, her diet changed dramatically. She was given eggs, potatoes and lamb chops for breakfast. Her mother would pack three sandwiches for her lunch. Shirley would give the sandwiches away to other children. Shirley was unhappy having to lie down during recess when she wanted to play with the other children. She felt different.

She did not die of a heart attack by age 14. Despite the wrong diagnosis and prognosis, she did not develop an eating disorder. She was a strong and healthy child with a curious interest in all things in life. Shirley grew into a beautiful teenager who would develop into a healthy young woman.

As a young mother, she began to gain weight with each new child. I remember her being not so thin, but she was tall and well built. Her health was always good except for a diagnosis of vertigo.

As an adult she visited a doctor to determine why she would get dizzy and pass out. After several tests, the doctor said, "You have vertigo." She told him, "I know that, but I want to know why." The doctor said, "I'm not sure." We never found out why.

In 1962 at a chemists' convention in Washington, D.C., which Dad attended and took the whole family with him, our car was rear-ended at a stop light. My brother Roy hit his head. My parents were very concerned about him and we all went to the emergency room. He was fine with just a little bump. However, the next morning Mom could not move. She had whiplash from the accident. This would be the start of many years of back pain, which would be aggravated, it seemed, every time we would go on a vacation.

Mom would fall down or trip on something. The running joke in the family was similar to the "Washington Slept Here" statement. It went like, this: "Mom fell here." It could be the rest stop on the Merritt Parkway in Connecticut on a trip to Boston to see Aunt Betty. It might be in North Carolina at a rest stop on the way to Florida.

One time with Parents without Partners she fell while roller skating. Everyone at the event piled into cars and followed the ambulance to the hospital. Imagine the waiting-room scene. A misdiagnosis resulted in more damage. She actually had a broken back and instead was given physical therapy. She ended up disabled and out of work for six months. When her disability benefits ran out, we were on welfare for a short time. When she recovered and went back to work, she paid the money back to welfare. Mom was a lesson in personal responsibility.

Another time, she was hanging a plant on the front porch. She was standing on a folding chair and it collapsed cutting her leg badly. She went to the emergency room and they wrapped it up and sent her home even though it was swelling. She was back the next day as the treatment was not adequate.

Despite these incidents, throughout her life she stayed active. She never belonged to a health club or "worked out." Her exercise was cleaning, lifting boxes, walking the dog for miles through the neighborhood and campaigning door to door. She also loved swimming and would do lap after lap at the local swimming pool. When we would go on vacations, we would walk for miles. Even in her 70's and early 80's Mom would walk when we went on vacations. In Chincoteague just a few years ago, she and I walked from our hotel to the downtown shopping area and back. This was about three miles roundtrip.

Mom took her vitamins. She ate well although I always told her she ate too much red meat and she liked it rare. A "steak tartar" sandwich was one of her favorites. This was merely uncooked hamburger on a bun. "Mom," I used to say,

"You can get sick eating that." Her answer was that people have been eating rare red meat for centuries. "Yes, Mom, but they all died," I would say.

Shirley Schriftman had a sharp mind and was an active person. Studies have shown that many Alzheimer's patients that were active in life develop the disease late. However, when they get it, there may be a sharp decline. This was Mom's case.

In late 2005 and early 2006 it was apparent that she wasn't as sharp as she used to be. She would tell me the computer didn't work the way it used to. She had trouble pushing the right buttons to turn on the oven. I first became concerned in May of 2005. We had traveled to the Harrisburg area to attend the confirmation of my friends Vince and Claudia's daughter Adrienne. When we got near the church, Mom said she had forgotten to bring her denture cream. I went into the grocery store and bought a tube. When I came back out to the car she had put vaginal cream on her false teeth and had put them in her mouth. We both laughed it off, but that was my first warning.

She began to lose weight and forget more things. Gradually, my trips home after work would be filled with apprehension. Some nights it would take two hours to clean up the wreckage of her daily activity.

I took her to a neurologist who performed the cognitive memory question test. Mom came out and told me that it wasn't fair that the doctor asked her questions, but had all the answers in front of her. Again, we laughed about this.

Then one Saturday night in December of 2006 Mom was making the grocery list. All of a sudden she started repeating herself. She kept writing the same word on the flyer from the grocery store and circling items over and over again. I thought she might be having a stroke. I called my brother Lee. I then called the ambulance. When they got to the house, she refused to go to the emergency room. With some coaxing by Lee, her son the dentist, she finally agreed to go. I drove her there. We spent most of the night with

Mother taking tests. There didn't appear to be any damage, but the doctor said there was atrophy in her brain.

After this incident it became difficult to convince her to go to doctors, but I would promise we would go out to lunch or do something afterwards. We went to a new neurologist who was all business. He ordered additional tests, but no treatments were recommended. She was beginning to develop dementia.

In late March of 2007, Mom and I were having breakfast. I was getting ready to leave to go to the Ocean Drive Marathon at the Jersey shore. Suddenly while eating, her head rolled back, her hand grasped the toast she was eating, food was in her mouth, and she was unresponsive. I quickly put my hand in her mouth and removed the food so she wouldn't choke. The period of unresponsiveness lasted about two minutes. Again, the ambulance arrived, and again she refused to go. Again Lee convinced her to let me drive her to the hospital. Again a bunch of tests were run and there was no serious problem detected. In hindsight, these might have been mini-strokes as a prelude to Alzheimer's disease.

Now the neurologist ordered a brain scan with wires attached to her head. She had to undergo this test for 48 hours so that they could see what was going on. She was to push a button if she felt a change. She kept telling me to "unhook it" when she went to sleep. She was very frustrated with this "nonsense." The results came back showing nothing unusual. What was unusual is that when I took her to the Diagnostic Center to remove the equipment, she told them that the people on television talk to her and that they smile at her.

Mom's eyesight and hearing were exceptionally good. One day in August of 2007 Mom and I went to visit Roy and Lera. When I got Mom in the car to leave, Roy and I were standing behind the vehicle. He asked me about the stove and the burners. I told him I had removed the knobs so Mom wouldn't leave the stove on. When I got back in the car, Mom turned to me and said, "We have to fix the stove. It isn't working anymore." In January of 2008 Nora needed to get an eye exam. So we took Mom as well to be examined. Dr. Koch examined Nora first. She needed new glasses. Then it was Mom's turn. Even though she was confused and was shouting, we maneuvered her into the chair. "Shirley, can you read the letters on the chart?" the doctor asked. "C-F-G- H-U-D." Mom read every letter at the very bottom of the chart. She loved reading, even if she didn't comprehend what was going on. Her eyes were perfect. The cataract surgery she had several years earlier at Wills Eye Outpatient Center was exceptional.

After her Alzheimer's disease had completely developed there were numerous visits to doctors and other health care providers. She was more compliant in going simply because it was a chance to be with me and a chance to go out and do something.

I took her for a bone density test. Explaining in simple terms I said, we are going over to the hospital and they are going to take a picture of your bones. "That's stupid" she said.

At one of the visits to her regular doctor, I momentarily forgot to turn Mom around while trying to get her into the passenger seat. She started going in forward. With her head down and her butt up in the air, I just started laughing. Nora looked at me as if I was crazy.

Mom would heal quickly. After falling and hitting her face on a table, she looked like a boxer who had lost a fight. The bruises healed in only a few weeks. She never complained. In fact, when we took her to Dr. Hirsch's office after that fall, we were sitting in the examination room and Mom was reading the doctor's diplomas on the wall despite her bruised face. She loved to read the words and still try to understand them.

Another time when we went to the doctor's office, Dr. Hirsch was not available. His associate Dr. Shomer examined Mom. While he worked he was recording his notes using a Dictaphone machine. Every time he would say something about Mom, she would hit me. "Why are you telling him this?" she shouted. "The patient, Shirley Schriftman has had trouble and is falling," he dictated. Wack! She would hit me again. "Stop talking about me," she yelled again while striking me. I found it funny. Dr. Schumer just looked at her.

Once, unknown to Nora and me she had dropped flooring on her foot in the dining room. Russell was putting in a floor and had piled them up in the dining room. We thought maybe she had slid it off and it fell. We didn't even know that she was injured until we went to change her socks and saw the bruises. Nothing was broken. There was no crying or screaming. She had good resistance to pain, but it might have also been the disease where the brain wasn't registering the pain so much.

Another time early in the morning, Nora and I were just about to get up when we heard a loud thud. We rushed into the bedroom. Mom had either rolled out of bed or had gotten up and slipped. She had hurt her back and her head. The ambulance came and we got her to the hospital. She was released two days later. She only had some bruises which again healed quickly.

We would take Mom to the geriatric psychiatrist at the local hospital for follow-up visits. During the drive, Mom would be saying her usual things, "Let me die; this is terrible; and I hate your guts. No! No! No!" We would get into the meeting with her doctor. He would say, "Shirley, how do you think your life is going?" "Oh, fine," she would respond. "Are you happy or sad?" he would inquire. "I'm happy" would be her response.

We would get back in the car and immediately her chatter would start up again, "Let me die. This is terrible. No! No! No!"

Dr. Waldfogel, her psychiatrist, had paintings of horses on the wall in his office. She would look at them intensely and just doing that would make her calm. I believe God made certain creatures to give humans comfort. Why some people treat these animal gifts so badly is unexplainable.

To try and break my mother's separation anxiety, Dr. Waldfogel asked Mom, "If Ross has to leave to go to Washington for a meeting for a few days, do you have any problem with that?" "No. I'm O.K. with that," Mom responded. Then there was a pause. "But I would want to go with him." She didn't get the point, but maybe she was remembering the times she would go with me. There was the Mother's Day Rally for Long-Term Care in Washington in 2002 and the State Legislative Hearing that Representative Dennis O'Brien conducted down at the Wister Institute at the University of Pennsylvania. In my mom's mind she couldn't be separated from me. We were a part of each other.

There was a clinical trial that I was hoping to get her into. However, she was already too far along with the loss of cognitive function. But some things still work. After the test, the doctor asked me to come in. He explained the difficulty of getting her into the study. He then asked her, "Shirley, what day is it?" Mom said, "It is Tuesday." "Mom, it is Thursday," I said. "Thursday, T-H-U-R-S-D-A-Y," she spelled in response.

She could also do simple math up until a few months from the end of her life. "Mom, what is 3 times 6?" "Eighteen," she would say quickly." She could still say, "Fuzzy Wuzzy was a bear. Fuzzy Wuzzy had no hair. Fuzzy Wuzzy wasn't fuzzy was he?" Through the first year of her disease she could say this in rapid cadence and then laugh. She could also still sing the prayers on Friday night for Shabbat. The rest was all slipping away.

Mom had been diagnosed with osteoporosis late in life. At her regular doctor's suggestion we arranged to have her get an injection at the rheumatologist's office. The office staff said it would take 15 minutes. They asked me what they should do to keep her calm. "One four-letter word," I said, "Sing!" So we got her in the chair and we had a sing-along.

"Fish gotta swim, birds gotta fly. I'm gonna love that man till I die."

Mom was yelling and upset before and after this visit, but she was singing through the whole infusion.

My mother was healthy most of her life. When she broke a bone in her jaw and they were ready to do the operation, I was asked if she ever had a reaction to general anesthesia. I could not remember a time when she had any operation requiring her to be put under. The operation went very well and remarkably she was eating solid food within 48 hours.

At home, from time to time she would hold onto the gate between the living room and kitchen where her body would become stiff. If you tried to move her she would cry out in pain.

At the end of her life, her left hand would curl up and make a fist so hard that her fingernails would tear into her palm. Nora would put a wash cloth in her hand to cushion the impact. I would gradually peel open her hand when I would sit with her. She would simply say, "Ouch," although there was no reason for pain.

I suspect she was experiencing mini-strokes throughout her disease. At the end, this could have been what resulted in her death.

The Worst Day of My Life

    I have always imagined that one of the hardest things any family member can do is institutionalize a loved one. It is even more difficult to institutionalize them in a locked-up facility. That is what I had to do with my mom for one terrible week in November of 2007.

    Two months into trying to manage with caregivers and medications to calm her, my mother was out of control. She was so desperately clinging to me that any aide worker was seen in her mind as a threat. She wanted them out of the way.

    Despite, her best efforts, Mary, who was filling in for Agnes, was my mom's target. It was the weekend before a local election. I was trying to campaign for our candidates. I had to bring Mom and Mary with me. They would sit in the car while I ran up and down the streets dropping off pamphlets and talking to voters. Mary had a tough time trying to keep Mom in the car.

    That Sunday morning, I needed to get groceries. Mom became very violent, trying to hit both me and Mary. We had to remove pictures from the hallway upstairs as Mom was knocking into them. They were falling off the wall and crashing to the floor.

    On Monday, I tried to get her to the doctor, but she refused to go. I had to get to work, so I left while Mary tried to manage the situation. Around 10:30, Leslie, the care manager called and said I needed to get home right away. Mom was choking Mary and they had to get Mary out of the situation.

    I arrived home and Leslie suggested I take Mom right to the hospital. Mom was walking around the house without a skirt on. She was confused and angry. I convinced her to help me take some items to the dry cleaners. However, I was really going to drive her to the hospital.

When we got to the emergency room parking lot, I made up a story that I wanted to visit a sick friend. She was very suspicious but this ruse convinced her to go inside. It seemed to take forever before they brought her into the emergency room. For almost one hour, she kept trying to leave. A security guard and I would walk up and down the hall with her.

Finally we got her into a bed in the emergency room and an entire afternoon went by with tests and discussions. Mom kept trying to leave. She was very afraid of what was going on and very disruptive. Finally, when the intake nurse started to approach her, Mom got up and tried to walk out. This is when several ER personnel and security people surrounded her. This only exacerbated her anxiety; she started screaming and yelling, "Ross! Ross! Help me! Help me!" She was fighting them with all her strength, kicking her feet and swinging her arms. They carried her to a bed and gave her a needle to sedate her. All the time, she was yelling my name.

At this point I lost it. I couldn't go to "help her." I felt so guilty and physically felt her fear in my chest." I never felt worse in all my life.

They sent me out to the waiting room. Then the intake nurse came out with a shocking statement, "You know we can't admit her unless she signs herself in or if you have a power of attorney that specifically allows you to make decisions on her mental care."

How would I handle her now if they simply released her in her condition? I didn't have the Power of Attorney document with me, but it was in my office. It would turn out to be a broad power that included all kinds of medical treatment decisions. I didn't need to go get it. Mom calmed down and signed the form, although it is unlikely she knew what she was signing.

This was only the beginning. After she was admitted to the Psychiatric Unit for observation and treatment, she fought them for the first two days. They had to medicate her.

They had to put her in restraints. She cursed. She screamed and she yelled for me. I didn't hear this, but was told by her doctors. The third day, she started to become more cooperative. She probably figured out if she played "their game" she could go home and everything would be O.K. I visited her everyday, but the doctors gave me only a short time for the visits. It was very hard leaving her. At home, the house was empty. K.C., the old dog, would stand at the family room door and wait and look, but there was no Mommy coming in after me. I imagined this is what it would be like years later when Mom would be gone.

Finally, the psychiatrist's office called me on Thursday saying that Mom was ready to go home the next day. On the way over, I did not know what to expect. Would she be angry with me? Would she no longer trust me? Would our wonderful relationship change?

I pulled into the hospital parking lot, parked and checked my voice messages. To my great surprise, one of the messages was from Mom. "Hi, Ross. I am ready to come home. Please come and get me?" Where was she calling from? Whose phone was she using? It turned out that the nurse in the unit let her use the phone in her office to call me.

When I came into the unit, I met with the floor nurse. "Your Mom is doing well. Here are the discharge notes." There were new medications, new dosages and all kinds of instructions. "Are you ready to see your Mom?"

As I came out of the office, Mom was coming down the hall. She was walking slowly. She raised her arm and waved at me. It broke my heart. She wanted to be with me more than anything in the world. I gave her a big hug.

As we walked through the dayroom she greeted the other patients. She said goodbye to each of them and wished them luck. Most were probably there for mental conditions, not dementia. She showed her concern for their welfare. Maybe listening to their problems during their sessions allowed her to focus on others rather than her great desire to go home and to be with me.

They gave me a wheelchair for Mom and I wheeled her out to the car and took her home. She was very tired. She went upstairs and lay down. Leslie came by and dropped off Agnes. When Mom saw Agnes she rolled her eyes. She thought she had been "cured" and that she was back to the old days when it was just me and her. Now everything was back to the way it was before she went to the hospital with someone living in the house telling her what to do and me going to work every day. She didn't talk to me again that evening. She was angry. But she was home.

Nora and Shirley

Caregiving is a difficult job. Professional caregiving, which usually is arranged through a home health agency, has a number of challenges. Caring for another person in their own home by a complete stranger (at first) is a difficult hurdle. All of a sudden someone you never met is coming into your home and telling you what to do. If the caregiver is a live-in, they are now becoming part of your family. If you are the patient, there may be a sense of resentment, fear and frustration. Your life is being taken over by someone else in the very place where you were always in charge. At first, you don't even know who this person is and you feel that you are losing control.

My mom used to announce, "I am leaving here, and you will never see me again." She wanted to escape. She was very unhappy.

The day before Thanksgiving in 2007, a new live-in companion was assigned to my mom by our new home health care agency, Intervention Associates. The caregiver's name was Nora. Nora had been born in the Louisiana settlement in Liberia in West Africa. She survived the horrific Civil War in her country in the 1990s and lived in a refugee camp in Ghana for three years before coming to the United States. While in the refugee camp she was assigned to take care of the children and the elderly and became well acquainted with the duties of a caregiver.

When Nora arrived at our house with Emily, the Care Manager, and Maxine, the Intake Coordinator, I knew right away that Nora would be good for my mom. She smiled at my mom and took her hand when they were introduced. She had kind eyes and a caring way about her. I would come to know that Nora had a special way with my mom. She had a great sense of what my mother needed and when to just let her do what she wanted to and give her space.

After Emily and Maxine left that first day, I didn't go back to work for a little while in order to see how things would go with our new arrangement. I showed Nora around, got her situated in her room and then the three of us sat and talked. Mom, of course, was not totally thrilled with a new person, and she protested when I told her I was leaving for work but I would be back later. Nora had a commanding way about her and took Mom into the TV room to settle down and watch television. I left for work feeling that maybe I could function a little better through my workday having confidence in Nora's ability to take care of things and manage Mom.

About 6:00 p.m. I got a call from Mike next door. Mom was over there. She decided to leave the house and go visiting. Nora was with her but didn't know what to do to get her to go back into our house. I drove home. By the time I got there Mom was back in the house. Nora told me later she was surprised at how fast Mom moved out the door to go to the neighbor's home. "Go back in the house," Mom had shouted at Nora. "I want to go over there!" She pointed towards the neighbor's house. "Shirley, it is cold. Come back inside and I will put your coat on," Nora had told my mom. "No, I'm going over there" was the response.

The next day, Mom, Nora and I went out for a Thanksgiving dinner at a local buffet. It would be Mom's first Thanksgiving without participating at a big family event. We had always done something with the family. For many years, Mom had hosted Thanksgiving. In later years it was a trip to Pittsburgh to my niece Deena's home with her husband Dan and later with their new son Owen. This year we were going to meet them at Dan's parents' home in York, but Deena felt it would be too difficult for Mom to travel, and she may have disruptive episodes as she had just been released from the Psychiatric Ward at the hospital. I agreed, but it was very sad to not have her involved in the holiday.

At the same time, it gave the three of us (Nora, Mom and me) a chance to get to know one another. That evening we watched a movie. I believe it was *Little Miss Sunshine*, which my mom had enjoyed seeing before. She loved movies. As usual that night it was difficult to get Mom to stay in bed and get some sleep. She was up and down. Nora kept her distance but gently coaxed Mom to go back to bed.

We had just completed the first two days of our lives together. This would last for almost two years. Nora related many interesting stories about her time alone with Mom. They were pleasant ones, disruptive ones, sad ones, and funny ones—all the things that life throws at us, especially when a person suffers from a disease like Alzheimer's.

Mom was still extremely fearful of my leaving her, even for a moment. I thought that if I could get her into adult day care for a couple days a week, she would enjoy being with others. This would give Nora and me a break. We took her up to a small center in Warrington. We spent a half hour there with Mom sitting and talking with the other people. Someone from the community had brought a dog and she got a chance to pet the animal. She seemed to enjoy herself. After doing all the paperwork and organizing, I dropped Mom off one day just before Christmas. She seemed to be O.K. However, by the time I drove the 10 minutes back to my office, there were several messages left by the director to come and get her. Mom had become very agitated and frightened and was pounding her fist on the front door screaming my name. When I arrived both the police and an ambulance were there. Mom was sitting in the ambulance. She saw me and said, "They were mean to the dog. I never want to go back there again." She made up a reason why there was a problem. After all that work setting this up, I brought her back home. Nora looked surprised. I told her what happen. She took Mom by the hand and they went back upstairs. Mom lay down on the bed. She had an upset look on her face, but she was back home in the place where she felt safe.

As time went by, Mom and Nora got to be good friends. Nora would spend most of the day following Mom around the house keeping her distance and picking up after her. Mom would remove china and glasses from the dining room cabinet and would take them upstairs. Nora would take them back downstairs. Both Nora and I were amazed that despite Mom's lack of sleep at night, she was active all day. Nora was usually exhausted by the time I got home, which would be around 7:00 most evenings. She would lie down in her room and then it was my time to watch Mom go up and down the stairs.

To get Mom to rest, Nora would say to her, "Shirley, I'm tired; I am going to lie down. Why don't you go in your room and rest also?" Mom would lie down but after a few minutes, she would get up and head toward the stairs to go back down. Usually it meant that she was looking for me or trying to do work at something that no longer had much sense. She would look into Nora's room as she passed by to see if she was sleeping. Nora wasn't. She was pretending. As Mom started for the stairs Nora would get up and tell Mom to rest. "Where are you going, Shirley? You need to rest," Nora would say. Mom, realizing that she hadn't put one over on Nora would say to her, "You're smart."

At night, Nora would close her door. Mom would get up to go downstairs. She would throw open Nora's door, look in and continue downstairs. We would find Mom sitting on a chair in the living room with her legs dangling over the side arm of the chair like a teenager. Sometimes she would be sitting on the sofa. Sometimes she would just be sitting or lying on the floor. We always worried that we both would be asleep and she would fall on the stairs. She never did.

Nora decided to put one of the trees that was in a planter in the doorways between the kitchen and the dining room and the kitchen and the living room to prevent Mom from reaching me at night. This didn't work as Mom got caught up in the branches of the tree. Mom was calling out, "Ross! Where are you? I can't find my way." I had to get Nora up to get Mom untangled from the branches as I couldn't get to her myself with the tree in the way. It was like she had gotten lost in the woods in her own living room.

Emily, the care manager, was very concerned about the dogs and cat defecating in the living room. Mom would pick up the droppings and carry it around. She would show Nora. Then she would drop it in the kitchen sink. At least she understood that the sink was a place to wash. Obviously it was the wrong place when it came to animal droppings. Nora then would have to clean up the mess, wash Mom's hands and get the animals downstairs. Caregivers are not supposed to be cleaning up after the client's pets.

"We need to do something about the animals," Emily said when she called me one day. The last thing I wanted to do is give away Mom's beloved pets, so we came up with a solution.

I decided to have Russell put in gates and keep the dogs downstairs. I also put a child gate at the bottom of the stairs to the family room to keep the cat downstairs. This change ended up making it easier for me to sleep. Mom could no longer reach me downstairs. She would come to the gate in the living room in the middle of the night. "Ross! Where are you? I can't see you," she would cry out. She would then violently shake the gate. After a while I would hear her go back upstairs. With each step, she pounded her foot in anger and frustration. She would be back at the gate later doing the same thing. I would hear Nora, "Shirley, come to bed. You need your rest." "I can't see him!" Mom would cry. Later, I would hear Mom shouting, "No! No! No!" Nora would try and calm her down, "Shirley, it's O.K.; Ross is there. He needs to sleep. You will see him in the morning."

As time went by Nora and I would find Mom at the gate with her hands clenched over the top. She was frozen to it. It would take both of us to peel her hands off the gate. Her body was stiff. Maybe she was having mini-strokes. She would cry in pain and then her body would become limber again and we would take her back upstairs.

Thoughts of restraining her in the bed came to mind. However, that only makes a person with Alzheimer's disease more agitated. They feel trapped. She still needed her movement, but our greatest fear was a fall. She had several. Fortunately, she never broke a hip, which makes caring for a person at home almost impossible.

Taking Mom out was always a challenge. We would take her to the Cherokee Indian Festival on the grounds of Temple University's Ambler Campus on Memorial Day. We would go to Democratic meetings and Ambler Area Running Club events. We would take her to doctors' offices and to the synagogue or out to Lancer's Diner. We would take her to Tony Davenport's home or Val's house or my office. Each time we didn't know what would happen. When we returned Nora and I would give each other a "high five" and then we could relax.

The procedure to get ready for a trip would start with washing Mom. Nora and I would put plastic sheets on the floor in the hall bathroom. We would then put bed padding down. We then would guide Mom into the bathroom, which many times she resisted. We would get her on the toilet after fighting with her to get her clothes off. After she toileted, Nora would take a wash bucket of soapy, lukewarm water and using a wash cloth, she would bathe Mom. "A Baath"! That's what Mom called it. Mom didn't like it at all. She would scream, "You're burning me. I hate you." Nora would have me test the water with my finger. "She's screaming and it isn't even hot" Nora would say. Mom was just frightened. I would hold her hands so she didn't strike Nora while she was bathing her. Mom would squeeze my hand so tightly while she was being washed it felt like a workman's wrench. She was very strong. Eventually we finished bathing her. Like the entire bathroom, all three of us were soaked.

We then would get her up and she would hold on to the towel rack. I would hold her, wrapping my arm around her waist and under her shoulders while Nora would dry her with the towels. Mom would then start walking to her bedroom. Nora had already covered her bed with other towels so we could dry her and she could lie down. "Dirty pig!" she shouted at us as we guided her to the bed.

While Nora dried her I cleaned up the bathroom. I put the bed padding and plastic sheet into the tub and squeezed the water out. Towels went down to the dryer. I cleaned the excess water off the floor so it wouldn't do damage. After putting the dirty clothes in the washer and cleaning the bathroom, I helped Nora get Mom dressed. Nora would be brushing Mom's hair. "Shirley, you know I love you." "No! No! No!" Mom would be protesting.

Finally, we had Mom dressed. I put her socks and shoes on and helped her up. We guided her to the top of the stairs and carefully we would walk her down to the kitchen; Nora behind her and me in front. In colder weather Nora would say, "Let's put on your red hat and your red coat and let's go." Nora would put the hat and coat on. "I'm beautiful," Mom would laugh facetiously. We would laugh as well. Then down through the family room to the garage we would guide her. Getting Mom into the car was another challenge. We had to guide her to make sure she ended up seated properly. If we made one error she would end up halfway in the car or lying down on the seat with half her buttocks partially hanging off the seat. We learned how to do this maneuver fairly well over time. While we were doing this Mom would be yelling, "I hate you. I hate your guts." Once we were driving down the road she would calm down. The traveling probably brought back good memories of other trips. She would look out the window. "Look at the beautiful flowers," she would say. "I want to go somewhere!" would be Mom's request during her illness.

Once we arrived at our destination we were faced with yet another challenge. Many times Mom would just sit in the car and not get out for a while. Nora would say, "Ross is going in. Don't you want to go with him?" "I don't care. Let him go" would be her response. Eventually, after several minutes, she would suddenly get up. We would go in to whatever event we had planned. Mom would usually be at her best behavior at the event but not always. The doctor's office was particularly challenging, especially if Nora and I had to take her into the bathroom.

When Nora and I would take Mom out when it was cold we would dress her in her favorite outfit. She had a red hat I bought for her at Target and a red coat that she had for many years. She loved wearing them. We would take her through the garage and I would have my red Ford Focus in the driveway so it would be easy to get her in the passenger side. As Nora and I walked her to the car through the garage she would look up, see the car and say, "Isn't that beautiful!"

Another time while sitting in Lancer's Diner Mom wanted to go to the bathroom. We were sitting in the backroom. Mom headed toward the kitchen since the restrooms were at the other end of the main room. Mary and Denise, two of the waitresses, tried to redirect her. She was insisting. They were concerned she would get hurt if she actually got into the kitchen. Eventually, we got her redirected around the salad bar and down the counter section to the restrooms. That was the last time we sat in the backroom with Mom. For future visits Nora and I would get the table closest to the restrooms. During her visits to Lancer's during the first year of her disease she would speak in Spanish to Juana, one of the workers. Juana would come over to our table, give Mom a hug, and say, "Como esta, mi amiga." Mom would answer, "Muy bien" and smile up at Juana. On leaving, Mom would want to go to the bakery display. We always had to buy her something sweet to take home. Janet or Helen or one of the other hostesses would help us. We also had to be careful as too much chocolate made her too active at night or would create problems with her digestion. Mom was a chocoholic.

Once when Mom was already bedridden, Nora got her some ice cream. She sat her up in the bed and gave her the spoon and bowl. After a few minutes, Nora asked, "Shirley, how is the ice cream?" Mom responded, "It's good. It's DAMN good!" We both laughed at her efforts to express how wonderful it tasted. Such a simple pleasure of life! So vitally important!

Coming out after any visit to a location was still more of a challenge for Nora and me. Many times Mom would try to get in the passenger side of the car. I had to guide her around to the other side. A treat was usually in order after a doctor's appointment. It might be a hot chocolate or some other item like a cookie. This would always calm Mom down.

We would take Mom to Roy and Lera's home early in her illness. Lera would give her something to eat and Roy would put on a movie such as "Hello Dolly". Mom would get up and dance. It was tough negotiating her to get there and back home, but she enjoyed herself, and that is what was important.

At Tony's house Mom went upstairs and lay down on his bed. She liked the house and felt comfortable there. When we were ready to leave I guided her out the door, but she wanted to go back in. "I want to go in the house!" she demanded. She must have thought she was home. Nora and I had a tough time getting her back to the car. She kept trying to open the door and get out. Eventually, she calmed down. When we got her in the car, she would not only put her feet on the dashboard, sometimes she would put them on the front window. She was very limber despite her illness.

Other times she would start taking off her clothes while we were driving home. One time Nora and I took her to the movies. By the time we got to our driveway, her pants were around her knees. We got her in the garage quickly, closed the door and walked her into the house. She was only wearing a bra and panties by then. Nora quickly got her dressed in the family room, and I got the car in the garage.

All of these challenges during our travels were worth it. These activities kept my mother involved in the world outside of our home.

"Ross?!" Mom would shout from the living room gate. "Ross went to work," Nora would remind her. "No he didn't. He's downstairs. He isn't answering." She would tell Nora. "O.K. Shirley," Nora would agree. "He is downstairs." That would make Mom more comfortable thinking I was at home. Mom would relax and go back upstairs. "I don't understand why he isn't answering me," she would tell Nora.

Early in my mother's illness, she would get the idea that she wanted to go somewhere. Of course Nora would follow to watch her. "You go back inside," Mom would say. "I'm going over there." Nora would coax her back into the house. "Shirley, come back in; I want you to show me how to fix the sink." Sometimes that would work.

In her clearer times, when Mom knew I was at work or out on appointments, she would tell Nora, "You know I worry when he isn't home." She really was saying that she felt more comfortable when I was around. She feared that something would happen to me and I would never return. Nora would tell me that when I would open the garage door and the dog would jump up, Mom knew I was home. "Thank God" Mom would say. "Ross is home." As soon as I got upstairs Mom would start with me. Obviously, she needed to get all her frustration out. When I came home from work I would want to get caught up with Nora on how the day went. Mom didn't like the two of us talking with each other. She would interrupt by yelling out, "I'm talking to you!" or yell "YAH, YAH, YAH" or "BAH, BAH, BAH." This was a throw-back to what she used to say when she thought you weren't listening. She would say, "I'm talking. You're not listening to me. Now you see what you did! I don't remember what I wanted to tell you. You always do that."

Nora would tell me that Mom had a very good appetite. For breakfast Mom would have juice, as many as seven pieces of toast, eggs and bacon. Eating seemed to comfort my mother. We would take her to Lancer's. She would polish off an entire plate of pancakes and bacon. Later on in July of 2009 when she forgot how to swallow, it was very sad as one of the last remaining things she could do on her own was to eat. Her inability to remember how to swallow was the beginning of the end of her life.

In the early days on a regular basis Nora would purposely mispronounce our last name in order to exercise Mom's brain. "Shirley, what is your last name?" she would ask. "Is it Shifman?" My mother would respond, "No. It's Schriftman?" Mom's response would accentuate the syllables. "Can you spell it?" Nora would ask. "S-C-H-R-I-F-T-M-A-N" Mom would respond. "Thank you, Shirley" Nora would say. Even with a disease, Mom felt she was helping to teach Nora, which made her feel good about herself. Nora was very wise to my mother and what she was all about.

One time Nora said she was watching television and a man was crying on the program. So Nora acted like she was crying. "Why are you crying?" my mother asked. "Because the man is crying." Mom said, "That's a fake."

Nora would always get a positive reaction from Mom when there would be a sweet treat available. (We didn't do this too often because it would affect Mom's digestive system and it would cause Nora and me a lot of extra work.) "Who likes chocolate? Who likes ice cream?" Nora would say. Mom would raise her arm quickly. "I do. I do." Then she would laugh.

Sometimes I liked teasing Nora. I would tell Happy Girl, "Give Nora a big kiss." "I don't want that dog kissing me," Nora would say. We would laugh. Mom would laugh, too. Happy Girl was perfectly willing to kiss her as she likes kissing everyone. This teasing would break the tension of a stressful day.

We had a cleaning service to remove the dog droppings in the backyard. This was important so that the likelihood of dirt being brought into the house was diminished. Mom would laugh when I said that the Poop man was coming. Nora said her friends in Liberia thought it funny and strange that Americans have someone who comes around and picks up the dog droppings.

Nora said that Mom used to tell her, "You're a good worker." Mom was always observant of what people were doing. As Nora got her breakfast, cleaned her room or picked up after her, Mom could tell that she was really working hard. When I would come home from work, Nora would take a break. We all would go to sleep at 9:00 p.m. That seemed to be the perfect time. If we put Mom to bed too early she would get up in the middle of the night and not go back to sleep. If we waited too late, that would result in a disastrous night of wandering. "I want to go to the machine," Mom would announce. That might be looking in the laundry room at the washing machine, dryer or heater. It would also mean opening the garage door and looking at the car. "Machine" became a very important word to Mom. Nora would tell me during the daytime that Mom would go up and down the stairs all day looking at the "machine."

I used to ask Mom, "What does Nora sound like when she talks?" "Ba, Ba, Ba, Ba," Mom would reply or "bum, bum, bum, bum" or "patchka, patchka, patchka." This is what Nora's fast cadence, West African accent sounded like to Mom. One time Nora was instructing Mom on something she wanted her to do. "Shirley, I want you to do one thing," Nora stated. "Ting! Ting! Ting!" was my mother's response.

One winter day, Nora asked Mom to look at the window. "Do you see the snow?" "Yes, it is beautiful." Nora and Mom together watched the seasons change over two years. Nora would get Mom to watch from the window, or when it was warm, they would sit on the back porch enjoying the beauty of nature together.

Another time I had just gotten home from work and heard a loud bang upstairs. I ran up the stairs. Nora and I rushed into the TV room. Mom had slammed the door closed so hard and fast that the rush of air and the vibration caused an entire area of shelves to come right out of the wall. Mom was on the bed and there were videotapes, shelves and brackets all over her. I quickly picked up Mom with all my strength and carried her into her bedroom and put her on the bed. Nora went into the bedroom to watch Mom while I cleaned up the damage. Fortunately, Mom had no injuries. This incident proves how quickly something can happen when caring for a person with Alzheimer's.

Many times, just to keep Mom talking and active, Nora would say, "Shirley." Mom would say, "What!" They would do this routine back and forth periodically throughout their day.

When Nora and I would walk into Mom's room late in her illness, sometimes she would look at us and say, "What am I supposed to be doing?" It was her way of saying I want to do something. I'm not doing anything and I must be doing something.

Nora told me once that Mom said to her, "I am sad." "Why are you sad, Shirley?" Nora inquired. "I'm sad because I died last night." "Who then am I talking to? "Nora asked. Mom responded, "You don't believe me? I did. I died last night." She probably dreamed about the way she used to be and then realized when she awakened that she was not the same anymore. Or maybe she foresaw her own death.

When Mom was in bed all the time late in her illness Nora would check on her frequently. "Shirley, are you all right?" Nora would ask. "I'm all right," Mom would respond. I am sure it was reassuring to my mom just to hear Nora's voice and know that she was close by.

Nora told me that several weeks before my mom died, she would look over at Nora from her bed while Nora was opening the window or cleaning up the room. Mom would say, "God bless you" to Nora. "Thank you, Shirley. You know I love you," Nora would respond. "I love you, too," Mom would say and then she would cry." "It's O.K. Shirley," Nora would reassure her. For two years, Mom gave Nora and me hell at times. From what Nora told me, it was apparent that my mom knew her life was ending soon and she wanted to say thank you.

A few days before she died, Nora was sitting in the TV room. She heard my mother shouting out, "Mom, Mom, Mom." "Who are you calling for?" Nora asked. Mom didn't say anything. Nora thinks she was calling for her own mother. Another day, she was looking down at the foot of the bed and saying, "What are you looking at?" "I am talking to the three of them." Nora thinks she was talking to family members who were long gone, maybe her mother, her father, Aunt Bettie or her sister Miriam. We will never know what she thought she saw, but maybe in her mind they were calling her home.

My mom remained in her own home as she had wished and as I had tried to fulfill my promise to her. I could not have done this without Nora. I am blessed that Nora came into our lives. She is and will always be my sister who helped me care for Mom. My mother loved Nora and Nora loved her Shirley. Even through her illness Shirley tried to express her gratitude to her Nora.

I Want to Go Over There!

Some Alzheimer's patients wander. My view is that they are actually trying to get back to what is familiar and safe because they no longer feel that way even in a place they have lived for many years.

My Mom did not wander. She knew exactly where she wanted to go. "I want to go over there!" she would point with definite emphasis. She would get in her mind that she wanted to visit a neighbor. Or she was leaving and never coming back. The first night that Nora was with us, Mom headed next door telling Nora, "Go back in the house. I know where I am going."

Once when Agnes was caring for her, I had to go to the pharmacy and we had Mom with us. I got out of the car and told Mom I would be right back. It was no more than five minutes when I came out. I heard my name being called from a distance. There was Agnes waving frantically from the front of the Giant Grocery Store. Mom had gotten out of the car and had gone looking for me. She was still very mobile and very fast at the time. She was all the way down a middle aisle in the store when we found her.

I used to come home from work and Mom would point, "I want to go to the end." For a while I couldn't figure out what she was trying to tell me. Then I realized she was pointing toward the garage. The end was where the car was. She wanted to get out of the house and go somewhere.

She had always wanted to go out and do things. Before she got sick, she would take the "Weekend" section of the Friday *Philadelphia Inquirer* and circle all the events coming up that weekend that she would like to go to. "I want to go somewhere!" she would demand. "I don't want to just sit around the house all weekend." Now, however, it was different. She wanted to get out of her present condition. In her mind, going to the "end" would somehow be better than where she was.

I tried to satisfy her need as much as possible. It was hard because we never knew what would happen. We had to keep her safe. We would go to events and she would want to get up and go somewhere else. She wouldn't sit still.

In August of 2008, Nora and I took her to a picnic and religious service at the Synagogue. She was fine during the meal. Once the service started, she kept trying to get up. We made the mistake of seating her on the end of the row. At one point she jumped up and started walking down the aisle toward the Bima (stage). "I want to go there," she shouted in a loud voice. Everyone was looking. We had to pull her outside while she was yelling.

She said, "I am never coming back here again," with disappointment in her voice. That broke my heart as she loved being there at Synagogue. She knew she had messed up. I realized later that she was enjoying the service and the music so much that she wanted to go down front like she always did with singing and dancing and be right in the middle of the activity.

I was sad that she might not be able to go back ever again. However, at Succoth (harvest) we took her to a children's musical service. We sat in the very back row near the exit. Nora sat on one side of her and I sat on the other. Every time there was music, she got up, put her arms in the air and swayed back and forth. At one point, she waved to the Rabbi. He waved back. Everyone turned to see who the Rabbi was waving to. It was Shirley who loved the service and loved the music. I was so glad we were able to do this.

Mom was always ready to go somewhere. I will always remember her words, "I want to go there!" with the finger jutting forward.

I Want to Die

Living with an illness like Alzheimer's disease is not only hard on family members, it is terribly hard for the patient. There is fear, depression and confusion. It is constant. I know now that for many patients that they actually do know what is going on. It really isn't that they don't know their situation. It may be a comfort to think so, but many times it isn't the case.

My mother kept up a continual plea. "I want to die. I died already. I don't want to live. I'm dead!" At the beginning of her last year she would lie in her bed and whisper, "Please God. Let me die." She recognized that she was no longer the way she used to be. She had already died in her mind. The Shirley she was didn't exist for her anymore. What she was really saying was that she didn't want to live the way she was anymore. She wanted to escape the pain and difficulty of her situation.

Mom used to laugh about the passage in the Torah about Jonah. When he went to Ninevah to tell the people to repent or God would destroy them and then God did not destroy them, Jonah was very unhappy. He sat under a vine God prepared and then destroyed so that he fainted. Jonah pleaded to God, "I would rather die than live." God then asked him, "Are you angry?" Mom thought that line was funny. Of course Jonah was angry. Why couldn't God recognize that?

Now Mom would say, "I died!" If this happened at meal time I would say to her, "I wish you would have told me that before I made you this wonderful dinner," Then she would laugh. Sometimes when she said she died, I would tease her and say, "You look pretty good for a dead person." Again there would be laughter, but sometimes she would flash a look of disgust at me as if to say, "What's wrong with you. This is serious." Other times, I would say, "If you die I will miss you."

One time Nora and I were taking her to Dr. Hirsch's office. As we drove down Dillon Road, Mom started, "Die! Die! Die!" I started to sing the Passover song, "*Dayenu.*" "Die, Die, *Dayenu.* Die, Die, *Dayenu,*" I started. Mom jumped right in, and we sang for the next 20 minutes all the way to the doctor's office. Mom had completely forgotten about dying and was enjoying the singing, which took her mind away from her fear and anxiety about her condition. The word "*Dayenu*" means "It would have been enough." One miracle from God would have been enough for the Israelites who were slaves in Egypt. Mom and I were always grateful for whatever blessings we had, but I still prayed for one more miracle—a cure for Alzheimer's before it would be too late for my mom.

She and I used to remember with humor my father's dad, Abe Schriftman, who also had a form of dementia. We went to visit him as often as we could. His language about dying was similar to hers. "I died. I died!" he would shout. His face would twist up with anger as he yelled out. One time he said, "If this were California, I would be dead already." Of course, he had the time zones backwards. It was very hard for Mom and me to see him that way, but she loved both Grandpa and Grandma Schriftman.

While Grandma Schriftman was alive and living with Grandpa Schriftman in a nursing home in Coney Island, she would look forward so much to our visits. One time we came to see them, Grandpa kept up his banter, "I died. I'm dead." Grandma finally lost it and hit him on the shoulder. (Grandma was tiny so it had no effect.) She yelled at him, "Die and shut up already." Then she felt embarrassed. Mom and I hugged her. It was so hard for her.

For my mom in a way things got better. Toward the end of her life, she stopped talking this way and became calm. I think she actually knew she was dying; she appeared to be waiting for the time to really come. She would look at me and say, "I'm terrible," meaning that she knew she was sick. I would simply respond, "Well, your head isn't working too well today, but I'm here for you."

Dying is never easy. But living with pain and discomfort and feelings of being a burden to others is worse. In the end Mom's death was a blessing. Her wish, "I want to die. Please God, let me die" was fulfilled and she passed into a beautiful memory of a meaningful life.

Loss: The Price for Freedom

Caregivers go through times when you look forward to the day when you will not be a caregiver, a time when your loved one no longer needs your constant attention—a time of freedom.

This desire can generate feelings of guilt. "How can I want my loved one to die?" Although guilt will surface, it is important to realize that you don't really want the person to die. You want the pressure to stop. Your entire life becomes focused on your responsibilities as a caregiver. You can't think of anything else. You can't plan to go away. You can't be involved in outside activities. You feel you are "on-call" at all times. You dread the cell phone or the office phone ringing. You fear the constant disruptions, the lack of concentration, the loss of sleep and the loss of a life of your own.

Caregiving is a form of prison.

Then suddenly that day comes. The day you dreamed of with all your guilt. But also the day you dread. The day your loved one dies.

Within a short time after the funeral and the final responsibilities, you are free. You have the time to do the things you couldn't do before. The guilt will NOT subside, but the pressure, the stress, will.

You must take comfort in knowing that you did all you could to keep your loved one healthy, safe and happy; you did as much as you could. It is now time to honor your loved one by living a full life, one that he or she would be proud of. Remember that you have been blessed with the opportunity to give of yourself to someone who gave so much to you.

Try not to feel guilty. Pick up and go away. Take a trip. Plant a new garden. Read a new book. Dance and sing.

Take a long walk with your dog. See a new place. Honor the memories that you have by creating new ones to last the rest of your life.

Sunday Morning's With Alzheimer's

For many years, Sunday morning would be grocery time. When I moved back home in 1992, Mom would make the list and the two of us would go to the store. It was a two-hour event.

Later on, she would have me go alone. However, it would be frequent that while I was shopping, I would hear my name announced. I would go to the counter. Mom had called. She forgot to tell me about XYZ that she wanted. "You left the house so quick that I didn't have time to tell you everything. You do that to me."

When I would come home there would be fights. You bought the wrong can of whatever or this isn't the brand I buy. I would then leave for work very upset. Calling her later in the day, she would have completely forgotten the argument. These were probably early dementia symptoms beginning to affect her reasoning. She would have flare-ups, but I didn't understand what I had done wrong. Now I know that I really didn't do anything wrong.

Later when the disease was in its full stage, Sunday mornings were no longer stressful. They actually became a pleasure. Now I would make the list knowing what Mom needed to eat (soft foods, vegetables and fruits) and what Nora liked (fish with its head still on, mangoes, certain kinds of nuts and the hottest spices I could find). I would try and get anything Nora wanted to make her as happy as possible. After all, she was the angel taking care of Mom. She was the stay-at-home sister taking care of her brother's Mom. That is how we felt.

When I got home from grocery shopping, the dogs would go out, the groceries would be put away, and I would make breakfast. When Mom was mobile we had to be careful to bring in only one bag at a time and put everything away. If we didn't follow this procedure, Mom would start pulling things out of the bags and you wouldn't know where they went.

After her fall in February of 2009, she would remain upstairs in the hospital bed. This gave Nora and me more relief as we could put everything away without concern for Shirley getting into things.

Breakfast would usually be lox (smoked salmon), something my mother always loved. Nora, who liked fish, didn't like lox. She thought it was too oily and didn't appreciate its slimy texture. Maybe you need to be Jewish or at least Eastern European to understand this delicacy.

Mom used to eat the lox on a bagel with sour cream. Now I would buy soft Jewish sandwich rolls.

We would get her out of bed and sit her in a lawn chair facing the window over the garage. We would cut the roll in half and give her one piece at a time. Nora and I would go into the TV room. We would watch Joel Olsteen's Christian Sunday service program from some huge facility. Nora liked the program. I liked it as well with its uplifting messages. I would then leave for work (yes, I worked Sunday and every other day of the week in my insurance business). I had a peaceful feeling when I left. Things were manageable. Mom was still home and; although we had to physically move her, she seemed comfortable. Nora made me feel comfortable because she knew exactly what needed to be done. Sundays were also visiting time for my mom's nurse Crystal, a cheerful and caring person who would brighten up my mom's day during her visits. Crystal would help Nora with the caregiving. When I would get home Sunday evening there would be a report from Crystal on her activities and observations.

We continued having Sundays like this through the spring and early summer of 2009. Mom began to toss her sandwich on the floor or tear pieces off. She also would lean forward putting her head almost on her feet (I never knew how flexible she was). Now we had to watch her even when she would eat. One time she tipped the chair over and fell on her face.

I asked Emily whether a harness would work when she was sitting in the chair. Emily suggested instead a reclining chair, such as one which Mom's father, Harry Goldman, sold—Berkline Chairs. I went to a client who owned a furniture warehouse. They didn't have a Berkline Chair, but they did have a chair that looked like it would work. It did. Mom was much more comfortable in her chair. "Do you like your chair?" I would ask her. "Yes," was the reply.

She would sit like a teenage girl with her legs dangling over one side and her head toward the other. The lox sandwich would be in one hand and she now was watching the Christian broadcast on TV with us.

When she would finish and it would be time to go, I would stand in front of her and say, "Up, up, up!" She would repeat, "Up, up, up!" She would be agitated as she knew I wanted to get her to her feet and that I would soon be leaving for work.

I would lean forward, wrap my arms around her waist, and rock backwards pulling her up in one motion. I would walk backwards from the TV room to the bedroom with her walking in synchronized steps with mine. I was able to do this for several months. However, more and more over time she could only take a few steps before her body went limp and she became dead weight. I wanted desperately to keep her legs working, as atrophy would result and blood clots might occur. However, it was a losing battle. Nora would be standing by with the wheelchair. As soon as she would become limp, I would pivot and we would plop her in the wheelchair and take her back to the bedroom.

Sunday mornings had changed. Mom was now in bed most of the time. She then stopped swallowing her food. Trips to the grocery now included baby food and nutritious drinks. Hospice services were now arranged by Emily.

Peculiar Behavior

Alzheimer's patients do strange and unexpected things. Mom was no different. She would walk through the upstairs hallway and open each door and look in as she passed. She would insist on blankets and sheets to be set in a certain way on her bed. She loved a beach blanket with silhouettes of runners on it. She had given me that beach blanket as a gift many years earlier. Now she insisted that the runners had to face a certain way on the bed. Even though it was a beach blanket she wanted it on the bed next to hers where my dad used to sleep. "Don't leave. You don't have it straight," she would say.

Before we had a caregiver, I would come home from work to a mess. She would fill every water glass and put them in the freezer. The dog and cat food cans had all been opened and put in dishes downstairs in the family room. The dogs were eating all of it and, as a result, were defecating all over the house. The cat was starving because she wouldn't eat on the floor with the dogs. It would take me at least two hours every evening to clean up.

Papers would be scattered all around. Mom would cut up paper towels and stuff them in the toilet. She would flush the toilet over and over again until it got clogged. Several times after cleaning up the flood in the bathroom that would spill out into the hallway or the bedroom, I would have to get the plumber to come over to repair the damage.

She would throw cat litter or other items in the dryer and turn it on. The dryer would be rotating for hours. I then had to clean out the dryer. The utility bills were skyrocketing.

In the late summer of 2007, she insisted on wearing several shirts, one on top of the other as well as several pairs of underpants. Despite Agnes' best efforts, Mom refused to remove any of the clothing, even though September of that year was very hot.

Mom would go through the breakfronts in the dining room and pull out all the china. She would take it upstairs and either the aide or I would take it back down.

During the nights when she was still walking well, she would get up and go into the living room or dining room. On her way up or back we would hear the piano. She would carefully hit every black key from the bottom notes to the top and then back down again. Maybe this gave her comfort since she loved the sound of music.

I tried to remain patient with her, but it was difficult. She would not listen. She would buy things in quantities. She wanted 12 Frisbees for the dog to play with. She wanted six dust pans and brushes. Because the dog collar needed a different number of latches, we would go to the pet store and she would try to explain to a clerk what she wanted. Of course it made no sense. She would buy 10 pairs of underwear or 12 pairs of socks. Even though time and expenses grew, I tried to make her happy, which was never possible because she always insisted on more; whatever we bought was not the right kind, the right size or the correct amount.

As her reasoning diminished, Mom would ask me impossible things. "Can you take the picture of Deena and Micah back to the artist and make them look at each other?" she asked. Mom would also imagine that objects were talking to her. She had a calendar of animals in her TV room. There was a cat named "Michelangelo" on one calendar. "I talk with him all the time," she would tell me. The contestants on "Dancing with the Stars" were asking her personally to call them. "She wants me to call her. Dial the phone now," she would demand. Mom really thought that the people looking at the camera on TV were actually talking directly to her.

Mom would walk down the hallway in our house and make a clicking sound with her tongue, "Cluck, cluck,

cluck." The sound was usually in threes. She would look at the dog or the cat and blow kisses. Her kisses were made by bringing her lips together and creating a puckering sound.

Are You Sleeping?

When my mom was still mobile and active, despite her disease she would come looking for me in the middle of the night. Nora and I realized that if Mom found me during her quest, she would not go back to sleep. I spent many sleepless nights walking her back to bed, kissing her goodnight and then finding her at the door to my bedroom down on the family level of our split-level home.

I would pretend to be asleep. Sometimes this would work. I would hear my door open. She would turn on the light, and I knew she was looking at me. If I kept pretending I was asleep, she would lean over me and ask, "Are you sleeping?" If I didn't answer, she would shake my shoulder. If I still didn't move, she would say to herself, "He is sleeping. He must be tired." Only then would she go back upstairs.

At other times I couldn't resist laughing; then I would open my eyes, and she would smile at me. "I knew you were faking," she would say. I would hug her and then end up sleep deprived, as she would sit on my bed and we would talk for a long while.

If I was successful in getting her to go back to bed, fifteen minutes later she would be back downstairs. Again she would not only ask me if I was sleeping, she would shake me. I couldn't help but open my eyes. We would both laugh again. "Mom, it is very late," I would say. "Why don't you go back to sleep?" "I just wanted to make sure you were O.K." she would answer. I knew she was really saying that she wanted to make sure SHE was O.K. and that everything was safe and that I was right there for her. I am proud to say that I was right there for her just as she was always right there for me.

The Funny Side of Alzheimer's Disease

Illnesses related to various forms of dementia are sad, difficult and terrible experiences for loving family members. However, there are many joyful moments of humor. My mom was no exception.

Since she liked to be the center of the party and loved a good joke, especially if she was involved in it, her humor didn't change even toward the end of her life. She used to laugh very hard when I would say to her, "What are your sons' names?" Then I would say, "Roy, RA-AAS, Lee and Barry." That was because she would call out for me using my name with two syllables.

When she was younger she loved when her sons would tell the story of how "Mom fell here." She would tell funny stories about her childhood and the silly things that happened.

About a year after she got Alzheimer's we were watching the videotape my nephew made of her 80th birthday party. We were now three years past that event. I had arranged through my friend Lawrence Curry, who is a State Representative, a Legislative Proclamation to be presented to her at the celebration. The proclamation contained all the wonderful achievements my mother had realized throughout her life. They included her service in the State Department, her assistance to Jews immigrating to the United States from the Soviet Union, and her work to establish the Bucks-Mont Chapter of Parents without Partners. After Larry read the proclamation and gave her a kiss, she grabbed the microphone and talked for 20 minutes. Three years later while watching the recording of this event, she started laughing and said, "I talked a lot."

At her 84th birthday party, which we held in the living room of our house, many neighbors, friends and family came to visit for the event. When we sang "Happy Birthday" to her, she blurted out "Happy Birthday, Damn It!" as we finished.

When I would arrive home from work around 7:00 p.m., I would give Nora a break. Many times I would go into my mom's bedroom and lie in the bed next to her and just talk with her. This was our quiet time together. One evening we were lying and talking. She looked past me at the wall. On the wall facing the street there are artists' sketches of her sons. "Mom, do you know who those people are?" I asked. She didn't answer. She just looked. "They are your sons. How many sons do you have?" I always tried to get her mind working by asking her simple questions. "Ten!" was her quick response. Of course she only had four. "You have ten sons? What are their names?" Without a second's hesitation and in rapid, quick and loud cadence she responded, "One! Two! Three! Four! Five! Six! Seven! Eight! Nine! Ten!"

During early 2009, I had read about a clinical trial for Alzheimer's patients. I took her to Jenkintown to meet with the doctor doing the clinical trial. Mom had to do a cognitive test which she did not do very well. At one point the doctor asked her, "Shirley, what day is it?" Mom responded, "Tuesday." "No," said the doctor. It is Thursday." Then Mom said, Thursday, T-H-U-R-S-D-A-Y, Thursday. She could still spell words, but didn't know what day it was. For other questions the doctor would ask her, Mom turned to me and said, "Tell him the answer." She didn't get it.

Her last visit to the Bethesda Project Dormitory for Homeless Men was in December of 2008. She had always conducted Hanukah services for the men. We would then serve a brunch which included latkes (potato pancakes) and play the dreidel (spinning top) game. It is now my tradition, which she started, to have each resident read the meaning of each of the eight candles of the menorah of Hanukah.

Penny was assisting me with Mom that weekend. We got her dressed and down the stairs. She had on her red coat and red soft hat. All the way from our house in the northern

Philadelphia suburbs to South Philadelphia, she was talking and very nervous. "Oh God. I am dying. I can't take it. Let me die." Interspersed with this banter she would blurt out, "turnpike up ahead" or "construction 2 miles." She was reading the road signs while she was yelling out her anxiety. There was both fear and joyful excitement just going on this little trip.

When Mom and I took care of our Aunt Bettie, we used to take her everywhere. Bettie had a mild form of dementia. She was in her mid-90s when we cared for her. I was the Democratic area leader at the time which is similar to a Ward Leader. There were very few elected Democratic officials in those days in Montgomery County, Pennsylvania. So to draw out people, we asked the District Attorney of Philadelphia to come and give a speech at one of our meetings. His name was Ed Rendell. He would eventually become Mayor and then Governor of Pennsylvania.

We did achieve a "crowd" of about 20 people that evening at the old McCann Building in Ambler. Rendell spoke about crime in Philadelphia and all the things his office was trying to do. When he finished, he asked if there were any questions. Betty raised her hand. "I wanted to know who is stealing my scissors!" she yelled out. (My mother had hid the scissors. My aunt would cut up her pictures and her dresses and there were also safety concerns. "Betty with the Scissors" is what my mom's family used to call her as she never liked the way she looked and would cut herself out of family photographs.)

Rendell had a puzzled look on his face from the question. Mom pointed to herself and winked. Rendell picked up on this and said, "I don't know who stole your scissors lady, but I will put a man on it right away."

Twenty-five years later, I took Mom to a Democratic committee meeting. Most of the other people there had known her for many years and knew her before she became ill. Some, if they were old enough, had walked the neighborhoods campaigning with Mom.

During this particular meeting there was a long discussion about the construction of the new high school in our community. Mom listened intently. All of a sudden, in a loud voice she yelled out, "A-B-C-D-E-F-G." I don't know if this was a comment as in "You all are just using a lot of words" or whether she felt like she wanted to participate but couldn't think of what to say.

One evening I came home from work. Mom came downstairs to the gate between the living room and the kitchen. She looked back upstairs where Nora was standing. Then she looked at me and said, "She's a mess." Nora must have told her to do something and she objected.

During the Christmas Holiday in 2008 I took Mom to my friend Val's house for lunch. Val ran an animal rescue and had a number of dogs and cats. Mom was dressed up in her red hat and red coat, very appropriate attire for the season.

After Mom sat down at the table, one of the cats jumped up on her and sat on her shoulder. Mom was overcome with laughter. Halfway through the meal, Mom put her head down on the table. She must have been tired we thought. Val said to me, "I guess Shirley is sleeping." "No I'm not," my mother blurted out as she sat straight up in the chair.

Mom would tease Nora about her accent. One of the vegetables that we all liked was brussel sprouts. Mom would tease Nora by saying, "Brussel sproot! Brussel sproot!"

We would watch movies after dinner if it wasn't too close to 9:00 p.m., our bedtime. (Nora and I found that perfect spot that Mom would fall asleep and not get up. It was late enough that she would be tired, but not early enough that she would get up in the middle of the night.) One evening we watched "Driving Miss Daisy." Nora had never seen it and loved it. Toward the end Jessica Tandy's character Daisy was very agitated and didn't seem to know what she was doing. Morgan Freeman's character Hoke was trying to help her remember that she no longer was a school teacher and everything was fine. My mom, who was already deep into her Alzheimer's, watched the scene intently. Finally she concluded, "She's confused." Mom could recognize moods on people's faces and their actions with emotional connection far into her own disease.

The gates I had Russell install between the kitchen and living room and the kitchen and dining room allowed me to sleep at night. Mom could not reach me, so she would go back upstairs. She would yell, "Ross! Ross! Ross!" for a long time and then give up. I would hear her walking heavily up the stairs and back to her bedroom. She would be angry. However, the activity would then make her tired and she would go back to sleep.

One night Mom must have decided to try a different strategy. She would use sweetness. I heard her at the gate. "Ross? Ross? Rossy Bossy?" Then out of nowhere she yelled, "Herb? Herb? Herb?" I sat straight up in bed. She hadn't called my father's name in years. The next day I told her about this. She started laughing.

She asked me, "Was I married?" I told her about her marriage. "Where is he now?" I told her that he had died many years ago but that she had been divorced for many years before. She thought for a minute. "Did I divorce him or did he divorce me?" I said, "He divorced you." She thought again for a moment. "I must have been upset."

While Mom was mobile and we were taking her places, we always had to be careful guiding her. Sometimes she would try to get into the car on the driver's side. "Do you plan to drive?" I would ask her. She would laugh. It would take us a while to guide her to the correct side of the car.

In the fall of 2008 we took her to get a flu shot. We came out of the pharmacy. I was holding her arm and walking with her to the car. All of a sudden she started to speed up. She looked over at me and demanded, "Slow down!" I'm not sure if she was really telling me or telling herself.

That's a Big House

"That's a big house." This is what my Mom would say when she had Alzheimer's and we passed the Brandywine Dresher Estates Assisted Living Community down the street from our house. In the fall of 2007, Agnes and I took her there for a community "Oktoberfest" celebration. They had a German Opa band and even though Mom already had Alzheimer's disease, she had the presence of mind to go up and tell the band director that it was my birthday. She and I danced together as the band played "Happy Birthday" to me.

Afterwards we walked around the facility. She kept saying that it was beautiful there. There was a fish aquarium and a well-decorated dining room. I asked her, "Would you want to live here?" I wanted to see what she thought of the idea. I didn't know what the future would hold if it got too difficult to manage her at home. "Oh no," she said. "I wouldn't want to live here; I have my own house. But this is really a very big house," she reiterated.

The next year, Nora and I took her again to the Oktoberfest. This time she couldn't dance. We brought her in the wheelchair. We got her a hotdog and something to drink. She liked to visit the "big house" down the street.

Lasts

After a loved one dies, we always remember the last time they did particular things in their life. With my mom, there are so many "Lasts" that I remember.

Last Birthday Party: Mom's 84th: Although she couldn't walk without assistance, Nora and I got Mom ready for her 84th birthday. We bathed her, got her dressed and put her in the wheelchair. We got her to the top of the stairs and walked her down to the living room. We then put her back in the chair and wheeled her to the middle of the room. I had sent lots of invitations to neighbors, friends and family. It seemed that everyone showed up.

We had plenty of food. People brought simple gifts for her to enjoy like books with pictures and videotapes. We sang "Happy Birthday." She even sang along. It was a simple tribute that so many people who loved her gave by just coming over and spending time with her.

Last Book Read—*Marley and Me*: Before she had gotten sick, I had given Mom *Marley and Me* for her birthday in 2006. This is a very special book about a dog and the family who loved him. I had met the author John Grogan when he was a writer for the *Philadelphia Inquirer*. John was covering the pay raise debacle in the Pennsylvania State Legislature. When he wasn't writing great tongue-in-cheek articles about the antics of elected officials, he would write about his "bad" dog Marley. When Marley died many people wrote to John about how sorry they were about his loss. I was one of them. He decided to write a book about the dog.

Mom, having loved so many dogs, really enjoyed reading the book. It touched her heart as she always understood the special bond between people and their pets.

Last Time at Synagogue: Hanukah 2008 was the last time my mother ever went to the Synagogue. It was the annual dinner and service. The year before they had a "Shultide" Chinese dinner and Klezmer Band playing on Christmas Eve. Mom was still very mobile in 2007 and was up dancing and swinging. She was standing so close to the band I thought she might fall into the instruments. She kept waving to Nora to get up and dance the Hora with us. Now a year later she could still walk, but with us holding on. We assisted her into the wheelchair and moved her to the table. By coincidence, there was a man at our table who had been a teacher at Abington High School North Campus when she was in the language department there. She was very different now. She would put her head down on the table and couldn't communicate too well. We knew late in the meal that the service would be too much. Before dinner she watched the candle lighting of the huge menorah in the lobby. She kept wanting to stand up. She talked with the Rabbis but didn't make much sense. Several weeks earlier we went to a luncheon in that same lobby. It was an opportunity for members to buy things at the gift shop for the holidays. As Mom walked by the tables, she picked up a tiny wooden driedel (a spinning top for a Hanukah game). I thought she was going to try and spin it as she had her fingers over the stem. Then suddenly she popped the wooden toy in her mouth. I guess she thought it was candy. I quickly pried open her mouth and removed it before she could swallow it. You never know what someone will do when they have Alzheimer's. Accidents can happen very quickly.

    All during the Hanukah dinner we knew that we would have to take her home at the end of dinner. We wheeled her out and she never returned. Her religion and Synagogue life were very important to her. From the time she was a little girl her parents took her to Synagogue. She would tell the story of how as a young girl she fainted during Passover. After feeling sick and trying to back out of the sanctuary so she would still face the Bema (stage) area and not insult God, she ended up passed out between the doors at the back of the room.

Hanukah 2008 would be her last visit.

Last Time Walking: In January and February of 2009 Mom had become unstable on her feet. It wasn't the vertigo that she had suffered from most of her life. It was her brain not being able to properly direct her legs and feet on how to move. She fell behind the door in her bedroom and had hit the door stop right above her eye. This was obviously fortunate in that it didn't affect her eye.

Nora and I would have to help her get up the stairs. She would be very unsure of herself, especially at the very top step where the railing would end. I would put my knee under her butt and push her up to keep her going. Nora would be at the top to guide her.

Then on February 28th, while Nora was on a break, I was just leaving the office around 7:00 p.m. when the phone rang. I thought it might be a client and I would return the call the next day. I didn't answer or check the message and left for home. What I didn't know was that the call was from Penny, Nora's temporary replacement. When I got home, Penny came down and told me that my mom had fallen. Penny had gotten Mom some juice. Mom threw it up in the air and it spilled all over Penny. Penny went into her bedroom to change her shirt, and in that short time, Mom got up, slammed the door closed and lost her balance. She fell against the wooden TV dinner tray right on her jaw and then to the floor. Penny had gotten her up and put her on the bed.

When I checked her it was obvious that she had a serious injury. Her mouth was not straight and there was a small amount of blood around the injured area. We applied first aid and walked her down to the car and got her to the emergency room at the hospital. Within two hours we knew she needed surgery to repair a small bone toward the mouth area of her jaw. She didn't complain and didn't indicate that she was in pain. Of course, it is hard to tell with Alzheimer's patients what they actually feel.

Penny felt terrible about the accident. She sat holding Mom's hand the entire first day in the hospital. She sat with her almost all night in the emergency room holding Mom's hand. There is something very special about those who care for the elderly and for sick children. They are truly angels.

Mom was put in a special private room for patients at risk of falling. They scheduled surgery two days into her stay. While she lay in bed, she enjoyed the television channel that showed rolling streams, mountains and meadows with soft music. She kept saying how beautiful it was.

The surgery went very well. Mom recovered quickly from her injury. She was eating regular food two days after the operation. However what never healed was her ability to walk. Even though physical therapy went well the day of her release, when the ambulance took her home and we got her upstairs, her life had changed dramatically. She could no longer walk on her own and even holding her while she walked became difficult.

Last Trip: As the months went by, my mom was less able to do things. Even moving her between the bedroom and the TV room became more difficult. Nora and I would try and get her moving on her feet. We would say, "Up, up, up" as we would wrap our arms around her front, lean toward her, and then move back and up to lift her. The agency got Nora a back brace so that she wouldn't strain herself while lifting Mom to her feet. Early on we were able to get her to walk between rooms holding her this way. We even still got her into the bathroom and onto the toilet. However, as time went on, we could only walk a few steps before Mom's whole body would stop. It wouldn't be that she would just stand in one place. Instead, she would just collapse as dead weight. Now the wheelchair would have to be right next to us, so we could quickly turn and get her into the chair before she would collapse to the floor. If we weren't quick enough, we then had to struggle to get her from a lying position to a sitting position and then lift her up and get her back in the chair.

We were still having her sit in a chair when we got her up, but even that became difficult as she would lean all the way forward touching her feet and then falling off. I spoke to Emily, the care manager about the idea of having her wear a harness. Instead, Emily suggested a recliner for the TV room. That was a great addition for a while. Mom could be comfortable and not fall out. She liked the chair. Sometimes she would hang her legs to one side like a teenager. However, after a while even moving her to the recliner became difficult.

As the warmer weather of 2009 approached I prayed that I would be able to take Mom for one last trip. June was a very wet and cold month. However, the weather broke and June 30th was a beautiful day with blue skies and temperatures in the 70's. Nora and I got Mom dressed. We got her in the wheelchair and moved it to the top of the stairs. Mom knew she was going out AND she wanted to go. I could tell she was determined to go, although she didn't know where she was headed. We did our "Up, up, up" routine and got her to a standing position. With much effort we got her down the stairs from the bedroom level to the living room. Nora was behind, holding her up and I was helping in the front getting her legs in the right position to make contact with each step of the stairs.

Into the kitchen and onto a chair for a rest. A glass of water. A break and then "UP, up, up." Moving her to the stairs to the family room level and down the six steps. We then swung her around and into the wheelchair. We had made it. We would have to worry later about how to get her back up the stairs.

We now wheeled her into the garage to the car. Again, the command "Up, up, up." Turn and put her butt on the seat in the back of the car. Nora came around from the other side and slid her in. I turned her legs to the floor. Nora propped her up next to her. I got in and we were on our way.

This was Nora's first trip to an American beach. She had never been to one since arriving from Liberia. She had always been in areas away from the shore since coming to this country. I thought this would be a nice day for all three of us . . . Me, taking a break from work to be with Mom and Nora . . . Nora experiencing South Jersey for the first time . . . And of course, Mom going on a trip which she always loved to do.

Through the expressways, over the bridge and down the back way through the South Jersey farmland we went. "Mom, how are you doing?" I called out to the back seat. "Fine," she answered.

We arrived. The weather was beautiful. We parked, got her in the wheelchair and moved along the sidewalk to the Promenade ramp. Up the ramp and to the spot under the awning we went...the spot where she had spent so many August Saturday afternoons and evenings watching me run the Sea Isle City 10 miler. It was her spot. She might not have recognized it, but we were there. The sun. The ocean. The people walking by. I took pictures of Nora and Mom. Nora took pictures of me and Mom. Mom ate a hotdog and had a drink of water. I went for a short run. We sat and watched the people. Late in the afternoon, the weather report predicted thunderstorms. So around 2:30 p.m., we wheeled Mom around the downtown area and then back to the car. "Up, up, up." We lifted Mom onto the seat in the back, slid her into position and drove out of town over the bridge ending her last visit to the shore. "Donna shore," Mom used to laugh at how people in the Philadelphia area would describe a visit "Down the shore" as in "You going donna shore this weekend?" No more for Mom.

We got home with only a little thundershower action. Now we had to get Mom back up the stairs. Out of the car, into the wheelchair, up the first flight. Rest in the kitchen. Now the eight steps to the bedroom floor. We made it. Put her back in the wheelchair at the top and wheeled her into the bed. Out of the chair and onto the bed.

"Mom, did you have a good time?" I asked. "Oh, yes!" she said. "I love you." I kissed her and she fell asleep. It was my best day all year.

Last trip to Sea Isle.

Mom and Nora in Sea Isle.

Last Time Out. Last Time Downstairs: July 4th, 2009. The Oreland parade. Two years earlier I had marched in the parade with the Democrats. Mom sat in a chair we brought from home from which she watched at a spot near the beginning of the parade. She was already having difficulty and when the group I was in completed the parade route, I ran the two miles back hoping she hadn't gotten up and moved somewhere. She was still there. We had gone out to lunch afterwards and had a good day. Now two years later and only a few days after Nora and I had taken Mom to the shore, I would attempt to take her out one more time.

Nora had taken a few days off so Ramatu was her replacement. Ramatu knew how to move my mother. Also, there was something about her that my mother liked. She would look at her and smile. Ramatu had a kind face.

Ramatu had no fear about handling Mom in her condition. Just like with Nora, we got Mom out of bed and into the car. This time, the trip was short, a few miles to Oreland from our house. We set Mom in the wheelchair along the parade route. She watched. She held her ears when the rifle corps fired their weapons. She waved to the fire personnel riding by in their engines. Then we went home. We wheeled Mom onto the back porch and we had lunch together. The dog played in the yard and I threw the Frisbee for her. Mom watched. The flowers were out; the trees were swaying gently. It was the peace we all dream about and it was July 4th. And my mom was still a part of it.

Our neighbors, the Healys, came over to the fence. Their daughter Gina and her husband were visiting. They waved to Mom. Mom looked, but didn't respond. Maybe she knew them, but just couldn't acknowledge. Maybe she didn't know them. She just looked.

Mom began to look tired. We wheeled her in the house. "Up, up, up." We got her up and helped her up the stairs to the kitchen and the chair for a rest. A little water. Then the harder part. Getting her upstairs. We did it; put her in the wheelchair and into the bedroom.

This was the last time my mother was ever out of her home and the last time she was ever downstairs again.

Final July 4ᵗʰ parade, Oreland, PA.

Last Religious Service: Erev (Evening) of Rosh Hashanah in 2007 I had come home and was running late for services. Since it was almost time for the service to begin, I decided instead to stay home and to conduct services for Mom and me. I read from the old Union Hebrew prayer book, the one that I had grown up with and that was most familiar to her. Mom was in bed. I sat at the foot of the bed next to her and read each prayer. She looked straight at me and listened. She could no longer respond. She could no longer sing the Hebrew prayers in her beautiful voice. She just listened. When I finished I asked her. "Did I do it right?" "Yes," she responded.

The next afternoon after services I returned home. Nora and I got Mom to a sitting position and put her in the wheelchair. We brought her into the TV room. I put the sacred music CD from Keneseth Israel into the disk drive and turned on the TV. This CD with Cantor Levy and other singers was a gift to the congregation by Jack and Sandy Glass. It was produced to give those people who could not attend services a chance to hear the sacred music. The Brotherhood of the congregation also sponsors a radio program for shut-ins. Earlier in the year, Sandy Glass had died from ALS. She had been a regional President of the Sisterhood and an inspiration to many. Jack and I had served as co-presidents of the Brotherhood at Rodeph Shalom many years before.

So now on a sunny Saturday afternoon in late September Mom was sitting in her wheelchair in her TV room listening to beautiful religious music. I was holding her hand and I was crying softly. Mom could hardly talk at this point in her illness, but she said, "You are crying." I just held her hand knowing that she was slipping away from the world. I wanted to continue giving her the joy of life she so much loved. At one point, Nora came into the room and opened the window as it was getting warm. As she passed by, my mom grabbed her arm and kissed her hand. She was showing how grateful she was for the love, companionship and caring that Nora had shown her the last two years. I think Mom knew her end was near.

Last Song ("Edelweiss"): Abington Hospice has a singing group called Breath of Dawn. These ladies travel to patients' homes and sing to them. When hospice told me about this I thought this would be good for Mom since she loved music and singing. There were two visits. During the first one, Mom was more alert and she sang with them a little. When they finished they each kissed her and she said, "Thank you." The second visit, Mom was just listening. They sang a variety of music. While they were singing she listened carefully. At one point she turned to me and said, "I can't make it." I know what she meant. She couldn't make herself sing anymore and she really wanted to. She did say the world Edelweiss while they were singing the famous "Sound of Music" song. I am grateful to these ladies for their visits to allow my mother the joy of hearing live singing one more time.

Last Words: "I'm not answering any more questions." About two weeks before she died, I came into Mother's bedroom after work one evening. Nora had given her some of her pudding from the baby food jar and some water. I gave her a kiss and a hug. Then I took the spoon and gave her a little baby food. Then I said, "Mom, would you like a little more? Do you want some water? How are you feeling? She looked up at me. Her eyes were wide. Her mouth opened and she said, "AH! AH! I'm not answering any more questions!" I realized the rapid list of three questions I gave her overwhelmed her brain. She hadn't spoken sentences for quiet awhile by then so this was a surprise. It was the last words she ever said, but appropriate for living life. Sometimes everyone is asking us questions that we are supposed to answer for them. When I get overwhelmed, especially in business with clients or coworkers calling asking me for advice and help, I will always remember my mother's last words.

Last Dance: Two days before her death, my friends took me out for my birthday. My co-worker Lee gave me a gift certificate to Barnes and Noble. I purchased the music CD, "Songs and Stories by George Benson." That night I put the CD on in the TV room and turned it up loud. The song "Nothing But A Party," which is a collaboration between Benson and Norman Brown came on. I went into Mom's bedroom, took her hand and rocked it back and forth to the funky beat of the music. She just looked at me. I knew she was enjoying her last dance. It was an appropriate one because Mom always loved a party and always loved to dance to good music.

Last Breath: It was the morning of Saturday, October 10, 2009. I was planning to leave for Scranton that day to run the Steamtown Marathon on Sunday. Mom had been calm but weak during the last couple days, so I felt safe to go away. I would be back Monday morning after recovering from my run.

As I slept that morning I had a dream that Mom was jumping up the stairs between the living room and the bedroom level. She was jumping two steps at a time. In my dream she had recovered her capacity to move.

Suddenly I heard Nora's voice at my door. "Ross! Something's going on with Shirley."

I jumped up and put on my pants. I followed Nora upstairs.

Mom was breathing rapidly with her eyes half open. She had done this about a week earlier just before she woke up and then she was fine. This time we shook her gently and kept saying, "Shirley, Mom," but she didn't come out of it. I thought it would take a little time for her to wake up. I told Nora I was going to go back downstairs and asked her to call me when Mom got back to her normal condition. This was at 5:30 a.m.

At about 6:15 Nora came down again. "Shirley's died," she cried. I ran back upstairs. Mom had stopped breathing. Her eyes were open and her mouth was open. Nora hugged me and cried. Then I hugged Mom. Sobbing I said, "I love you. I love you."

My immediate thoughts were how in one instance in her entire life everything she was, everything she had done, was gone. I closed her eyes and hugged her again.

Nora called the hospice service number and a nurse came around 7:30 and declared that Mom had died. The funeral home staff came to take her. Mom left her bedroom and her home for the last time. No more planting flowers. No more singing and dancing. No more loving her animals. No more hugs. No more discussing politics and events of the day. No more cataloging movies or preparing holiday meals or vacations. All is now a wonderful memory.

Mourning along the Way

With any disease that gets progressively worse, when death finally comes many family members are doubly surprised—that they don't have a feeling of shock and that they seem to be all right. This can cause guilt feelings. "Why am I feeling so calm and not so upset?" they question themselves.

This was the case with my mother's death. I soon realized within days after she was gone that I had already been grieving for more than two years. Each step along the way to the end of her life . . . I was in mourning. I mourned the loss of her intellect and reasoning. I mourned the mood changes that were not reflective of her, but of the disease. I mourned the loss of her ability to dress, bathe and toilette. I mourned the loss of her ability to walk. I mourned the loss of her ability to eat.

So when the end came, I had already done a bunch of mourning. The immediate weeks after her death were filled with details and work to "take care of things." This can be overwhelming for some people. However, she and I had planned ahead for this time and the activity kept me focused.

It was only weeks later that I resumed my mourning, which indeed will never end. It is a sweet feeling of remembrance with the bitterness of her not being present that I am left with.

I guess we who lose family members slowly get the opportunity to spend time with our loved ones and plan for the eventual day. It must be a terrible thing to have someone disappear from your life without warning and never get the opportunity to say goodbye. At least I am blessed to have had that time. I am also blessed that as far as I can tell my mom was not in physical pain at the end. This was not the case with my brother Roy who went through so much pain and discomfort at the end of his life. It was also not the case for Roy's first wife, my wonderful sister-in-law Tobey, who suffered for five years. We all go through mourning for those we loved throughout our life. I pray that you can bear your pain and sorrow and that you can hold on to the sweet memories of your loved ones as I do.

My Mother's Synagogue

Shemini Atzeret: The Day Mom Died

My mother died on the morning of Shemini Atzeret. This is the time on the Jewish calendar when Simchat Torah, the celebration of the laws of Judaism is celebrated. Study, learning and education were a big part of my mother's life. Shemini Atzeret also marks the beginning of the rainy season following the harvest in Israel. It signifies gathering of all the production of one's works. My mother's work on earth had come to a close. Everything she was—all memory, all meaning—had left her body that morning. What remained were all the good works she had done.

Judaism was very important to her. The earliest stories of her religious experience were attending services in the synagogue in Brooklyn, Massachusetts. I believe she had attended Congregation Kahillath Israel on Harvard Street. She would go with the entire family. Once at Passover she felt dizzy. She wanted to go outside, but she was afraid to face away from the open Ark revealing the Torah while everyone stood.

So she tried to back out down the aisle. She was not successful as she passed out between the doors of the sanctuary and the lobby, causing a large commotion. From what she told me she loved going to synagogue.

When the family moved to Washington, D.C., they joined Washington Hebrew Congregation in the Northwest part of the city. This is where my grandmother, Freda Goldman, became very involved in the City of Hope charitable program. She was the chair. My mother would help her with her projects. My grandmother was a task master whose co-volunteers loved her. She would lecture errant volunteers who had taken on projects and had not completed the work. She would phone them and say, "You took on this committee position. I expect you to get your work done and report back to me."

My mother became active in Young Judea, a group that promoted the establishment of the State of Israel. It was a very exciting time when in 1948 the United Nations recognized the establishment of the new nation. It was also a difficult time as war broke out immediately. My grandparents and my mom worked to help the beleaguered State of Israel until the war ended.

After marrying and moving to Baltimore, my parents joined Baltimore Hebrew Congregation. My earliest recollection is walking through the front door of the huge entrance way. The Rabbi appeared to be godly as the sermons were done in a booming voice. At four or five years old I couldn't understand it, but it was still awe-inspiring.

After moving to Springfield, Delaware County in Pennsylvania, my parents joined a small suburban congregation in Broomall. It was Temple Shalom. They had a converted barn as their sanctuary. Our time there didn't last long. My mother felt that the board was not kind to the Rabbi, so they went "synagogue shopping" again. They asked the Rabbi at Baltimore Hebrew if he had any recommendations. He spoke highly of his colleague, Rabbi David Wice, at Rodeph Shalom in Philadelphia. So we joined that congregation in the late 1950s.

A BOOK OF PRAYERS
FOR THE HOME

presented to

The Schriftman Family

by the Rabbi, Officers
and Board of Trustees of

TEMPLE SHOLOM IN BROOMALL

A Reform Congregation
Affiliated with the Union of American Hebrew Congregations

_____
Rabbi

_____
President

1959

    Shirley Schriftman was never just a member of any congregation. She became an involved participant. All of her four sons became active in the Children's Choir under the direction of Cantor Harry Stanley. My mother joined the parents' group. When my youngest brother was still a baby, Mom would nurse him in one of the empty classrooms while her other sons were attending class.

    The children's choir and the religious school on Sunday were a big part of our life for many years. The hardest part was the lack of food until our Sunday dinners. As we got older Mom would stay at home on Sunday. Dad would drive us to the synagogue located on Broad Street just north of Center City, Philadelphia. All the other children in the choir would eat their lunch after school and before choir practice. But Mom didn't want us to "spoil" our Sunday dinner by eating early. I never could figure how food would be spoiled if you eat something else before the meal. Dad would stop at Pechter's Bakery in Drexel Hill on the way home, and we would all split a roll. "Don't tell Mom," he would say. "I don't want us to get in trouble."

As her children grew, each of us approached the time for our Bar Mitzvah. My parents were not the kind who would throw elaborate celebrations. The religious meaning and the importance of the experience of the service was their focus. They would sit with us and help us with our speech. They would make sure we were prepared to read the Hebrew in the Torah with training from Cantor Stanley and Hebrew tutors. The party afterwards would be big celebrations with all our relatives and friends at our home. For my Bar Mitzvah one of Roy's friends (Bob Stremme) from high school prepared a wonderful chicken dinner. Bob was studying to be a chef.

My mother took Adult Education courses through the Old York Road Consortium. She loved studying Judaism and could discuss the beliefs of such great thinkers as Hillel and Moses Maimonides. The ten levels of charitable giving was among the subjects she taught me. The highest level of charity is to help another person raise themselves out of poverty by teaching them a trade or putting them in the way of business.

Mom would enjoy the sermons and the speakers and would always be one to stay late at the Oneg Shabbat to discuss the subject with the presenters. She would also be one of the most welcoming and involved congregants when guests were attending. They might have been congregants from the church in the neighborhood or a musical group performing with their parents in attendance or simply anyone new to the synagogue. I would also be involuntarily recruited to drive people home. "My son can take you home," she would tell them. I was always glad to do so. The discussions of the evening would continue as I drove Mom's new friend home.

Mom became chair of the Soviet Jewry Committee at Rodeph Shalom. She organized writing campaigns and petitions and helped immigrants settle in Philadelphia.

As Mom got older, I would leave her by the side door of the Synagogue and then go around and park the car. The security people got to know her well, especially Mario, who would watch her for me before and after services. She would go get a seat and when I would arrive, she would wave furiously for me to find her. Of course, she would always sit near the front so everyone would turn around to see who this lady was waving to.

The older she got the more difficult it became for her to be involved in all the activities. She still went with me to many Brotherhood events, especially when I became Regional President. I would take her with me to Scranton or Allentown or other locations where I would be speaking or participating at that congregation's Brotherhood program. She loved to be there and would strike up conversations with everyone she met.

Throughout her life, Mom enjoyed the music accompanying the services. She had a beautiful voice and would sing out. Sometimes she would get dirty looks from other people who didn't know her. They seemed to feel that her singing was ruining the experience of the "performance" by the professional Cantor and choir. Today, the synagogue experience that I have seen is much more participatory than it was 20 years ago.

When Rodeph Shalom closed its Suburban Center in Elkins Park, I decided to join Congregation Keneseth Israel. At first Mom was reluctant. "You have been at Rodeph Shalom most of your life," she said. "How can you do this?"

However, when she found out that many of her friends had transferred, she agreed to join. Keneseth Israel was the synagogue that my Brother Roy and his first wife Tobey had joined when they got married. Tobey, who was an art historian, had worked on the museum there. Mom and I had been there many times for either family events or Brotherhood meetings. The change was to a family-friendly place. Also, the change was made more comfortable by the welcoming professional staff of Rabbi Sussman and Cantor

Levy. Here was a synagogue where Mom could do her singing.

In May of 2007 Mom and I were among the last to help write the new Torah, which was a project of the Congregation. Each congregant helped the scribe write a Hebrew letter for our donation to the project. We then helped march the new Torah around the building. Mom was already having difficulty with her illness and had to be watched closely as we walked. I took her hand and guided her. We started toward the front but were the last to re-enter the sanctuary for the service that followed. However, she wanted so much to participate.

Mom's beliefs carried her through life. She participated with joy and enthusiasm. Involvement and kindness with action and education are the lessons she taught me through her beliefs; these will be part of my life until my last day.

Mom, the scribe writing the Torah.

The Funeral

Knowing my mom, she would have wanted to make sure all her friends and family would be invited to her funeral. She also would have wanted people to talk about all the things she did during her life. Jewish funerals usually take place within a day or two after death but can take place later. We decided to have the funeral on Friday, October 16th. Mom had died on Saturday, October 10th. Throughout the weekend and week after her death I called as many people as possible.

Before the ceremony began close family members were ushered into the funeral home's chapel. Mom's casket was open for viewing for only immediately family. I whispered in her ear, "I'm right here with you. I will always be right here with you. I love."

The doors of the chapel were open and people came to the front to give their condolences. About 150 people came to honor her life and I am grateful to them.

The ceremony began. Cantor Amy sang and Rabbi Sussman talked about his tall and vibrant congregant. My brother Lee spoke about all the vacations and holiday meals and the feelings of love in our family. Then it was my turn. After thanking all the people who helped make my mom's days during her illness less difficult with a special thank-you to our angel Nora, I said the following:

> Our parents taught us that it didn't matter if we won some contest or got the top grade in school so long as we tried our best. Mom, I hope you know that I tried to do my best for you.
>
> I am so grateful for having been given the opportunity to care for my mom during the last several years. In some small measure I was able

to give back to her some of the wonderful things she did for me.

Mom, you taught me how I should live my life. You were my good friend and my biggest supporter and fan. I love you and I will miss you.

Mom would have been happy with the ceremony.

At the gravesite it was cold and rainy. The noise of traffic whizzing by on Roosevelt Boulevard only twenty yards behind our little prayer service forced the Rabbi to speak loudly. The traditional shoveling of dirt by family and friends onto the grave took place and then it was over. The final resting place. The last moments to honor a life well lived.

At the Shiva house at Lee and Nan's many people came and told "Shirley stories." This continued at my home on Sunday evening with neighbors, friends, family and longtime Democratic volunteers who had worked beside my mom.

As the weeks went by, I began to enter into a new pattern of life. It became less painful to be by myself in the house where many years ago six people lived together. It now was quiet, except for Happy Girl barking to go out or Helen Keller meowing. But the house is full of beautiful memories and remains so today.

Epilogue

*"To love someone deeply gives you strength.
Being loved by someone deeply gives you courage."*

-- Lao Tzu

Today I will buy a plot next to Mom's. Even though it is just a piece of dirt to put my body into when I die, it will fulfill my mother's constant request: "Don't go anywhere." I was moved to whisper to her unhearing ear on the day of her funeral, "I am right here with you. I am not going anywhere. I am right here."

I few weeks after she died, I had a dream. Mom came back from Heaven. (I don't believe in a physical heaven, so this was a rather unusual dream.) So what do you ask someone who has been to Heaven? "What is it like?" I asked. "I had the fish," she answered. That is typical of my mom. She would describe events by zeroing in on one aspect of the experience. It might be the food she ate or the furniture in the corner of the room, or what someone said or did. It would take her a long time to describe the whole experience. "I had the fish," would be a description of a vacation.

A few weeks later I had another dream. Mom was gardening in the far corner of the back yard where several years ago she and I had planted a "Forget Me Not" garden as a memorial for her pets. In the dream she stopped gardening, stood up and waved back toward the house while I looked out the kitchen window. The garden was important to her. We used to tease each other: "What is the name of that flower? Forget-me-not." Then we would both laugh. We had to go and buy forget-me-nots for each of Mother's pets during her life. The spring before she died, Nora and I took her to the little roadside garden shop in Fort Washington. Joe, the owner, remembered her. He walked to the car and handed Mom a bunch of forget-me-nots through the window. Mom couldn't communicate very well by then, but she smiled at him. I plan to expand that garden this spring and put a little marker in the ground for each pet, just as my mother had always planned. Here is a picture of the garden.

My mother's shoes are still next to her bed. I put them there to remind me that she was always ready to go somewhere and to do something new, interesting, and exciting. Mom loved life. It hurts to know that she can no longer be part of it. The only comfort we have when someone dies is that we keep their memories in our heart for as long as we live. This is the most important gift that they can give us.

Mom taught me the courage to be able to go on and live life with as much joy as possible. She made me strong and even though I will always miss her she will always be right here in my heart. I am so grateful to have had Shirley Ruth Goldman Schriftman as my mom. She not only gave me life, she gave me a life worth living.

Rabbi Jacob Rudin once wrote, "When we are gone, and people weep for us and grieve, let it be because we touched their lives with beauty and simplicity. Let it not be said that life was good to us, but, rather, we were good to life." My mother pursued life. She felt it slipping away from her in the final years. But hers was a life worth living. I am so grateful to her for giving me a life worth living as well.

I wrote this book because I remember all of it and want you to know what kind of a joyous, loving and giving person my mother was. Knowing my mom she would be very happy that I wrote this book. While writing this book, I kept hearing my mother say, "When are you going to finish the book?!" "After the next election," I would have liked to answer her. This was our little joke as I always had election time as the excuse for not finishing something that she wanted me to do.

Mom would be so pleased to know that I have continued living my life to the fullest. Mom taught me how to be strong so I could continue enjoying life and pursuing new dreams even if it meant continuing without her. I will continue to honor her memory in this way.

Yes, I miss her deeply, especially when I listen to music. New songs like Peter White's song "Bright" and Kenny G's "Heart and Soul" bring back sweet memories and melancholy that always makes me cry. I think of the trips Mom and I would take, the animals she loved, the babies she would hold, the parties she would attend, and the tears that would come; but the smiles would come as well.

Hold on to the people who mean the most to you in your life. Treasure the times together, both the difficult and the happy, both the tragic and the uplifting. Through my mother's example I found the meaning of life. It is one word—LOVE.

Advice for Caregivers

If you are caring for a loved one with Alzheimer's here is some advice from my experience. First, you must take good care of your own health. Meet with your doctor and get an exam. Get advice on exercise, stress reduction, nutrition and rest. Attention to all these factors is a must for optimum care of others. Remember, care for self first assures that you can stand up to caring for others. If you are in poor health, you will be less likely to give your loved one the kind of care they need.

Surround yourself with friends and family who will be willing to share the burden, but realize that you will be the one that most of the work and stress will fall upon, even if you have contracted for professional help. Don't assume that others will help if they haven't done so in the past. Everyone has their limits and you need to recognize this. A good support system is essential to allow you some time to restore your strength of purpose so come up with flexible ideas of who can be of help.

Work smartly and plan ahead. You must be able to learn how to anticipate so that you can meet the health and safety needs of your loved one. Make the home Alzheimer's friendly. Allow movement for the patient but in a safe environment. Feeling safe will allow the patient to relax and be more comfortable. Safety-proof the home. Grab bars, railings, stair-masters, special hiding places or pass codes for outside doors and other items will be a work in progress. As the patient's condition worsens, you may have to change the equipment and modify the home to meet these new challenges. Take joy in the success of knowing your proactive safety measures have worked and relish in the peace of mind that your family member is safe in the comfort of his or her own home.

Keep your loved one as active and involved as possible. Keep them "In the World" as much as possible. Take joy in each "victory" of going somewhere and coming home safely with no major incidents.

Give your loved one the dignity and respect he or she disserves. You are caring for the same person who has loved you all your life. They are still the same deep inside. In their Alzheimer's state, they just can't express it anymore and what comes out seems angry or distant or confused. Look deep inside of them. You will still find your loved one there. Be patient and understanding, although it can be very hard to do at times. Allow your loved one to have something that gives them pleasure. It might be a chocolate or a small dish of ice cream. It will be a sweet memory and will make them calm.

Create opportunities for your loved one to help you. This will give them pleasure and comfort even though Alzheimer's patients are very limited in the things they can do. I would ask my mom to rub my back even toward the end of her life. "Mom, my back itches," I would say. "Can you rub it?" She would reach up and rub my back for only seconds before her arm would drop back down on the bed. I would look back at her and she would have a calm, satisfied look on her face. She had done something for her son whom she loved. I wanted her to know that she could still take care of me like she used to just like I was now caring for her.

When she was mobile I would take her to my office. "Would you like to help me at work today?" I would ask. "Oh, yes," would be her response. "Be ready; I will pick you up at 2:00 p.m." was my response. It would take Nora and me 20 minutes just to get her up the two sets of stairs to the second floor of my office building. One time, she turned to Nora and said about me, "He is a good man." She was still so appreciative of being able to go to work.

Make sure you have a good care manager who has the experience, knowledge and a caring attitude to consistently look out for the best interests of the patient. Look on this person as your coach, and you are the quarterback of the care your family member is getting.

Plan out the financial, legal and emotional needs for yourself and your family BEFORE the need arises. It is extremely difficult to be thinking and planning for the need when it has already happened. Make sure you have your will, power of attorney, medical directives and living will in place when you are still able to competently make those decisions. Discuss these needs with other family members in advance. Make sure your parents have this planned out in advance and have told you what their desires and expectations are. Remember, they will not be able to assist you once they have developed this mind-altering, terrible disease.

Make sure you and your family purchase adequate and appropriate private long-term care insurance as soon as you can. Remember, you can't buy this kind of insurance when you need it. By then you will be uninsurable. You have to buy it BEFORE you need it, just like other forms of insurance.

Purchase the coverage from an agent who specializes in long-term care issues and ask for his credentials and references. Buy at least as much coverage as the current daily costs of care for all types of care in your area. There are surveys that are updated annually for the various regions in the country. You can also contact nursing homes, adult day care centers, assisted living communities and home health agencies to get their current prices. Make sure you ask the home health agencies about their fees for live-in care, which is a 24-hour cycle charge. Make sure the policy you purchase has built-in guaranteed inflation protection coverage, as the cost of care will continue to rise and most likely rise faster than the consumer price index. Having insurance to pay for professional care will allow you time to spend with your loved one doing the things that give you both joy—talking together, playing games, watching television or singing. Instead of trying to do everything on your own, the professional caregiver will be your partner. The long-term coverage that you so thoughtfully provide will pay so that you can have the pleasure of being your loved one's buddy.

Do not rely on the government to provide care for you and your loved ones. As of now the Federal Government is over $14 trillion in debt. Any new government programs to address the cost of providing long term-care services will be a dismal failure. They will simply not have enough money to pay for all the expensive care that so many people will need in the future. You must plan ahead and fund your own program now through insurance, savings, and investments.

As a caregiver you need to take breaks. Make sure you can get away and that you are comfortable that your support system can work adequately.

Take up a hobby, maybe one you can do at home when your loved one is sleeping or resting or being cared for by the professional caregiver. This will keep your mind active and allow you to experience a mental break away from your primary job as caregiver.

Realize that you may try out the services of several home companions to find the right fit for the care and needs of your family member. Don't be afraid of telling the home health agency that the person they sent isn't working out. Good agencies will work with you to find the right person as this will be a long, protracted experience for everyone concerned. It is important to understand that the caregiver becomes part of the family in this live-in companion situation. Your loved one must feel comfortable with this person coming into their home. It is expected that the family member will resent this new person coming into their home and telling them what to do. This is a work in progress that will take some time for everyone to get comfortable with.

Realize that it will take time for you and your parent to adjust to the role-reversal. Elderly parents are still used to telling their adult children what to do. You should gradually work with them to reverse the role where you will be making decisions for them. This is very difficult. When I would come home from work during the early days of my mother's disease, I would go into her bedroom and she would whisper, "Close the door." I would do so and then she would lecture me. "You have no right telling me what to do. When is she leaving? If she doesn't leave, I swear, I am walking out and you will never see me again." I would promise her I would look into it, give her a kiss and sit with her. She felt, and rightly so, that I was taking over her life and she hated it. I had no choice; I could not leave her alone. There were many fights and arguments during those early months, but gradually she got used to the caregivers.

Keep a sense of humor and enjoy the good moments when your loved one does or says something funny. Try to enjoy your new role as caregiver. It is truly an honor to care for someone, especially a parent, one who cared for you. People say to me, "It must have been hard taking care of your mom for those two years." My response would be and still is, "She cared for me for 57 years. I will never repay her in two years what she did for me for my entire life." You may sacrifice a lot for your loved one, but you will get so much more from the joy of giving back to one who cared so much for you during your lifetime.

Gratitude

There are so many people to thank for making the last years of my mother's life comfortable, healthy and safe as well as the joy so many friends and family brought to her during her lifetime. If I miss anyone, please let me know so that I can acknowledge you.

First and foremost is Nora whose love and kindness for my Mom was a wonderful blessing. A special thank you to all of the other caregivers, including Agnes, Ramatu, Evadny, Mary, Tata, Queena, Penny, Marianne, and Amanatu

Thank you to all the medical professionals and their staffs, including Mom's cheerful and caring nurse Crystal Tuffy, Dr. Hirsch, Dr. Waldfogel, Dr. Gordon, Dr. Meyers, Intervention Associates, Emily Lowe, Mom's Care Manager, Fine Care, Linder Opticians, Dr. David Koch, the CVS Pharmacy staff, the staff at Quest Diagnostics in Horsham, the Abington Hospice nursing staff and volunteers from Breath of Dawn singers.

I also extend a thank you to Horsham Veterinary Hospital, Metropolitan and Bucks County Vets for providing great care to Mom's pets and to dog trainer Cindy for helping Happy Girl become a 'house trained" dog.

A special thank you to our wonderful neighbors: The Healys, The Wydans, Deb Crowe and her children, Elizabeth Bogle, Mary Grace Allen, Dolores Kershaw, The Covers, The Carouthers, The Ryeskys, The Almonds, The Ungers, Wayne and Mary Winslow, Carol Bonet and The Minnigs.

To Russ Combs for the work he did to make the house livable and safe for my Mom. To Courtney and Jim for making sure the place stayed clean, and to all the other workers, including Adam Hoffman of Pet Butler, Kevin Schmidt of Clean Scoop, Jeff of Brandon Electric, Gary of Rainman, Greg and Paul of DelBar, Dennis Pearsall Plumbing, Bryan's Appliance, Jack Pittinger Paving, Pat Cornely, Shabi and his son Oren, Pete Williams of Brooks Barber, Mike of Mr. Landscaper and the crew from Saw Mill Fence Company.

A very special thank you to our friends Cathy Buckwalter, Bill Kearn, Bill and Florie Craig, George and Gloria Falk, Nan Rosner, Valarie Nave, Kass Hermann, Tony Davenport, the Phillips Family and Lee Jefferson for their kindness and support.

To Rabbi Sussman and Cantor Levy for conducting such a beautiful memorial service and to Kevin Block and Levine's Chapel for making the arrangements for Mom's funeral.

A special thank you to Jack Glass and the late Sandy Glass who arranged for sacred music for people who are homebound and gave my mom so much joy in listening to sacred music toward the end of her life.

Thank you to Ellen Fischer, Mom's attorney and Larry Aurbach my attorney, for their excellent legal work and to Corinna Tini of Mortgage Mobility for arranging the reverse mortgage, Bill Pearson at Gateway Mortgage and Julie Van Duyne-King at Univest and C.N.A. Insurance and Aetna for helping with the financing of Mom's care and living expenses. To the Catanzaro Family of Nationwide Insurance for protecting our home and being so helpful to Mom over the years.

To my brothers Roy (of blessed memory), Lee and Barry, sisters-in-law Lera, Nan and Tobey (of blessed memory), Mom's grandchildren who she loved very much including Micah who helped me take Mom on her last vacation, and Mom's nieces, nephews and cousins. A special thank you to Aunt Bea, Uncle Paul and Cousins Rona and Edye and Cousin Lisa for visiting Mom when she was sick and for being good family to my mom throughout her life. Finally, thank you to Harry and Freda Goldman for raising such a wonderful daughter who became such a great Mom.

About the Author

At age 3 helping Mom water her garden

Ross Schriftman was a devoted son. In addition to his love of family, Ross has been active in politics for more than 40 years. He ran for Pennsylvania State Representative in 1974, 1976 and 2004 and Montgomery County Controller in 1979. He has been an insurance agent since 1975 and specializes in Medicare and long-term care insurance. Professionally, he served as the Associate Chair for Long-Term Care for the National Association of Health Underwriters from 2001 to 2003 and Legislative Chair of the Pennsylvania Association of Health Underwriters from 1994 to 2003.

Ross served as Regional President of the National Federation of Temple Brotherhoods in the 1980s. He has run marathons since 1970. Though Ross is a frequent speaker and writer on health care issues and public policy, *My Million Dollar Mom* is his first published book.

CPSIA information can be obtained
at www.ICGtesting.com
Printed in the USA
BVHW01s2116280118
506367BV00005B/8/P